EXECUTIVE PRESENCE

"*Executive Presence* takes one of the most elusive qualities of leadership and makes it concrete and practical. The nine components of executive presence will give leaders at every level the guidance and confidence to up their game."

Daniel H. Pink, #1 New York Times bestselling author of
The Power Of Regret, To Sell is Human, and Drive

"If you've ever wanted to have a more powerful presence in all interactions, *Executive Presence* is the book for you. With a focus on specific behaviors, Joel explains how the most powerful leaders project that presence in every situation. You'll learn to command the room using the tools and strategies he shares throughout the book."

Dr. Marshall Goldsmith is the *Thinkers50* #1 Executive Coach and New York Times bestselling author of *Triggers, Mojo,* and *What Got You Here Won't Get You There.*

"Few people understand what executive presence is and how to demonstrate it as well as Joel Garfinkle. In *Executive Presence,* Joel draws on his deep executive coaching experience to provide self-assessments, case studies and specific action steps for any leader who wants to show up with more gravitas, authority and full expression."

Scott Eblin, best-selling author of
The Next Level; What Insiders Know About Executive Success.

"This book takes the mystery out of executive presence and offers a practical path to learning to enhance your influence."

David Burkus, author of *Leading From Anywhere*

"You don't often find a book that empowers you to immediately improve others' perception of you. But Joel Garfinkle's new book *Executive Presence* clearly explains how to radiate power and charisma, even if you weren't born with these qualities. This book is an indispensable guide for up-and-coming leaders, providing the tools to emanate an executive presence in every interaction. Whether you're an extrovert or introvert, and whether you work in a very social setting or remotely, this book provides incredibly useful ideas on how to present yourself as a commanding leader to those who matter most in your work. This book is a great find for any professional. I highly recommend it!"

Maya Hu-Chan, author of *Saving Face: How to Preserve Dignity and Build Trust*

"Ready to accomplish more in your current role or rise higher through the ranks? *Executive Presence* will guide you to adopt specific practices of successful leaders who consistently deliver results. Joel Garfinkle's new book is the guide you need reach greater heights of influence, service, and success."

Ron Kaufman
New York Times bestselling author of *Uplifting Service*

"Much has been written about the presence executives must display as they lead. In his newest book, *Executive Presence*, Joel Garfinkle provides insights into what this *presence* truly is. An experienced executive coach, he articulates its three core domains—gravitas, authority, and expression—by building upon his research conducted with thousands of clients and workshop participants. *Executive Presence* is a book that will open the eyes of those looking to advance their careers the right way with dignity, respect, and confidence."

John Baldoni, author of many books on leadership, including
"Grace Notes: Leading in an Upside-Down World."

"Whether driving a team or directing an enterprise, everybody wants to know your purpose, applaud your presence, and value your narrative. Drawing on years of executive coaching, Joel Garfinkle sets forward a compelling formula for doing so. His *Executive Presence* offers the roadmap for upping your confidence, decisiveness, and forcefulness."

Michael Useem, Faculty Director of the McNulty Leadership Program,
Wharton School, University of Pennsylvania,
and author of *The Edge: How 10 CEOs Learned to Lead*

"As a long time thought leader in the world of career development, I say with conviction that everyone needs presence to get ahead. Joel Garfinkle outlines, with wonderful credible examples, a model for how to think about your own presence and how to take the next step in improving it. Bravo."

Dr. Beverly Kaye, Author, Consultant, Thought Leader
Recipient of ATD Lifetime Contribution Award

"In *Executive Presence*, Joel Garfinkle explains how to demonstrate the traits of leaders who people want to follow. His well-researched advice and practical action steps show how to lead by inspiring others through gravitas, authority, and expression. This book is a must-read for any leader—or anyone who wants their employees to achieve their full potential."

Mike Figliuolo, Managing Director, *thought*LEADERS, LLC and author of
One Piece of Paper, Lead Inside the Box, and *The Elegant Pitch*

"With inspiring stories, self-assessments, and clear strategies, *Executive Presence* explains how to step into your full power as a leader—even when navigating crisis. You'll learn to inspire your team to embrace positive change by cultivating a bold, commanding, and charismatic presence."

Mike Robbins, author of *Bring Your Whole Self to Work*

"Executive Presence is the go-to playbook for developing or enhancing your executive presence to maximize your leadership success. He provides a road map, step by step, on what you need to do to improve your executive presence. Joel's model is understandable, clear and what I find most helpful is that he provides insights on how to practice, develop and sharpen your executive presence. Practicing new tactics and skills is a must to improve and Executive Presence is *the* authoritative guide."

Nancy Parsons
CEO of CDR Companies, LLC, and author of
Women Are Creating the Glass Ceiling and Have the Power to End It

"In *Executive Presence*, Joel shows you how to cultivate the power and presence of top leaders. As you read this book, you'll identify which qualities you're lacking and how to immediately begin adopting specific new behaviors that radiate executive presence. This book will show you how to have the executive presence qualities that all next level leaders utilize for impact and success."

Eileen He, Vice President, Software Development and Operations
Oracle

"Joel's approach presented in Executive Presence is a robust roadmap for navigating a career into the next level. One thing I love about this book is that it approaches supporting people with compassion and empowerment. This is not a book modeled on the "winner take all" philosophy, but rather in enabling everything to present their best self, to help themselves and their organization excel."

Noah Goldstein, Senior Sustainability Program Manager
Google

"Executive presence is a critical attribute of successful leaders. You can see it not only in how they exude confidence, but in how they show up in a way that builds, inspires, and challenges people to be their best. Applicable to those leading teams and individual contributors alike, Joel's insight on executive presence captures what we can and should learn for it to become a core strength to more effectively influence others. Highly recommended."

Kevin Morrison, Managing Director, Chief Information Security Officer
Alaska Airlines

"If you want to become a more inspiring and impressive leader who catalyzes change and influences at scale, *Executive Presence* will guide you in doing just that in your professional and personal life. Using stories from his hundreds of coaching engagements, Joel Garfinkle shows the reader that any leader with a passion for their work can develop executive presence. I highly recommend this book to any individual who aspires to become an influential and effective leader!"

Kevin Nembhard, Senior Manager, Corporate Accounting
Walmart

"This is an excellent book from Joel Garfinkle who is one of the nation's top executive coaches and a world recognized expert on Executive Presence (EP). The book clearly explains main EP concepts via an innovative model, provides a series of tests and questions for measurement of your own current EP level, and gives you valuable suggestions on how to create and expand your EP based on your individual personality and working style. I am glad to see that now Joel's powerful work is available to influence thousands executive leaders in many organizations across the entire world"

Igor Kozlov, Global Head, Reagent Research and Design
Roche

"This thoroughly researched book provides a clear blueprint to developing executive presence. He debunks myths about this elusive quality and illustrates how three key domains—gravitas, authority, and expression—merge together to imbue a leader with executive presence. If you have ever felt confused about what executive presence truly is, you will be grateful for this book."

Omkar Pendse, Senior Director of Engineering
PayPal

"I can't recommend Executive Presence highly enough. Joel helps you gauge your level of executive presence—and then improve it—like no other resource I've found. His self-assessment exercises for each of the 9 executive presence qualities help you see exactly where you stand, so you can focus on the most critical areas for improvement. From Joel's clarity of writing and to his ability to distill down an opaque area into actionable steps, this book leaves the reader feeling emboldened to develop the powerful presence of a great leader."

Former VP, Policy Development and Research
Lyft

EXECUTIVE PRESENCE

STEP INTO YOUR **POWER**, CONVEY **CONFIDENCE**, & LEAD WITH **CONVICTION**

• • • • • • • • • • • • • • • ★ • • • • • • • • • • • • • • •

JOEL A. GARFINKLE

Publisher name: JAG Press

ISBN (print): 979-8-9859366-0-5
ISBN (ebook): 979-8-9859366-1-2

© 2022 by Joel Garfinkle

CONTENTS

PART 1
The Importance of Executive Presence

PART 2
Gravitas, Authority, Expression

Section 1: GRAVITAS

Section 2: AUTHORITY

Section 3: EXPRESSION

Part 1

The Importance of Executive Presence

Introduction

Executive Presence Is a Prerequisite to Leadership Success

"The most dangerous leadership myth is that leaders are born—that there is a genetic factor to leadership. That's nonsense; in fact, the opposite is true. Leaders are made rather than born."

— Warren Bennis

No one can realize their full potential as a leader without executive presence. But the good news is that executive presence can be learned. In fact, 98% of senior leaders say they didn't innately possess executive presence[i]. Instead, they had to cultivate it. This book will show you how to do this, through clear and actionable steps focusing on building specific competencies.

Executive presence is something that can—and *must*—be learned. As Michael Useem, director of the Center for Leadership and Change Management at Wharton, says:

"Leadership at the front, mid and top lines alike is not innate. It is true some people have a huge head start. They're exceptionally clear minded. They communicate well. They're exceptionally persuasive. They look physically like a leader should, at least in the idealized Hollywood version. But the real skills of leadership at every level must be acquired in our lifetimes. There are no biological advantages. You have to learn those skills. And any organization, by implication, has to provide a chance for everybody to be a leader."[ii]

This book gives you the tools to develop and hone your own executive presence and become an elite performer who influences outcomes and drives change. You'll learn how to convey confidence, command respect, and exude a professional magnetism that influences others at every level. You'll learn new strategies for projecting conviction, asserting your opinions, and leading with gravitas, trading in passivity and self-doubt for self-assurance, decisiveness, and bold decision-making.

No one can realize their full potential as
a leader without executive presence.

Fortunately, you don't need to wait for anyone's permission to begin developing executive presence. Rather, you can start right here and now. In fact, the onus is on *you* to develop it within yourself. Don't wait for a superior to point you toward a workshop or an executive presence coach.

In Part 1 of this book, we'll first take a deeper look at what executive presence is and how growing it will benefit you as a leader. You'll learn how executive presence enhances leadership, and how to avoid undermining it within yourself. You'll also take a quiz to assess your current level of executive presence, and you'll learn how to gauge whether others perceive you as having it. Most importantly, you'll begin to learn my 3x3 Executive Presence Model, which will serve as your guide in developing these indispensable qualities. In Part 2, we'll then examine each of the nine key components of executive presence and how to develop them one by one.

Here's the 3x3 Executive Presence Model which provides an overview of the nine competencies. As you read this book, you can use this model as a reference and return to this page again and again.

THE 3X3 EXECUTIVE PRESENCE MODEL

GRAVITAS	AUTHORITY	EXPRESSION
CONFIDENT You lead with the assuredness that you can do it. You're assertive, decisive, and willing to take risks. You state your opinions strongly. You believe in what you know and who you are.	**DECISIVE** You take initiative and move things forward. You act with conviction. You make up your mind quickly and arrive at a clear decision with certainty. You don't waver or hesitate.	**VOCAL** You share your thoughts and ideas without hesitation. You're forthcoming with your opinions. Your voice and presence are visible to others. You make your expertise, competence, and talents known.
COMMANDING You take charge, driving toward outcomes. People look to you for leadership. They defer to you. When you speak, people pay attention. Others perceive your presence and power.	**BOLD** You are willing to make bold decisions—then put a stake in the ground and own your position. You stand by your beliefs and convictions. You are willing to challenge and push back.	**INSIGHTFUL** You make great recommendations. You ask excellent questions and share ideas precisely, confidently, and with conviction. You are known for smart thinking and critical analysis.
CHARISMATIC You radiate enthusiasm, personal charm, and an optimistic attitude. You motivate and inspire others. People are drawn to you. You feel approachable.	**INFLUENTIAL** You are convincing, compelling, and forceful. You incite and encourage others toward action. Your articulate and assertive points of view persuade others. You can effectively counter-argue.	**CLEAR** When you communicate, you are succinct and to the point. Your message is clear and crisp; you are straightforward and direct. You're polished and express yourself without qualifier or filler words.

If you're a leader working to help your employees develop executive presence, this book will assist you in teaching them to leverage it more effectively, propelling them forward in their careers. By embodying the qualities of executive presence and applying them wisely, your people will achieve and sustain a high level of success and impact.

When you or your employees begin exuding the confidence that executive presence entails, top leadership will more easily envision you becoming next-level leaders. These senior leaders will be naturally drawn to you, opening new doorways to increased responsibility.

As you rise in your organization, you'll realize how much greater your executive presence must become. When 400 CEOs were asked how they chose their next-level leaders, 100% of them said that executive presence can differentiate a person from the crowd, and 89% said it plays a key role in getting ahead.[iii] Leaders are paying attention to who has enhanced executive presence. Those who do are the ones who get promoted. This quality clearly plays a central role in a leader's career progression and promotional opportunities. The higher the stakes, the more you need that power and presence.

This book will provide you with a step-by-step process for how to build and leverage your executive presence in any role. *Executive Presence* will teach you how to:

Radiate Gravitas: Be confident, commanding, and charismatic.
Act with Authority: Be decisive, bold, and influential.
Express Yourself Fully: Be vocal, insightful, and clear.

As you master the lessons in this book, you'll expand what is possible for you to achieve. And as you teach them to your employees, you'll develop a core group of capable leaders who know how to influence others and drive results.

Creating your executive presence brand.

If you don't establish your own brand, someone else will do it for you. As a rising leader, executive presence must be the central focus of that brand.

Most of the time, your brand is created by others. They will project onto you what they believe is there. They will develop a particular perception of you—an image of what they think they see. This perception may not be accurate or favorable. However, you can control your own narrative by intentionally and systematically establishing your own executive presence brand.

The manager of one of my executive coaching clients said this to me:

> "His ability to become a next-level leader is tied to his brand—to his *executive presence* brand. I asked the higher-level leaders what they think of when they see him, and they drew a blank. Nothing. They knew who he was, but they didn't know what he *did*. They didn't know his value to the company at all."

The advice shared in this book helped this leader to come up with an executive presence brand that got the attention of all senior leaders. He learned how to fill in the blank with all the key qualities of executive presence—and you will too.

Who is this book for?

This book will help you to not only cultivate your own executive presence (EP); it will also teach you how to coach your employees to success. Here are five key audiences who will benefit from this book.

Top-level leaders and senior executives. The higher you rise in an organization, the more executive presence becomes a necessity. At the senior executive level, you are already expected to have executive presence. If you haven't fully developed your executive presence or are underutilizing it, you'll have less credibility and garner less respect. Senior executives spend the majority of their time in meetings where they constantly need to speak up to influence others. Their employees, peers, C-level executives, and clients all expect them to present themselves and their ideas with conviction, authority, confidence, and command. When top leaders lack executive presence, they immediately lose credibility and persuasiveness.

The higher you go in an organization, the more you need the confidence, authority, and presence that you notice in great leaders.

Future company leaders. Maybe you're one of the fast-rising, high-potential employees who are the up-and-coming stars of the organization. As an aspiring or emerging leader, you need to have executive presence to succeed in advanced positions. I am continuously working with leaders whose career success came to an abrupt halt because they didn't develop and improve their executive presence as they advanced up the company ladder. Often they were highly competent and assumed they would naturally continue rising in rank. However, having a high degree of skill and expertise isn't enough. The higher you go in an organization, the more you need the confidence, authority, and presence that you notice in great leaders.

To ensure the company's continued success, you have the responsibility to master the qualities of executive presence. It's also the only way to continue your personal trajectory toward heightened success.

Managers who want to help employees grow into leaders. As a leader, you need your employees to develop executive presence to elevate their potential and impact. Think about all the people you oversee in your role as a manager. Your direct reports, the employees working for your direct reports, and the employees below them. Right now, identify the employees you manage who lack executive presence. Apply what you are learning in this book to help them improve their EP, and consider giving them a copy to read.

Employees with a solid performance who are ready for the next level. As a solid performer, you receive good performance reviews, have a strong skillset, and execute your responsibilities well. With this strong foundation of performance and results, you are ready to begin developing your executive presence. If you don't have a solid foundation as a good performer, you'll need to shore this up first by eliminating all performance issues before focusing on executive presence.

People in the STEM fields. In these professions, leaders often advance due to engineering, IT, or research skills without receiving executive presence development. Introverts are often drawn to these fields. While introverts are fully capable of cultivating executive presence, their organization may not guide them in developing the leadership abilities that will allow them to command a team and lead with conviction. Executive presence will allow them to show up with the confidence and charisma needed.

Marginalized employees, including women. If you're a budding leader of a marginalized racial group, ethnicity, gender, or ability, you will benefit from cultivating executive presence. Women, people of color, and other employees from marginalized groups are too often overlooked and underappreciated, which causes companies to miss out on their full range of talent. If you're in one of these demographics, growing your executive presence will allow you to leap over the barriers you may encounter in your career.

As the diversity of a company grows, management needs to reflect a similar level of diversity. A highly diversified management team provides a vast array of insights and perspectives, rather than an echo chamber. While women have lacked adequate leadership roles inside companies for decades, now organizations are viewing women as a vital ingredient for sustained success. Women, people of color, and other marginalized employees need a competitive advantage to get the positions they deserve, and it's called—you guessed it—executive presence.

You may wonder, "Will women be perceived negatively when they display the qualities of executive presence?" After all, studies have shown that women are often viewed as unlikeable for embodying qualities that are lauded in men, like ambition and toughness.[iv] These double standards may raise concerns about being perceived as *too* assertive or even bossy. But you won't get where you want to go by staying on the sidelines. Executive presence is vital for anyone who wants to get into the game. And, guided by the increasing focus on servant leadership, you can work to balance nurturing qualities with the ability to command a team—as men should do, too.

In short, don't dial back your confidence because of how you fear others may perceive you. Own your power and strength, while also working to convey empathy and compassion. You can't necessarily change people's biases, but you *can* control how you show up. Again, this advice applies equally to men, who also benefit greatly from consciously working to show more empathy and emotional intelligence in their daily work.

Ways of approaching this book.

You can review, digest, and implement what you learn in this book in two different ways:

1. A leadership lens
2. A personal lens

When you bring the principles outlined in this book to your team, you are applying the leadership lens by focusing on the growth of the people you manage.

When you read this book for your own benefit, you are investing in yourself and applying the personal lens by working toward your own professional development.

Executive presence is as important as your current job.

Look at the training programs offered by your company. Is developing executive presence on the list? Probably not. Very few companies educate employees on how to develop EP. They fail to recognize its vital importance—so it's up to you to pursue this goal. Creating executive presence doesn't happen by accident. You need to mentally, intellectually, and emotionally challenge yourself to step into the shoes of the leader you want to become. Executive presence sometimes doesn't feel natural and easy. It must be practiced and learned over time. What will it take for you to commit to making executive presence a vital part of your work life?

Developing executive presence is a separate part-time job that deserves almost as much attention as your current assignment. Phylis Esposito, former executive vice president and chief strategy officer at Omaha-based TD Ameritrade, emphasizes the need to take a proactive approach to advancement. "Doing nothing and just hoping your next promotion will somehow take care of itself is really the biggest risk," says Esposito. "Don't forget that there are people coming up behind you who want your job."[v]

While cultivating executive presence requires a tremendous amount of time, effort, and energy, it will result in an extraordinary career. You will fully realize your professional, personal, and financial goals and improve the quality and quantity of your contributions to your company. As Roger Enrico, PepsiCo's former CEO, noted in *Business Week*: "The way I look upon it is that leadership is a skill like many others. Whatever leadership ability an individual has can be made better through practice and honing."[vi]

Practicing the core qualities of executive presence will directly increase your competence and confidence, as well as your level of contribution to your organization. Just as an athlete may run several additional miles per week to build endurance, strengthening your executive presence is an undertaking that requires dedication, repetition of key elements, and time spent beyond the typical workweek.

Practicing the skills that support a strong executive presence will lay the groundwork for becoming the best leader possible.

Few people have embodied the power of persistent, tenacious training as well as Kobe Bryant. His fellow players recount how at the 2008 Olympics, when the rest of the team was just waking up for breakfast, Bryant came in drenched in sweat after a three-hour workout.[vii] For him, that was just the norm. He routinely worked out and practiced in the wee hours of the morning, long before most people were even up. He made no excuses—not even for a broken wrist, fellow player John Celestand recalls, speaking of the 1999 season:

> "'The first time I began to understand why he was the best was in the pre-season. In a game against the Wizards, Kobe broke the wrist on his shooting hand. He was always the first person to practice every day, arriving at least an hour and a half early. This would infuriate me because I wanted to be the first person to practice,' says Celestand. 'As I walked through the training room, I became stricken with fear when I heard a ball bouncing. No, no, it couldn't be! Yes it could. Kobe was already in a full sweat with a cast on his right arm and dribbling and shooting with his left.'"[viii]

Bryant meticulously scrutinized footage of the games he played, even bringing out his laptop at half-time. "He often corrals teammates, fires up the laptop, and shows them precisely how they can carve out easier shots for themselves," ESPN once said.[ix] A soccer player as a child, Bryant focused on learning to use his lower body better than most of his fellow players—through strict self-discipline and rigorous practice.[x]

Just as practicing fundamentals provided a strong foundation upon which Bryant built his basketball skills, practicing the skills that support a strong executive presence will lay the groundwork for becoming the best leader possible.

Developing your executive presence may seem like a daunting task. It involves a lot of work, but it's the kind of work that will have far-reaching, long-lasting benefits. You will become more motivated, you'll learn to recognize and promote your own value, and you'll develop a meaningful and effective career plan. And you'll enjoy more fulfillment on a daily basis as you see yourself progress.

Frequently asked questions at my corporate trainings on executive presence.

You may be asking some of these common questions yourself. Read on for a better understanding of how executive presence applies to you.

Is executive presence something you are born with or something you can develop?

Some people come into the world with a certain vibe, energy, or charisma that allows them to show up in a way that naturally draws others to them. They exude an easy confidence and a natural gravitas. These individuals do have an advantage over others who have to work at it. However, the majority of people in the world aren't born with executive presence. It's something they must build and grow throughout their career.

Is executive presence only for extroverts?

Extroverts sometimes have an advantage when it comes to displaying their executive presence. They naturally come across as more confident, outgoing, and at ease with interpersonal dynamics. They tend to speak more loudly, enjoy taking the spotlight, and dominate conversations.

"The loudest person in the room is not always right, or even the best qualified."
Ben Lyttleton

But often the best players aren't the ones we'd expect them to be. Just look at the 2006 World Cup Final: Marcello Lippi, the coach for Italy, had to decide which player to give Italy's last penalty shot in the shoot-out. Rather than giving it to one of the most esteemed and well-known players, he gave it to Fabio Grosso, a quiet, unassuming left-back. Grosso succeeded, bringing Italy to victory. This story shows how talent can emerge in unexpected places, says Ben Lyttleton, author of *Twelve Yards: The Art and Psychology of the Perfect Penalty Kick*. "We may recognize from our own workplace (or, indeed, public life) that the loudest person in the room is not always right, or even the best qualified," he asserts.[xi] I see this point confirmed in my executive coaching work time and again, watching introverts master the art (or sport) of becoming a strong leader. LinkedIn has recognized this idea with its Quiet Ambassadors program, identifying leaders who don't fit the stereotypical extroverted profile.[xii]

The key to success for introverts is to dedicate the necessary time to developing their executive presence.

Even if they're not the loudest, introverts can learn to exude a steady confidence and presence that speaks volumes. They may struggle to speak up, stand out, and show confidence, which are key elements of EP. However, they can learn to speak with conviction, be decisive, put a stake in the ground and own their position, and assume a take-charge attitude. They don't need to be the most loquacious person to do any of that—in fact, brevity is one of the essential qualities of executive presence. The key to success for introverts is to dedicate the necessary time to developing their executive presence, because it's a competitive advantage they can't afford not to have.

Do you have to be an executive to work on your executive presence?

No, you definitely do *not* have to be an executive to work on your executive presence. Don't take the word "executive" literally. If you are stuck on the word "executive" ("I'm not an executive, so I can't relate to the concept of 'executive presence'"), I recommend thinking of it as "leadership presence."

All employees need to improve how they show up, act, and communicate with others. No matter what role you have or what level you've reached, you can constantly be working toward radiating more gravitas, acting with more authority, and expressing yourself more fully. If you do this early in your career, all the better!

What is the line between being confident and cocky? Commanding and a bully?

Being confident and in command are two cornerstones of executive presence, as we'll explore in this book. But where does confidence stray into being cocky, and where does being commanding stray into becoming too pushy?

Authentic confidence does *not* come across as arrogant. Truly confident people are comfortable admitting their weaknesses and shortcomings, whereas cocky people are hiding behind a veneer of false self-assuredness. They are putting on an act fueled by insecurity. If you're honest with yourself about your flaws as well as your strengths, you'll learn to project a natural confidence that does not come across as condescending. The same goes for showing that you're in command—you'll learn to radiate capability and inspire others to have confidence in you without being domineering. Most people tend to come across as lacking confidence or the ability to be in command, rather than too arrogant or pushy. However, if you believe those words describe you, cultivating executive presence will help you develop a more people-centered approach grounded in *true* confidence and command rather than an attempt to hide your weaknesses.

Does executive presence matter as much in the virtual world? Does the same advice for displaying it still apply?

Executive presence matters just as much, if not more, on teams working virtually. Holding people's attention proves even more challenging in a Zoom meeting than in person. And because you're not seeing people throughout the day, you need to really make an impression when you do interact with them. Those few moments go a long way toward inspiring engagement, instilling a sense of purpose, and keeping people driven to fulfill a shared vision. The 3x3 Executive Presence Model applies equally to those who work virtually and in person, and the advice I'll share in this book can be employed across all contexts. In certain cases, I'll share particular tips for making qualities known in virtual settings.

How much does appearance matter for executive presence—in the virtual world and in person?

It's essential to project a professional appearance, both virtually and in person. While dress norms are shifting in many companies, you also need to consider how clients and other people outside of your immediate workplace culture will perceive you. Plus, you need to bear in mind how your superiors will view you. If working from home, dress like you're back in the office, and follow the same dress standards as people at your boss's level (unless they're wearing sweatpants!). You'll set yourself apart from the crowd, especially if others have become more lax about dress.

Appearance is not one of the core qualities in the 3x3 Executive Presence Model because it takes relatively little effort to get this right. In this book, we're going to spend time exploring the qualities that take more effort to develop, helping you to express yourself well and show up fully as a leader. Dress is an important but superficial matter in comparison.

Do cultural differences affect whether you should demonstrate executive presence?

Cultural differences may affect exactly *how* your executive presence shows up, but in general, executive presence benefits leaders across cultures. Be sensitive to your audience and culture. For example, if your culture doesn't engage in a lot of direct eye contact, you can follow that cultural norm (although you can consider changing your approach when interacting with people outside of your own culture). Confidence may be tempered with more humility in certain cultures, like Japan—but even when making humble statements, one might project confidence as calm self-assuredness through body language and tone of voice. Keep your particular cultural context in mind, working to portray the executive presence qualities in a way that will resonate with the people you work with.

Does executive presence mesh with servant leadership?

Today's leaders are realizing the value of servant leadership, Teal organizations, and an agile mindset, which focus less on showing authority and more on empowering individuals. It follows that many will wonder if executive presence applies in these contexts. My answer is a resounding *yes*. Executive presence is not about intimidating people or dominating groups. Rather, it is about stepping into your potential as a leader who can effectively guide your team to success. And power is not about bossing others around—it's about bringing out their highest potential. Being a confident person whom people trust and respect will allow you to influence them in positive ways and draw out their best qualities. Thus, it will enable you to become a better servant leader rather than flying under the radar and missing opportunities to make a difference. You can model the humbleness of a great servant leader while radiating all of the nine executive presence qualities discussed in this book—and I encourage you to strive toward this goal.

The sweet spot of executive presence lies between "too nice" and "arrogant."

Executive presence is not about intimidating others *or* appeasing them. People who don't have executive presence often come across as being very nice but unassertive. Conversely, those who possess a high level of certain qualities but not others can seem arrogant or aggressive, as we'll discuss further in the coming chapters. These two extremes *both* come from not possessing a balanced range of all core executive presence qualities. The sweet spot you are trying to find lies in between being too nice and too aggressive, and it comes from achieving that ideal balance.

Great leaders are committed to nurturing others, leveraging all of their executive presence qualities for the good of the team rather than just personal gain.

A narcissistic person *can* project the appearance of executive presence at first glance. They can talk a good game and may even rise up through the ranks because some leaders perceive their arrogance as confidence. However, they lack essential qualities of executive presence that will make them a truly great leader, and most experienced leaders will see through them. Great leaders are committed to nurturing others, leveraging all of their executive presence qualities for the good of the team rather than just personal gain.

Take a look at this scale, which shows the two extremes some people may find themselves at. Where do you fall on the continuum?

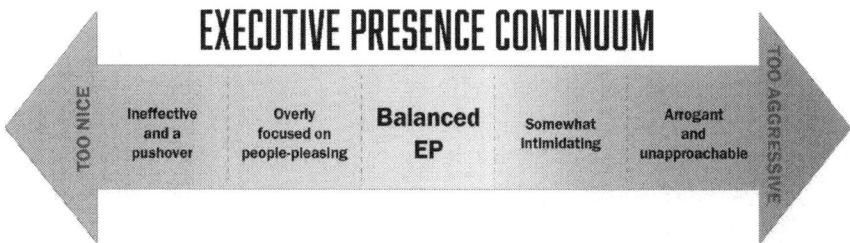

EXECUTIVE PRESENCE CONTINUUM

TOO NICE

| Ineffective and a pushover | Overly focused on people-pleasing | **Balanced EP** | Somewhat intimidating | Arrogant and unapproachable |

TOO AGGRESSIVE

Whether you're a seasoned leader who wants to get more from your team, or you're wondering why you haven't yet been promoted to a next-level leadership role, this book can help. As you work your way through it, use the action steps and exercises in this book to apply the lessons you're learning right away, while they're fresh in your mind. And don't rush. Growing executive presence is a journey that must be taken one step at a time, so be patient with yourself as you diligently implement these lessons. Give each step the time it deserves, and you'll become a truly inspiring and impressive leader who commands respect, exudes charisma, and radiates gravitas in all of your presentations, discussions, and interactions.

DO YOU HAVE EXECUTIVE PRESENCE?
ASSESS YOUR CURRENT LEVEL OF EP.

Place a checkmark next to each statement that describes you. If it somewhat describes you, put a checkmark. When you're finished, tally up your total number of checkmarks.

1. When I speak, I am long-winded and tend to share my unedited train of thought.
2. When I have new, creative, and unbaked ideas, I rarely share them at meetings.
3. I don't present ideas persuasively to senior leaders.
4. I avoid confronting challenges head-on and without delay.
5. I have trouble making decisions and feeling conviction in my choices.
6. I don't naturally draw people to me and build excitement for my ideas.
7. I often overanalyze what I'm going to say, and then I don't speak up.
8. I am laidback and casual, going with the flow and lacking conviction.
9. I'm too nice and accommodating, making decisions based on appeasing people.
10. I don't feel or act equal to people at higher levels than me.
11. I get consumed by day-to-day responsibilities and don't spend much time setting the strategic direction.
12. I don't share my full breadth of experience and expertise.
13. I don't boldly speak the truth when I know it will feel uncomfortable for others.
14. In situations that lack leadership, I don't take control of the situation and lead.
15. I struggle to make my presence felt, in each space I step into, by voicing my opinions.

16. I don't persuasively advocate for an idea even when I believe in its merit.

17. I refrain from taking risks, afraid of making mistakes.

18. When others push back or disagree, I tend to back down.

19. My words lack energy when I want to move people toward action.

20. I don't influence groups or people across the organization.

21. I don't take action in the face of uncertainty, pushing boundaries beyond what feels safe.

22. I rarely raise concerns that could lead to improvement of a plan.

23. I often show up unprepared to meetings.

24. I don't ignite interactive discussions that draw out others' ideas by asking great questions.

25. I often focus on data, facts, process, and background details instead of getting to the point.

These are all common flaws that people experience in the work-place—even high-level leaders. In many cases, while leaders have been promoted to positions of authority, they've never had any support in cultivating the abilities that will give them real power and influence. People with a great deal of talent often feel trapped at a certain rung of the leadership ladder because they lack that power and influence.

WHAT DOES YOUR SCORE MEAN?

Tally up the number of items you checked, and find the corresponding number below:

1-6: *Your executive presence is beginning to make itself known, even if you're not aware of it yet. You are probably getting noticed for your great ideas, talents, and leadership potential. Your organization likely sees you as someone who knows how to take charge, rally others behind an idea, and drive change.*

7-16: *You show promise in certain areas of leadership, but you're falling short in other ways that are keeping you from growing the visibility and influence you deserve. The good news is that you do have a leadership skill set that you can further cultivate in order to reach the next level—and this book will show you how.*

17-25: *You urgently need to take action to step into your power as a leader. You shrink back as others learn to assert themselves as leaders—even though they aren't more talented and capable than you. Fortunately, this book will help you change that. Your low level of gravitas, authority, and expression are holding you back in your career, and it's time to correct course so you can achieve the career you deserve.*

Chapter 1

How Executive Presence Enhances Leadership

"We convince by our presence."

— Walt Whitman

If you're an aspiring leader wondering whether you have what it takes to reach the next level, *you do*. You may be lacking executive presence now, but you have the skills and intelligence to build it step by step—just like nearly every great leader who has come before you.

How does executive presence benefit your own success? It will allow you to step into your full potential and drive your team toward your goals with grace and skill. People throughout your organization will recognize you as a leader, and thus, new opportunities will continuously open up.

How does executive presence benefit your company's success? As you cultivate your own executive presence, you'll become a stronger, more influential and convincing leader who guides others to reach their full potential.

If you're already a high-level leader, you must focus on helping your employees develop executive presence. As a senior leader striving to win the talent war, it's not about finding the right employees: You already have the best talent. Now it is time to uncover the high-value people inside your organization who are being overlooked. They are the competitive advantage you can't afford to lose.

What will move your hidden talent up
to superstar status?

What will move your hidden talent up to superstar status? Engaging, empowering, and leveraging them effectively. They are waiting for the development of their executive potential. Dedicate time, training, and coaching on how to improve their executive presence, and you'll release the untapped potential of your underutilized leaders.

Let's examine now why executive presence is critical to companies' success, as well as individual leaders' ability to thrive.

Why do companies need employees with executive presence?

By helping your people cultivate their executive presence, you'll accomplish each of these objectives:

- Build a leadership pipeline.
- Gain the most from your hidden leaders.
- Dramatically boost retention and engagement.
- Know the value each leader is contributing.
- Benefit from a diverse pool of talent.

Fifteen years ago, most companies didn't focus on executive presence as a leadership development area. A few years ago, it didn't even make the list of the top 20 traits for a leader to have. But across the board, company executives have come to realize that executive presence can make or break their leaders' success. In a survey conducted by Gartner, EP came in second on the list of the top 20 leadership traits that make a difference.[i]

Executive presence is not just a nice-to-have perk. Here's why every company should be focusing on helping its people cultivate executive presence—and why you need to start developing it in yourself, no matter what level you're at today.

> When your people are equipped with executive presence, they will become the high-impact leaders who move the organization forward.

Build a leadership pipeline.

Executive presence is essential to preparing employees for higher levels of leadership. As companies come to this realization, they're focusing more heavily on EP. They are requiring their people to have a strong foundation of executive presence as they move into middle management and beyond. Stepping up to the next levels of leadership requires a higher and higher degree of executive presence.

As you prepare for succession, work to grow leadership at scale. Don't just focus on a couple of people—build a cadre of leaders, as Claudio Feser, senior partner with McKinsey & Co., urges. "Organizations that built a significant number of leaders tend to outperform those that focus in on the very few," he explains.[ii]

In a survey by the Association for Talent Development, 47% of organizations said they expect to have a skills gap at the executive level in future years.[iii] Robert Half found that 52% of CFOs don't have a successor lined up for their position.[iv] "A company that doesn't engage in executive mentoring and knowledge-sharing can struggle with retention and potentially lose institutional expertise," Robert Half emphasizes. By providing targeted support to budding leaders, your company can fill these talent gaps and grow a leadership talent pipeline. You'll be helping each employee create a roadmap for future success, and your company will have a solid succession plan in place. When your people are equipped with executive presence, they will become the high-impact leaders who move the organization forward.

You'll gain the most from your hidden leaders.

Every company has hidden leaders. These low-profile leaders remain unrecognized and unappreciated, leading them to feel invisible. During talent reviews, executives will say, "I have no idea who that person is" or "I've been in meetings with them, but I never hear from them." When these leaders remain hidden, the company loses out on all that unused talent. They may even promote people with far *less* talent just because they're more visible. Gallup has found that companies miss the mark in their promotional and hiring decisions for leadership positions *82% of the time.* Allowing talent to remain invisible has serious repercussions for productivity and engagement as well.[v]

Don't fall into (or stay in) this trap. You must focus on bringing out the latent potential of your talented people so they'll become motivated, valued, and sought-after leaders. When these hidden leaders know how to convey confidence, command respect, and exude a professional magnetism that influences others, they'll inspire those around them and drive change.

Enable ordinary people to do extraordinary things.

Peter Drucker said, "The purpose of an organization is to enable ordinary people to do extraordinary things." Hidden leaders can become extraordinary when they grow and leverage a top-notch executive presence.

WHO are the hidden leaders?

+ Those in *a department that's low-profile* or far from the center of the action.
+ Those who are *quiet and reluctant to push themselves forward*, eclipsed by more forceful peers.
+ Those who *display some leadership potential, though it remains untapped because senior managers don't know they exist.*
+ Those who *took part in a project that failed*, which damaged their reputation.
+ Those *assigned to an unsupportive manager* who doesn't know how to encourage them to grow.
+ Those with *unconventional backgrounds.*
+ Those who *stepped off the upward mobility track for personal reasons*, transferring onto the children track, the back-to-school track, or the spouse relocation track.

The whole company, not just the individual, benefits when you find and identify these hidden leaders.

Dramatically boost retention and engagement.

How do you make sure your employees feel like an integral part of your company? Cultivate executive presence and provide the visibility they desire and deserve. Gartner has found that high-potential employees are 15% more likely than other employees to seek out new job opportunities if they don't believe you're grooming them for succession.[vi] Training your people to exude executive presence says, "You matter to us." It makes employees feel emotionally involved with the company. When you proactively work to identify and train your overlooked leaders, you'll also show them that you aim to promote from within. They'll envision an exciting future with your company, rather than thinking they'll only find opportunities for advancement elsewhere. People will want to be on your team, which will save you time and money by reducing recruitment costs and increasing employee retention rates.

Elevating your leaders' executive presence will also greatly improve engagement. When people feel valued, they'll produce better results. They'll have the confidence to bring great ideas to fruition and excited about what they are accomplishing. This creates a positive feedback loop in which the successes they experience fuel their desire to achieve more. As they enjoy the recognition that comes with strong performance, they'll feel driven to reach higher and higher, motivating their team to accomplish more ambitious goals.

> A leader's impact isn't just the end product of their work—it's their ability to shine as a confident, commanding, bold, decisive, and expressive leader.

When Intuit noticed it was experiencing a serious engagement problem, it began focusing on providing high-quality coaching for managers and giving them greater autonomy in solving problems.[vii] Within two years, engagement improved by 16%, reports the Society for Human Resource Management (SHRM). Intuit's stock rose in turn by almost 300%, and the company achieved the highest growth rate it had seen in four years. As this example clearly shows, your company's success depends on its employee retention and engagement.

Know the value each leader is contributing.

Oftentimes, the hidden leaders are the worker bees who put their heads down and get the work done. They let their work speak for itself, but that means senior leaders may have no idea what they actually contribute. Organizations cannot engage in effective decision-making when they don't have all the information about what their leaders are doing.

A leader's impact isn't just the end product of their work—it's their ability to shine as a confident, commanding, bold, decisive, and expressive leader. Letting their work speak for itself will directly undermine their executive presence and cause their company to gain less value from their efforts—partly because the company doesn't know what they've achieved. As each leader develops executive presence, others will know who they are and will appreciate the value they bring to the table.

Benefit from a diverse pool of talent.

Women, people of color, introverts, and those whose gender or sexual orientation is outside of the norm are prone to being overlooked and undervalued. Too often, companies miss out on leveraging their potential even when they have a phenomenal skill set. If you're underutilizing those who don't fit the traditional mold of a leader in your company, you're missing out on a vast pool of talent. Building a culturally diverse and inclusive leadership pool will give you access to an incredible range of insights, experience, and wisdom from which to draw. You'll avoid the groupthink that can result from operating in a silo, while helping your company to create an inclusive leadership pipeline. By supporting these leaders' executive-level growth, you'll fully leverage them and inspire their loyalty to your organization.

In today's competitive environment, focusing on diversity and inclusion is a must. Since 47% of the workers in this country are women[viii] and 37% are persons of color,[ix] it's time to stop overlooking these underrepresented groups. Providing executive presence training will allow these individuals to rise to their full potential, stepping into the leadership positions they deserve.

Many of these potential leaders would probably answer "yes" to most of the following questions:

+ Does top management often *overlook your insights and perspectives?*
+ Do you accomplish significant victories on key projects, yet your *low visibility prevents you from receiving the recognition you deserve?*
+ Do you believe that your *work should speak for itself*—that you shouldn't need to promote yourself to gain respect and influence within your company?

- Are your *colleagues getting more respect and influence than you are?*
- Do you realize that *talent, results, and competence aren't enough* to achieve career success?
- Do you wish your colleagues and managers *would value and appreciate your contributions?*
- Would you like to be *recognized as being highly capable and credible by upper management?*

For myriad reasons, people of marginalized groups may not put themselves forward or draw attention to themselves—and when they do, they may be overlooked. Exuding confidence doesn't come naturally to everyone. However, leaders from marginalized groups can absolutely learn to radiate conviction in their ideas and command respect from everyone at the table. Executive presence is the key to making their abilities so widely known that advancement is not just likely, but inevitable.

To encourage them along this journey, organizations must embrace six signature qualities of inclusive leadership, Deloitte explains.[x] These six qualities will help you mentor your diverse leaders as they rise to their full potential:

- Commitment
- Courage
- Cognizance of bias
- Curiosity
- Cultural intelligence
- Collaboration

Through commitment to inclusion, the courage to challenge the status quo, cognizance of their personal bias, curiosity about how other people view the world, an effort to become culturally intelligent, and proficiency in collaborating within diverse groups, you can nurture the development of all your rising stars.

This commitment to an inclusive leadership pipeline will benefit everyone within your organization. In a Deloitte study, 75% of respondents said they thrive in a diverse and inclusive environment. Many said such a workplace culture helps them to grow professionally and encourages creativity. Smart organizations are responding by making inclusiveness a priority through the recruitment of diverse employees for higher-level positions.

Executive presence is critical to leadership success.

78% of business leaders state that a low level of executive presence paralyzes career advancement.

Executive presence will propel you forward in all of these ways:

- Marking you as a next-level leader.
- Transforming self-doubt into confidence.
- Leading you to love your work more.
- Driving your team to accomplish bigger and bigger goals.

Let's consider how EP will benefit you in each of these ways.

Position you as a next-level leader.

The employees who are most likely to be chosen for next-level roles are the ones who are already viewed as capable and competent leaders. Because they exude confidence, senior executives see them as the leaders who will ensure the company's future success. They regularly receive opportunities for growth and advancement, including the training and mentoring that will help them continue honing their leadership abilities.

Just as executive presence is a prerequisite for next-level success, diminished executive presence will bring career advancement to a screeching halt. Seventy-eight percent of business leaders state that a low level of executive presence paralyzes career advancement.[xi] Leaders who lack executive presence will find themselves hitting an impenetrable ceiling. They'll fail to achieve their potential, become frustrated, and appear to lack conviction and power.

By taking the time to cultivate executive presence, you'll clear a path for yourself that ultimately leads to the upper echelons of leadership, if that's where you want to go. You'll see new doors opening for you as senior leaders become your advocates who nominate you for high-level projects and promotions. Other leaders will see you as an equal, believe in your abilities, and as a result, feel invested in your success.

Transform self-doubt into confidence.

With executive presence, self-doubt and uncertainty will transform into self-assurance, energy, and the confidence to successfully navigate the corporate landscape. You'll learn to think in new ways that will help you reframe your relationship to work, creating a more positive and productive attitude and belief system.

Don't worry if you can't imagine how that will look and feel right now. Executive presence can only be grown one step at a time, and through steady practice, you'll build your confidence to become a powerful leader you may not even recognize right now!

Love your work more.

As your executive presence grows, you'll gain more satisfaction from your daily work. You'll be more deeply engaged and excited about what you are doing.

As your executive presence starts to shine, you'll notice yourself doing these four things:

- Building meaningful relationships with peers and superiors across the organization, making your work more enjoyable.
- Lending your perspective and insight to others who seek it out, helping shape the success of company initiatives.
- Taking ownership of more complex and challenging projects, making your work more interesting.
- Becoming more fully seen for your contributions, making your work more satisfying.

Your work will become more dynamic and rewarding, giving you a higher level of fulfillment from your job.

Drive your team to accomplish bigger and bigger goals.

Cultivating executive presence won't just transform you as an individual—it will transform your team as well. The people you lead will benefit from the enhanced motivation they receive from you, and your whole team will flourish. You'll help people create a roadmap to their goals and stay the course to achieve them. When dealing with change, your calm, confident presence will help everyone around you to navigate the transition with grace and composure. Your peers and superiors will rely on you more fully as you further develop your executive presence.

As you reach your full potential as a leader, you'll tap into the hidden leadership qualities within your own people. You'll help them to awaken their own latent abilities and supercharge their strengths. As a result, you'll become a cherished mentor who helps create a leadership pipeline for your organization.

Eloise Strategically Grows Her Executive Presence

Problem:

Eloise, who'd been passed up twice for a promotion, finally realized she'd been leaving the fate of her career in someone else's hands. We discussed how she could demonstrate a stronger presence among her peers, to show she was ready for advancement.

Eloise needed to start leading from where she was rather than waiting for a golden opportunity to come along. She had been far too passive about letting her strengths shine, and she needed to take initiative to develop her own brand as a leader with executive presence.

Action:

Together, we determined ways that Eloise could make her expertise visible to colleagues and senior leaders rather than keeping it hidden. We also discussed how she could take more ownership of projects she was involved in by closely tracking their results and sharing them with senior leaders in an easily digestible way, rather than waiting for her boss to do it.

Results:

As she began to share her expertise with conviction in ways that benefited others, she built her influence among her coworkers and across functions. She also gained more attention for the results of her projects as she shared them directly with leaders. Her boss took note. Eloise was finally ready to move on to the next level, because she'd begun displaying the key ingredient for leadership success: executive presence.

Let's now dive deeper into what executive presence actually is, so you can learn to recognize it in yourself and others.

Chapter 2

What Executive Presence Entails

You probably have an image in mind of a leader with executive presence—even if the details are a bit vague. This person masterfully commands a room, exuding a magnetic force that makes everyone at the table seek her input and approval. Whether this leader has a gregarious personality or is quiet, poised, and self-possessed, her innate self-assurance reverberates throughout any space she inhabits.

Can you imagine yourself embodying the same behaviors as this powerful leader? Maybe you can, but you know you're still a few steps away from fully stepping into your potential. Or maybe it feels like an impossible goal. But as you methodically build the core qualities of executive presence, the impossible will become a reality.

Executive presence is easy to recognize, but hard to define.

I've asked over 150 leaders how they would define executive presence, and they named over 75 different attributes. These findings demonstrate that people have difficulty defining its core components.

Executive presence is an elusive quality—yet if it's lacking, you really notice its absence. A leader who lacks executive presence stands out in ways that don't feel elusive at all. Here are just a few examples:

- Rambling on and on, compulsively speaking with no clear purpose.
- Appearing quiet and reserved, rarely speaking up.

+ Being tentative and indecisive in decision-making.
+ Engaging in unassertive and passive behavior.

People who display these behaviors stand out for all the wrong reasons, sabotaging their achievement of their full potential. In a survey I conducted with 245 business leaders at a workshop on executive presence, 76% said that people who lack EP stand out from the crowd—but not for the reasons they hope.

> Executive presence is an elusive quality—yet if it's lacking, you really notice its absence.

Karen Captivates Leaders with Her Executive Presence

Problem:

In a talent review meeting, three different names came up. The executives at the table were working to create a succession plan that would replace a soon-to-retire leader. They concurred on the following points:

• One of the candidates displayed excellent performance.
• The other was extremely talented.
• The last one was very smart.

All executives said **SOMETHING was missing** from each of them. They couldn't put their finger on it, though. They argued and argued, and finally someone said, "*Executive presence!*" "Yes, that's it!" they all agreed.

Then, they argued over their individual interpretations of what executive presence is for the next hour. But ultimately, they all agreed that the winning candidate would need to speak with conviction, command respect, and demonstrate influence throughout the organization. They compared how each person led a meeting and presented ideas. None of them had that charisma and aura of authority that an inspiring leader carries.

Action:

Karen, the "talented one," happened to have an advocate sitting at that table. Her advocate emphasized why she needed to hone in on her executive presence. That's why Karen reached out for executive coaching assistance. We came up with a plan for how she could assert herself with conviction in meetings and discussions with leaders. We also outlined some actions she could take to present herself as more charismatic and grow her influence, like displaying more enthusiasm for her work and supporting her colleagues in their endeavors.

Results:

Six months down the road, the senior leaders held another talent review. Karen's name came up again, and this time, there was no contest. "She captures everyone's attention from the moment she walks into a room," said one leader. "When people have an idea, they want to hear what Karen thinks," said another. "She speaks boldly and directly, voicing her ideas with confidence," said a third. After this rave review, Karen is now preparing to assume her boss's job when he retires in the next year.

"She speaks boldly and directly, voicing her ideas with confidence."

As this story shows, even experienced leaders have difficulty describing executive presence—yet they all recognize it in action. People intuitively follow a leader who has EP, without even questioning whether they have it. Putting executive presence into words can be tough, since it's made up of various qualities that all work together. When we see it in practice, though, there's no question of whether a leader has it.

Subtle executive presence: Learn to recognize its nascent signs.

Executive presence can begin to show up in subtle ways as people build their confidence. Sometimes they've possessed a nascent form of executive presence all along. Often they have elements of EP in certain domains but not in others, and the domains where they're lacking cause those positive qualities to go unnoticed.

Do any of these statements ring true to you? If so, you may possess subtle elements of executive presence.

- I have a very high level of expertise in my industry, but I am insecure and self-doubting, which can cause others to think I lack knowledge and intelligence.
- I am a quiet and soft-spoken person, and that causes people who don't know me well to assume that I am not engaging and passionate. Within my own team, however, I'm very inspiring and enthusiastic.
- I am sometimes unorganized and unprepared when coming to meetings. This can cause others to think I am easily flustered and unstable, when I'm actually a clear, composed, and grounded communicator.
- I often appear indecisive because I weigh all of my options carefully. That causes others to think I lack confidence when I actually don't.
- I can be unassertive and complacent in group settings, especially in the presence of dominant personalities. This causes others to perceive me as not caring or not being willing to take a stand, when I actually do care. I will show my persuasive side when something extremely important needs to be communicated.
- I am an easygoing and laid-back person, and that causes others to overlook my strength, power, and conviction.
- I am usually very agreeable, which causes others to not notice when I am bold, convincing, and forceful.
- I don't get easily excited and show much emotion in meetings. This leads others to see me as uninspiring, when I'm actually encouraging and energizing with people one-on-one.
- I am extremely proficient and knowledgeable, and I love sharing my knowledge with others. However, I don't naturally hold their attention and make them excited to learn more.
- I am great at summarizing concepts concisely in a way that's easy to understand. However, I don't communicate with the strength and power that really drives ideas home.

- I tend to fly under the radar, which leads people to overlook how I have mentored many direct reports and even peers to success. I excel at inspiring and motivating others behind the scenes, even though I don't usually take center stage.
- I am often unclear, meandering, and confusing when communicating, which causes others to question whether I have conviction, can take accountability, and can be decisive. These three areas are strengths of mine, but they don't get noticed.
- I am a rambling, verbose, long-winded talker, which causes others to not just tune me out, but also to not notice when I am being decisive and confident.

When we think of executive presence, we tend to think of someone with an outgoing, dominant, and loud personality. However, executive presence isn't just about being the loudest person in the room. In the 2016 true-story film *Hidden Figures*, Katherine Johnson is put on the spot by her boss in a room filled with top-brass NASA officials—all of them male, all of them white.[i] Johnson, an African American woman vying for a seat at the table in the space race, is asked to lay out the math to bring John Glenn's space capsule out of orbit and back to Earth. She calmly strides up to the chalkboard to display not only her mathematical brilliance, but also her *aura of authority*.

As she explains the math, Johnson skillfully demonstrates each of the three main areas of executive presence:

- She shows gravitas in how she handles the situation by stepping up to the challenge, unfazed and in command.
- She claims authority by being bold and convincing in her speech.
- She makes herself understood by communicating concisely, with well-prepared and expressive words that establish her as credible and trustworthy.

Executive presence isn't just about being the loudest person in the room.

Johnson does not hesitate to seize the moment. Though she undoubtedly isn't immune to nervousness, she remains poised and in control, showing a clear self-assuredness that leads others to trust her conclusions. By doing so, she signals that she not only possesses incredible mathematical abilities, but also the markings of a great leader.

So, what exactly is executive presence?

Leaders with executive presence exude a certain magnetism that grabs people's attention. People lean in and want to listen to them.

Having this presence means radiating confidence in all of your interactions. It means communicating with conviction and clarity, avoiding ambiguity. And it means being a bold and decisive decision-maker and coming across as professional and competent.

People with executive presence have a reputation for making things happen. They're admired for exemplary leadership and respected as an authority. They earn people's respect—not because they demand it, but because they *command* it.

To cultivate executive presence, you need to look closely at how you show up at work, how you speak, and how you make decisions.

Telegraphing that you're in charge.

In its seminal definition of executive presence, the Center for Talent Innovation (CTI) characterizes EP as "a mixture of qualities that true leaders exude, culminating in an aura that telegraphs you're in charge or deserve to be."[ii] Without that aura of authority, it's hard to advance beyond a certain point in your career.

People with executive presence often come across as being in charge even when they're not the official leader. If working on a project with their boss's boss, their power and conviction makes it seem like they're at least a peer—and possibly the leader of the initiative. It's like when a supporting actor outshines the person with the lead role and gets all the praise in the reviews of the film. These people have the *It* factor that keeps all eyes on them, even if they're not the loudest ones in the room. Through all of their words and actions, they telegraph that they're in charge, meaning they're in the know, self-possessed, and poised to lead the team to success.

Take a close look at your ability to radiate that aura of authority.

+ Do you speak decisively when announcing a decision?
+ When an opportunity arises to show leadership, do you step up to the plate without hesitation, owning the role?
+ Do you share a clear rationale for your ideas, so you immediately gain buy-in?
+ Are you highly engaging in your speech, exuding a charisma that draws others to listen to you?

Practice seizing the opportunity to demonstrate your leadership in both large and small ways throughout your daily work. Rather than just going through your day in the same way you always do, ask yourself, "How does a leader with executive presence approach this situation?" Here are a few examples:

+ When your boss asks for a volunteer to lead a challenging new project, you offer to take the reins.
+ You mentally rehearse how you'll present a project proposal in a meeting with a compelling story and factual evidence.
+ Before your quarterly performance review, you create a draft career plan to share with your boss, as well as a list of points to get feedback on.

To grow or enhance these qualities, practice taking steps like these to exude authority and charisma in all your interactions.

> "...a mixture of qualities that true leaders exude, culminating in an aura that telegraphs you're in charge or deserve to be."
> Center for Talent Innovation (CTI)

Winning the confidence of those around you.

Employees throughout your company need to see you as a leader they believe in. A leader they respect. A leader with credibility. A leader who inspires confidence and whom others feel confident around. This is executive presence in action.

If you want to lead others, you can't just go through your daily work without an awareness of how every action and interaction comes across to them. How do they experience you? Do they view you as confident, bold, charismatic, in command, and radiating gravitas?

Take a close look at all of your behaviors, asking what qualities they radiate.

- How does your voice sound when you share an idea at a meeting? Do you stumble over your words or waver in your speech, or communicate clearly and powerfully?
- What does your body language say about you? Do you slouch or cross your arms, looking unsure or closed off—or do you put your shoulders back, sit up straight, and make direct eye contact?
- When speaking to senior leaders, does your approach change? Or do you speak with the same ease and confidence you use with peers?
- How do you enter a room? Do you immediately acknowledge people, boldly and without hesitation?

How do you feel about your own ideas? Do you believe in your own brilliance, or do you constantly doubt yourself? If you have a lot of insecurity, work to bolster your confidence by tackling increasingly bigger challenges. That approach will help you work through any of these confidence issues. Determine where you struggle, and at every opportunity, push yourself to step a little further outside of your comfort zone to exude confidence. This will get easier the more you do it, because it creates a positive feedback loop—you notice others responding to your confidence, which makes you *feel even more confident.*

Employees throughout your company
need to see you as a leader they
believe in. A leader they respect.

Painting a picture of yourself as a compelling force inside your organization.

To shine as a leader with executive presence, you need to become known as someone who influences outcomes, contributes to major decisions, and drives change. Don't wait for someone to bestow a certain title on you. Instead, leverage your influence now to positively shape outcomes. As you demonstrate your ability to influence others for the good of the organization, your colleagues, subordinates, and superiors will rely on your strength and wisdom.

Ask yourself how well you do all of the following:

+ Give others useful advice that helps them make the best decisions possible.
+ Coach and mentor others to success, including both direct reports and peers.
+ Follow through on the ideas you suggest, guiding them to fruition.
+ Voice ideas to people at all levels of the organization and across functions.
+ Build the trust with others that leads them to truly value your ideas and input.

Practice sharing your insights and opinions strategically and following up on the results. Take the time to check in on how projects are going, finding out if more advice is needed. By doing so, you'll show your investment in creating positive change and your commitment to seeing it through.

> To shine as a leader with executive presence, you need to become known as someone who influences outcomes, contributes to major decisions, and drives change.

Graham Grows an Aura of Authority

Problem:

A new GEC client, Graham, received this input from executives during a 360 survey: "People don't consider you a strong leader—the type to lead the charge or drive toward the future. Whenever a big initiative or transformation comes forward, leaders' names are thrown out to see which person would be best to lead that change. You are presented as part of the team that can support versus the one who can take charge."

"How important is it for him to be the one in charge?" one senior leader asked. "Deep down, does he really want this but doesn't know how to do it because it's not his personality type?" Only Graham himself could answer these questions, of course—and in fact, he *did* really want to learn to lead the charge.

Action:

Graham adopted a handful of go-to tactics for speaking up in meetings, and he practiced his delivery until he could voice his thoughts with authority. Graham also practiced reaching out to senior leaders on a weekly basis to offer insights, assistance, or updates on initiatives. By doing so, Graham established himself as a dynamic presence who could motivate others to achieve impressive outcomes.

Results:

Several months down the road, one exec nominated Graham to head up a project they were discussing. Another voiced skepticism, but a third advocated strongly for Graham, explaining how he'd really come into his own. The skeptic agreed to give him a shot—and Graham blew them away with the results his team achieved.

Notice executive presence in others.

Since most of us tend to have a hard time assessing ourselves, it's easier to start with noticing executive presence in others. Begin learning to identify what executive presence *is* and is *not* by looking for it in the people you work with. This exercise will help you learn to observe executive presence in action, so you know what qualities to emulate.

Identify the following four people in your company.

#1 and #2 – Two people with a high level of executive presence.
#3 – A person with a low degree of executive presence.
#4 – Anyone else who comes to mind.

1. _____

2. _____

3. _____

4. _____

Rate how well they each demonstrate executive presence.

Name of Employee Chosen	Poor	Below Average	Average	Above Average	Excellent
	O	O	O	O	O
	O	O	O	O	O
	O	O	O	O	O
	O	O	O	O	O

Now answer the following questions for each of the four people chosen.

+ Why did I give (*name of employee*) that specific rating?
+ What behaviors of theirs show they have executive presence?
+ What do they do to undermine their executive presence?

Person #1:
_____
_____
_____
_____

Person #2:
_____
_____
_____
_____

Person #3:

_____

_____

_____

_____

Person #4:

_____

_____

_____

_____

Why do you want to improve your executive presence?

People are motivated to develop executive presence for a number of reasons. The pie chart below shows a quick glance at the seven most important ones. We'll take a look at each of them in this section.

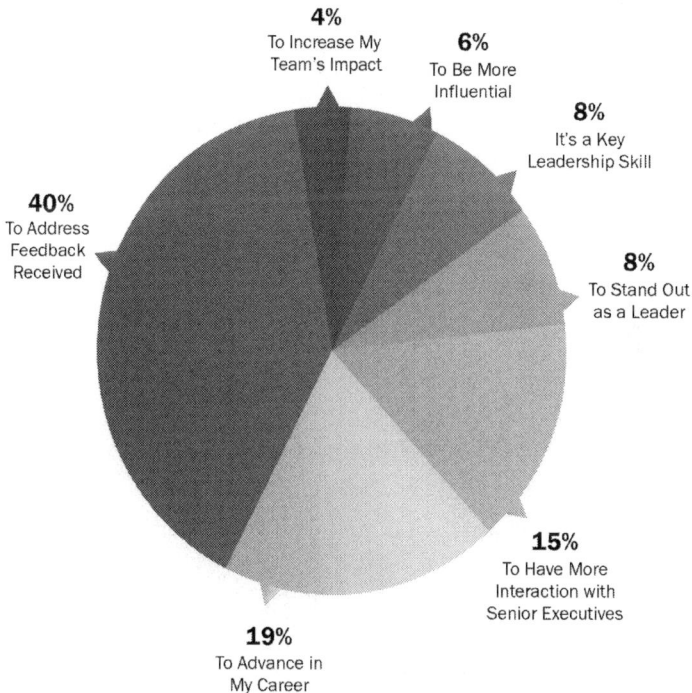

4%
To Increase My
Team's Impact

6%
To Be More
Influential

8%
It's a Key
Leadership Skill

8%
To Stand Out
as a Leader

40%
To Address
Feedback
Received

15%
To Have More
Interaction with
Senior Executives

19%
To Advance in
My Career

Source: GEC Research Center Survey, Poll of 425 U.S. Workers.

Feedback received from superiors.

The majority of professionals who want to improve their executive presence have been urged to do so by a boss or senior leader. This feedback is often vague, as the other person may not even know how to define EP—they just know it when they see it. If you've received this feedback, you may feel confused about what to do about it. The 3x3 EP Model will clarify exactly how to address this feedback.

If you're fortunate, executive presence makes up part of your existing development plan, and your boss may have suggested focusing on this area. Though you may be receiving higher-quality feedback than most, the 3x3 Model will still help you focus your efforts to build the most critical EP competencies.

Career advancement.

You may be proactively seeking to cultivate EP in order to move up in your organization. You know it's a key to advancement, as reaching and excelling at the next level requires an entirely new skill set. You want to cultivate executive presence to gain the confidence and competence to take the next steps.

Making an impact at the executive level.

You may wish to make a greater impact at the highest levels of your company. You want to be heard and understood by senior management, gaining respect among their ranks. To get there, you must present yourself as a next-level leader and influence upward. You know you'll gain great satisfaction from guiding company strategy and vision, which executive presence will allow you to do more effectively.

Standing out as a leader.

You may know that you need to improve your executive presence to build your visibility as a leader. Improving your presentation in both groups and one-on-one settings will help you make a lasting impression, you realize. Recognizing that you fall under the radar too often, you've learned that executive presence will get you noticed in positive ways.

To show that you're the confident, commanding leader whom others can rely on, you need to cultivate executive presence.

Improving leadership skills.

You may think about executive presence in broader terms, realizing the vital role it plays in leadership. To thrive as a leader, you know you need to grow your EP. This will help you become recognized as an effective leader, allowing you to take on increased responsibility.

Becoming more influential.

You may also wish to develop executive presence specifically to exert better command of a room and persuade people at all levels to believe in your ideas. You know that building influence through EP will help you win over peers, senior leaders, direct reports, clients, and others, so they will seek out and listen to your input.

Enhancing team capabilities.

People often wish to grow their EP to increase the impact of their team. They know that a leader with EP can guide their team to greater success, and they take great satisfaction from helping their team achieve ambitious goals.

As the survey results show, not everyone is motivated by a desire for advancement. Some people want to achieve more in their current role—or they may have already made their way to the top, and they want to leverage their position as effectively as possible. Other people *do* ultimately want a promotion, but more importantly, they wish to enhance their job satisfaction by excelling as a leader. They want more responsibility, influence, and engagement; they want a seat at the decision-making table. To grow this influence and show that you're the confident, commanding leader whom others can rely on, you need to cultivate executive presence.

Assess what motivates you to cultivate executive presence.

Now it's your turn to assess what motivates you to cultivate executive presence. Rate your level of agreement with each of the following statements to tune into what fuels your desire to grow your EP.

WHY DO YOU WANT TO GROW YOUR EP?

Select one of the following answers to each of these questions.

I have been advised by a superior to work on my EP.

Strongly Disagree	Disagree	Neutral	Agree	Strongly Agree
1	2	3	4	5

I wish to open new doors in my career, which will require a new skillset.

Strongly Disagree	Disagree	Neutral	Agree	Strongly Agree
1	2	3	4	5

I wish to have a greater impact at the highest levels of my company and be taken seriously by senior leaders.

Strongly Disagree	Disagree	Neutral	Agree	Strongly Agree
1	2	3	4	5

I need to boost my visibility and stand out— too often, I blend in too much.

Strongly Disagree	Disagree	Neutral	Agree	Strongly Agree
1	2	3	4	5

I want to grow a strong leadership skill set so I can truly thrive in my career.				
Strongly Disagree	Disagree	Neutral	Agree	Strongly Agree
1	2	3	4	5

I need to build my influence in all directions.				
Strongly Disagree	Disagree	Neutral	Agree	Strongly Agree
1	2	3	4	5

I want to become a more effective team leader.				
Strongly Disagree	Disagree	Neutral	Agree	Strongly Agree
1	2	3	4	5

Your answers most likely show that a combination of several factors is driving you to improve your executive presence. There's no "score" for this exercise—hopefully it has simply helped you zero in on your own motivation for doing so, which can continue to propel you forward on this transformative journey.

Common situations where having executive presence matters.

You're being continuously judged and evaluated at work on whether you have executive presence or not—even if people aren't aware that they're judging you. Here are some of the main situations where an enhanced executive presence matters. Think of them as opportunities to gain exposure for your EP.

+ Attending regular staff meetings
+ Giving team updates
+ Having discussions with clients
+ Sharing a new vision
+ Leading a project
+ Advocating for your team or employee
+ Attending community events
+ Making presentations to superiors
+ Guiding your team in a new direction
+ Meeting with external stakeholders
+ Giving a presentation
+ Influencing others (in any direction)
+ Implementing organizational changes
+ Presenting a business case when seeking funding
+ Conducting performance reviews
+ Coping with setbacks
+ Managing a crisis
+ Running into senior executives
+ Mediating a disagreement or conflict
+ Holding one-on-ones with direct reports
+ Getting the necessary resources for your team
+ Chatting informally in the hallway
+ Participating in cross-departmental meetings
+ Discussing ideas with colleagues over coffee
+ Joining all-hands meetings

This list covers quite a range of situations, as you've probably noticed. That's why executive presence has to become a part of who you *are,* not just something you turn on once in a while. In fact, executive presence must become part of your DNA, because there is no situation where your performance will not improve dramatically from having a high level of EP.

Which audience needs to see your executive presence?

The quick answer: everyone. Here's a more detailed breakdown of the various audiences who need to see you as having EP:

- Subordinates
- Coworkers
- Your boss
- Peers across functions
- Superiors
- Senior leadership
- Customers
- Clients
- Vendors

Lack of EP isn't something that can be hidden. It will be clearly noted and filed away. Strive to establish your EP in your interactions with all of these groups.

Let's take a look at a variety of situations that every leader faces at one point or another. The following two exercises will help you to notice and evaluate your own level of executive presence, and to recognize it in others.

Would you show executive presence in these scenarios?

As you read through these 10 common circumstances where executive presence is critical, ask yourself this: "Would I display executive presence in this situation?" Rate yourself on a scale of 1 to 5 for each of them.

1. *You have an important presentation to give to five leaders who are a couple levels above you. Since you've never spoken to this group before, you want to make an excellent first impression. Consider whether you come across as confident and articulate in your delivery.*

Would I display executive presence in this situation?				
Strongly Disagree	Disagree	Neutral	Agree	Strongly Agree
1	2	3	4	5

2. *You need to make a decision on a high-profile project. Other leaders and subordinates are awaiting your verdict. Consider whether you feel sure of yourself or uncertain, and how you come across to others.*

Would I display executive presence in this situation?				
Strongly Disagree	Disagree	Neutral	Agree	Strongly Agree
1	2	3	4	5

3. *You're sitting in a meeting where you have an opinion to share. Around you sit a mixed group of peers and leaders. Everyone is talking animatedly; there's hardly a break in the conversation. Consider whether you make your ideas known, and how others perceive you when—or if—you speak up.*

Would I display executive presence in this situation?				
Strongly Disagree	Disagree	Neutral	Agree	Strongly Agree
1	2	3	4	5

4. *Your boss's boss drops by while you're convening a team meeting, wanting to see what's happening on the ground. Consider how you conduct yourself at this meeting, and whether your team responds with enthusiasm.*

Would I display executive presence in this situation?				
Strongly Disagree	Disagree	Neutral	Agree	Strongly Agree
1	2	3	4	5

5. *You run into a top leader in the elevator. She asks for an update on your current project. Consider whether you share a concise overview with conviction, or whether your reply sounds confused or hum-drum.*

Would I display executive presence in this situation?				
Strongly Disagree	Disagree	Neutral	Agree	Strongly Agree
1	2	3	4	5

6. *Your boss announces an important new initiative that senior leadership has been planning and asks who is interested in leading it. Consider whether you step forward and take the reins, or whether you second-guess your abilities and let someone else take charge.*

Would I display executive presence in this situation?				
Strongly Disagree	Disagree	Neutral	Agree	Strongly Agree
1	2	3	4	5

7. *You need to have a tough conversation with a direct report who isn't meeting expectations. Consider whether you feel so anxious that it shows, or whether you master your emotions and remain poised and in command.*

Would I display executive presence in this situation?				
Strongly Disagree	Disagree	Neutral	Agree	Strongly Agree
1	2	3	4	5

8. *An advocate invites you to lunch with several superiors. This is a great chance to build a rapport with them. Consider how you interact with them— whether you relate to them as a peer or feel like a subordinate.*

Would I display executive presence in this situation?				
Strongly Disagree	Disagree	Neutral	Agree	Strongly Agree
1	2	3	4	5

9. *You're announcing a new initiative to your team. They're gathered around you, listening. Consider whether they are on the edge of their seats, hanging on your every word and waiting for the chance to sign up—or whether they look unenthused or even skeptical.*

Would I display executive presence in this situation?				
Strongly Disagree	Disagree	Neutral	Agree	Strongly Agree
1	2	3	4	5

10. *You're speaking to a large group of superiors, peers, and subordinates about the results of your latest project. Consider whether you command attention the moment you take the stage, emanating charisma, or whether you cower in the spotlight and muddle through your presentation.*

Would I display executive presence in this situation?				
Strongly Disagree	Disagree	Neutral	Agree	Strongly Agree
1	2	3	4	5

Tally up your total score. If you got 44–50, you're doing fantastic. You may have some work to do, but you're well on your way to radiating executive presence on a daily basis. If you scored from 36–43, you sometimes show executive presence—either in certain situations where you feel the most confident, or in subtle ways. If you got 26–35, you occasionally show certain executive presence qualities, although people have to be paying close attention to notice them. If you scored from 10–25, you haven't yet begun to exude a noticeable executive presence—but you'll see changes before very long as you put the lessons in this book to work.

Chapter 3

Learn the 3x3 Executive Presence Model

Executive presence doesn't have to be a mystery. The 3x3 Executive Presence Model outlines 3 domains that each encompass 3 qualities of executive presence, for a total of 9 core competencies. This model breaks down exactly what makes up executive presence, giving you an easy-to-use guide to growing your EP.

These 9 competencies distinguish the best
executives from others.
The remarkable from the ordinary. The
exceptional from the average.

The 3x3 Executive Presence Model is based on solid research.

I created the 3x3 Executive Presence Model based on 15 years of studying executive presence. To solidify the information I share in the model, my company, GEC Research Center, conducted research with over 1,400 of my executive coaching clients and 7,500 workshop participants. These established leaders provided feedback that lent great clarity on what makes a leader with executive presence. Ultimately, GEC isolated the executive presence (EP) characteristics that showed up in the top-performing leaders time after time, so others can follow in their footsteps.

The leaders attending the workshops and participating in 1:1 executive coaching hail from many of the most successful companies in the world:

Amazon	Autodesk	The Federal
Starbucks	Boeing	Reserve Bank
Toyota	Kohl's	National Basketball
Eli Lilly	Starbucks	Association (NBA)
NBC Universal	NASA	The Ritz-Carlton
Hewlett-Packard	Comcast	Hotels
Cisco Systems	Novartis	Levi Strauss &
Google	Gap Inc.	Company
Oracle	PG&E	The Peninsula Hotels
Pricewaterhouse	Gensler	IBM
Coopers	Citibank	Motorola
Procter & Gamble	Gilead	New York Times
Shell Chemicals	CVS Pharmacy	Brother International
Wells Fargo Bank	VMware	Corporation
Blue Cross Blue Shield	Takeda	BEA Systems
Microsoft	Aramark	Intuit
Deloitte	Fidelity	Nestle USA
Genentech	Bank of America	Ebay
Accenture	Marriott Hotels	Macy's
Sanofi	Warner Bros.	Visa International
Nissan	Entertainment	Union Bank of
Corning	Charles Schwab	California
Netflix	Electronic Arts	Sapient Corporation
Oracle	Morgan Stanley	Coldwell Banker
Portland Parks	Verizon	Kaiser Permanente
Foundation	Williams-Sonoma Inc.	Aetna
Henkel		

As an executive coach, I've had the opportunity to learn firsthand what a leader at this type of company does to project a top-notch executive presence. And as you can see, the research conducted by GEC with these leaders spans a wide variety of industries.

The results shone a spotlight on 312 behaviors: 145 positive and 167 negative. My team conducted cluster analysis, a method of organizing related behaviors into the same groups, called clusters. Ultimately, this brought us to a total of 30 behaviors: 15 showing strong executive presence, and 15 showing a lack of executive presence. Then, we tracked patterns for these 30 behaviors. From this analysis, we saw that exceptional leaders with executive presence exhibit 9 recurring positive behaviors. We then narrowed the final positive executive presence competencies to the 9 qualities that now make up the 3x3 Executive Presence Model. These 9 competencies distinguish the best executives from the rest. The remarkable from the ordinary. The exceptional from the average.

This research showed that the leaders who shine the most, achieve greatness for themselves, and create immense success for their organizations are the ones who embrace and utilize *gravitas*, *authority*, and *expression*. These 3 domains are the foundational pillars holding up the 9 executive presence competencies: confident, commanding, charismatic, decisive, bold, influential, vocal, insightful, and clear. These are the qualities you must dedicate yourself to growing so you can exude and embody them for far-reaching impact and success.

Learn which executive presence behaviors matter most.

Let's take a more detailed look at each of the three executive presence (EP) domains. To be a leader with executive presence, you must:

- *Radiate gravitas.* Leaders with executive presence demonstrate an innate self-assurance that leads others to trust them implicitly. They exude charisma and passion for what they do, and their belief in their work acts as a powerful driving force that motivates all those around them. They step up to the plate whenever strong leadership is needed, and they command a room just by showing up.

- *Act with authority.* Leaders who model executive presence are assertive and persuasive, projecting an aura of being in charge. They lead by example and act decisively, taking strategic risks. The strength and resolve that emanates from these leaders makes others naturally follow them and seek their input.
- *Express yourself fully.* Leaders with executive presence make their ideas and opinions known. They speak candidly and eloquently, and their concise, polished words resonate widely. They are outspoken but share the most essential ideas rather than rambling, and thus, when they speak, people pay close attention.

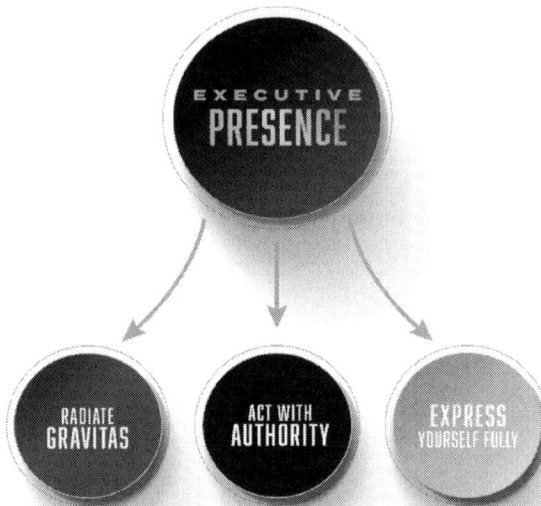

Each of these three key executive presence domains is made up of three core EP qualities. Now, let's take a closer look at the most essential behaviors within each of those domains.

In our survey, the GEC Research team asked a sample of 1,400 middle managers, high-level leaders, and other employees which specific behaviors are most crucial in helping leaders exude executive presence. From the data collected via both workshops and one-on-one executive coaching, here are the qualities they found most important to executive presence.

WHICH EXECUTIVE PRESENCE BEHAVIORS MATTER MOST?

% of leaders who say it is absolutely essential for a leader to be ...

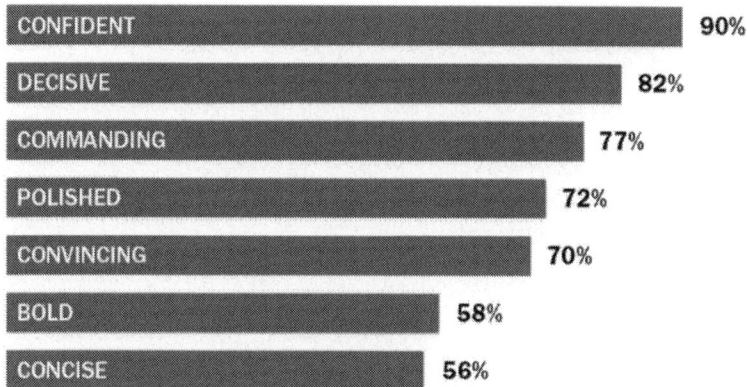

Behavior	%
CONFIDENT	90%
DECISIVE	82%
COMMANDING	77%
POLISHED	72%
CONVINCING	70%
BOLD	58%
CONCISE	56%

Source: GEC Research Center Survey, poll of 1,400 U.S. Workers

As you can see, the majority of participants in this survey said that *confident*, *decisive*, and *commanding* are the top three executive presence qualities a leader needs to radiate. But each quality in this chart is essential, contributing to the perception that a leader has what it takes to guide the team to success in any situation[1]. As discussed previously, having a *balanced* range of these competencies is essential. If you're extremely decisive or bold, but neglectful of the interpersonal skills that build charisma or allow you to effectively express yourself, you'll probably rub people the wrong way.

> Confident, decisive, and commanding
> are the top three executive presence
> qualities a leader needs to radiate.

The study identified nine total qualities that reveal executive presence, grouped by the three key EP domains in the following chart.

---

1   While analyzing the results of this survey, the research team surmised that "polished" and "concise" both strongly pertain to one of the nine core EP competencies, "clear." Additionally, we found "convincing" to be strongly associated with "influential," another of the nine core competencies.

COMPETENCIES FOR EACH OF THE EXECUTIVE PRESENCE DOMAINS

The results of the study also revealed nine behaviors of a leader with strong executive presence.

DOMAINS	COMPETENCIES
GRAVITAS	Confident
	Commanding
	Charismatic
AUTHORITY	Decisive
	Bold
	Influential
EXPRESSION	Vocal
	Insightful
	Clear

Learn which behaviors most undermine executive presence.

As you work to become a stronger leader, it's important to understand what an ineffective leader looks like. In the survey, participants were asked which specific behaviors most hinder leaders and prevent them from exuding executive presence. Here's what they said.

WHICH BEHAVIORS MOST UNDERMINE EXECUTIVE PRESENCE?

% saying these behaviors show a lack of EP

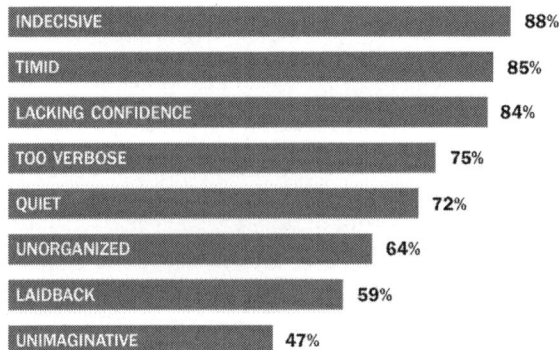

Behavior	%
INDECISIVE	88%
TIMID	85%
LACKING CONFIDENCE	84%
TOO VERBOSE	75%
QUIET	72%
UNORGANIZED	64%
LAIDBACK	59%
UNIMAGINATIVE	47%

Source: GEC Research Center Survey, Poll of 1,400 U.S. Workers.

People often display these behaviors unintentionally, without realizing they are undermining their executive presence. Overall, the study revealed nine key behaviors that show a lack of executive presence, as outlined in the following chart, which illustrates how each of these behaviors undermines one of the three core domains of executive presence.

QUALITIES SHOWING A LACK OF EXECUTIVE PRESENCE

The results of the study revealed nine behaviors that show a lack of executive presence.

DOMAINS	INADEQUACIES
GRAVITAS	Unconfident
	Easygoing
	Dull
AUTHORITY	Indecisive
	Timid
	Uninfluential
EXPRESSION	Nonvocal
	Uninformed
	Unclear

We'll be taking a deep dive into the 3x3 Executive Presence Model within the chapters that follow. However, this can all sound a bit abstract until you examine how you display (or don't display) these qualities in a particular situation. Let's take a look at how you show up with or without EP in the context of meetings.

How do you show up at meetings—with or without executive presence?

Why meetings? Analyzing your behavior in meetings is the easiest way to understand and quickly assess how well you show up with executive presence in your daily work. Meetings are an excellent environment in which to evaluate yourself and others because you participate in them regularly and can therefore notice clear patterns in how you show up.

Think of two recent meetings. Jot down the theme or objective of those meetings and who was in attendance.

MEETING #1

Theme:

_____

_____

_____

_____

Participants:

_____

_____

_____

_____

Which executive presence competencies did YOU display in the meeting? Refer to the table "Competencies for Each of the Executive Presence Domains" and jot down the ones you exhibited.

_____

_____

_____

_____

Next, reflect on the behaviors of others in attendance. **Jot down the executive presence competencies THEY displayed in the meeting.**

_____

_____

_____

_____

Which executive presence competencies did you LACK in the meeting? Refer to the table "Qualities Showing a Lack of Executive Presence" and jot down these competencies.

_____

_____

_____

_____

Next, reflect on the behaviors of others in attendance. **Jot down the executive presence competencies THEY lacked in the meeting.**

_____

_____

_____

_____

MEETING #2

Theme:

_____

_____

_____

Participants:

_____

_____

_____

Which executive presence competencies did YOU display in the meeting? Refer to the table "Competencies for Each of the Executive Presence Domains" and jot down these competencies.

_____

_____

_____

Next, reflect on the behaviors of others in attendance. **Jot down the executive presence competencies THEY displayed in the meeting.**

_____

_____

_____

_____

Which executive presence competencies did you LACK in the meeting? Refer to the table "Qualities Showing a Lack of Executive Presence" and jot down these competencies.

_____

_____

_____

_____

Next, reflect on the behaviors of others in attendance. **Jot down the executive presence competencies THEY lacked in the meeting.**

_____

_____

_____

_____

Tracking how you show up at meetings (with or without EP) will help you clearly evaluate your development. Your regular work meetings give you an easy way to benchmark your progress and determine where you need to focus your efforts.

Now we'll delve into the 3x3 Model, which will serve as your roadmap to honing your executive presence and maximizing your impact.

Chapter 4

Avoid Undermining Your Executive Presence

No one else can limit your executive presence or decide what is possible for you to achieve. You can only undermine it yourself—and when you allow it to flourish, no one else can hold you back.

How are you limiting your executive presence in your daily work? Perhaps you are realizing that you back down too quickly when someone disagrees with you, which is undermining your influence (and thus, your authority). Perhaps you are realizing that you don't step up to the plate often enough when a situation calls for a strong leader, lessening your ability to be in command (and thus, your gravitas). Or perhaps you are not choosing your words carefully before you begin speaking, preventing you from being a clear communicator and undermining your expression. After you come to these realizations, you can forge a pathway forward. But along the way, you'll find that the greatest obstacles are within. To overcome these challenges, you need to confront the greatest barrier of all: internal limiting beliefs. Let's take a close look at what these beliefs are, and how they undermine your executive presence.

You'll find that the greatest obstacles are within.

The biggest barrier to executive presence is self-doubt.

Internal limiting beliefs are the thoughts and preconceptions you have about yourself, which guide your behavior. Our internal limiting beliefs can be incredibly powerful even when based on false premises. Often, though, people aren't even aware of what their limiting beliefs are—and they remain oblivious to how these limiting beliefs are hindering their executive presence.

These beliefs have an especially strong hold on us when we don't consciously recognize them. Many people go through life being controlled by their internal limiting beliefs without becoming aware of them and realizing that they are false—and that the real issue lies in their self-confidence. To flourish as a leader with executive presence, you need to meet these beliefs head-on to challenge, unpack, and overcome them.

Tania Taps Into Her Strengths as a Leader

Problem:

Tania had been a graphic designer before becoming creative director of her department, and she'd never gone through formal leadership training of any kind. Unfortunately, her technical prowess didn't translate into managerial success.

In meetings, Tania always sounded tentative and unsure of herself. Even her direct reports characterized her as meek and unassertive. She would overanalyze a decision to no end, requesting input from everyone else but not sharing any of her own. Tania spoke in a quiet voice that lacked conviction, which didn't inspire much confidence in her direct reports. She lacked authority and urgently needed to develop it in order to effectively lead. But deep within, she felt she was not naturally a confident, authoritative leader and could never develop executive presence.

However, Tania had a number of positive qualities as well. She knew how to prepare well for a project and how to keep the workflow organized, since she'd been deeply immersed in the process for years herself. Thus, she *knew* how to direct her team. She just needed to trust herself to do it, and to learn to give directives rather than soft-spoken suggestions. She also had an inner passion for the work that did reveal itself to those who knew her well.

Action:

Through executive coaching, Tania learned to identify and challenge the false beliefs she held about her own abilities. She agreed to practice putting a stake in the ground for the smaller decisions and to work her way up to the big ones. She also promised to use her impeccable organizational skills to prepare her thoughts on key agenda topics *before* meetings. Through coaching on how to effectively make decisions, she learned to stop trying to gain 100% of the information every time she made a choice. She learned to trust her gut and gain input from a few people instead of fifteen. She also practiced using language that conveyed authority, such as saying "I know" rather than "I think" and cutting out filler phrases before getting to her main point.

Results:

Tania's boss confided that while he'd had some initial concerns about her ability to lead, these improvements had blown him away. Tania's team became more energized than ever, fueled by her contagious enthusiasm for the work—which she'd now learned to convey to all those around her. She'd overcome her internal limiting beliefs to truly thrive as a leader with a growing executive presence.

You may possess deep-seated feelings of inadequacy that keep you locked into the same unhealthy thinking patterns, which translates into behaviors that undermine your executive presence. Everyone has experienced the limiting power of self-doubt at one time or another in their career. These internal beliefs can hinder your career success in a major way, unless you correct them. They can bring your ability to develop executive presence to a halt, preventing you from trying new things and stepping out of your comfort zone.

Remember that one of the core competencies of executive presence is confidence. All of the other eight competencies actually rely on confidence as a foundation. It is very difficult to be commanding, charismatic, bold, decisive, and vocal (to name a few) if you don't have a strong foundation of confidence.

While it's important to think critically about the areas you need to develop, you need a strong foundation of confidence to actually be able to take action. And that confidence comes from healthy, balanced self-talk that acknowledges and celebrates your strengths.

"Self-doubt is the mortal enemy of executive presence," says Chris

Westfall in *Forbes*[i]. However, you can counteract insecure thinking with another point of view, as he notes. Most of us have multiple perspectives of our own skills and talents. Often we tune into the self-doubting voice rather than the soft, still one that says, "You've done incredible things before. You have what it takes." However, it's still there, and you can encourage it to speak more loudly by genuinely tuning in to what it has to say. Imagine how a trusted friend or colleague who knows your work well would speak to you. What assurances would they give about your performance and potential? Give this reassurance to yourself, and really take it in.

"Self-doubt is the mortal enemy of executive presence."
Chris Westfall

Jeanette Takes a Seat at the Table

Problem:

Jeanette, an HR director, was at a meeting with all the company VPs and the CEO. The VPs left to discuss something for 10 minutes. Jeanette went over to the CEO to ask him a question about the agenda and sat in the chair next to him. As the VPs began coming back into the room, she started getting up to give her seat back to them. However, the CEO said, "Stay where you are." He saw her and valued her. He didn't feel she needed to leave her seat at the table.

Jeanette didn't yet see herself in the same way the CEO saw her. She began to realize that how she presented herself—what space she felt she could take up, and how—reflected her level of confidence. While a select few people like the CEO might see her actual competencies despite her lack of confidence, most would not. She needed to portray confidence in order to inspire others to feel confident in her.

Action:

In future meetings, Jeanette began arriving early and taking a seat by a high-level leader. As they chatted before the meeting, she spoke to them like peers rather than superiors. She sounded more relaxed and sparked genuine conversation about their current projects and areas of interest. She casually mentioned important developments in her own work.

Results:

Jeanette had changed her own mindset so that she was no longer viewing these leaders as more important than herself, but as peers. In doing so, she'd claimed a real seat at the table.

Think of the situations that bring up feelings of self-doubt for you. Chances are, you experience self-doubt when in meetings with people who are more influential and powerful than you are right now. This self-doubt destabilizes your executive presence, becoming a self-fulfilling prophecy. How can you be fully in your power in a room full of strong, confident leaders?

You probably already have some level of confidence in your skill set and expertise. You might even rate your technical prowess very highly. Now you need to translate that confidence into the ability to command a room and influence senior leaders.

> Be fully in your power in a room
> full of strong, confident leaders.

Gunther Grows His Presentation Skills

Problem:

Gunther had a strong belief in his technical knowledge and abilities. In fact, his peers had recently rated him a 9.5 out of 10 in terms of skill level. When he spoke to senior leaders, though, his confidence plummeted. He felt like he couldn't articulate his ideas, or even formulate them. Later on, he would think of the perfect thing to say—but it was too late. Gunther began clamming up in those interactions. His confidence level and executive presence were about a 3 out of 10.

After one particularly unsuccessful encounter, his boss called him into her office. "I didn't just invite you to that meeting to give you a chance to build a rapport with a senior leader," she said. "I knew you could actually explain the project results better than I could. You know that stuff like the back of your hand. There's no one I'd trust more to relay that info–not even myself."

Action:

Gunther's boss didn't give up on him just yet. A week later, she asked him to pretend she was a senior leader and to prepare to deliver a three-minute overview of project results to her. Gunther spent 15 minutes outlining his thoughts beforehand, as directed. Then he went to her office and delivered the report. His boss gave him pointers on strengthening his performance, and he tried it again. "That was excellent. You are ready," she told him.

His boss invited him to present the project update at a senior-level meeting later that week. Gunther realized he'd felt a bit awkward about the idea of role-playing before, but now he knew it was critical to growing his confidence. He practiced with two of his peers, inviting them to ask him tough questions that leaders might pose. By the day of the presentation, he had a solid response to each of them.

Results:

Finally the moment came. Gunther stepped into the conference room and took a seat at the table. He reminded himself that he deserved to be there, as senior leaders needed his knowledge and perspective. It wasn't a personal favor to him. It was for the good of the company. When Gunther's turn came to speak, he eloquently delivered his message. The leaders sounded truly appreciative as they thanked him for sharing his thoughts, and he knew he'd nailed it. He also felt much less nervous about the idea of doing it again! Something had shifted for him. Gunther had begun projecting executive presence, and now that he knew he could carry himself with it, his self-doubt continued to subside.

The success you've experienced thus far in your career may have relied on your expertise and technical knowledge. Your future success, however, will draw much more upon your confidence and ability to lead, influence others, and exude a strong executive presence. Like the clients in these case studies, you need to realize that you deserve a seat at the table. You're there for a reason, not by happenstance. You bring a great deal of value, and you are needed there.

You deserve a seat at the table.

The movie *Hoosiers* shares a great lesson about recognizing your own capabilities. A small-town basketball team that has only played for hometown crowds in very small venues holding 30 to 50 people makes it all the way to the state finals. They'll be playing for a crowd of twenty thousand, against bigger, far more accomplished players. They're understandably petrified. Their coach brings them to the gigantic arena where they'll be playing and asks them to stand on a chair and measure the hoop's height. They tell him that it's 10 feet high. Their coach then asks them how tall the hoop in their home gym is. Ten feet, they tell him. There's no difference between playing at home and playing here in front of tens of thousands of people, he's showing them.

Every leader needs to learn the same lesson as these small-town high school basketball players. There's no difference between talking with a peer and talking with a senior leader in the board room, unless you *allow* there to be a difference. The players in *Hoosiers* remembered that they were on that court for a reason, just as you're at the table for a reason. Seize the moment by showing your fellow leaders that you have the confidence to speak to them as equals.

Imposter syndrome: Why it strikes and how to combat it.

Experiencing imposter syndrome means doubting whether you actually have the skills, competence, or qualifications to excel in a particular role. Many people suffer from imposter syndrome as they move up to a new position with increased responsibilities. It especially shows up when leaders advance quickly, taking on new roles and identities that they don't quite feel confident about filling—even if they felt highly confident in their previous position. They feel like they don't quite belong in the new role or trust themselves to carry it out. Feeling like an imposter seriously undermines their ability to exude executive presence. It's hard to radiate gravitas, carry yourself with an aura of authority, or express yourself powerfully when you don't truly believe you deserve to be where you are today.

Over 70% of the U.S.
population has experienced
imposter syndrome.

This dilemma is incredibly common: Over 70% of the U.S. population has experienced imposter syndrome (IS), a study in the *Journal of Behavioral Science* says.[ii] Most of us will experience it at one point or another. However, some people work through it as they begin to fully identify with their new role, while for others, it lingers for months or even years.

Psychologists Suzanne Imes and Pauline Rose Clance first described imposter syndrome in the 1970s. It often causes high-level achievers to attribute their success more to luck than to skill, leaving them afraid of being found out a fraud.[iii] If you have imposter syndrome, you may find yourself suddenly lacking confidence even if you had it in your previous role. Here are some of the symptoms you may experience as a result.

+ Feeling incompetent to fulfill your new role
+ Experiencing self-doubt
+ Lacking conviction
+ Feeling insecure
+ Believing you don't deserve to be here
+ Not speaking up (even if you used to do so)

You may lose trust in yourself, even if you used to trust your intuition and speak your mind. That experience can feel disorienting. A negative feedback loop begins: You feel anxious about the fact that you are experiencing imposter syndrome, believing this signals that something is wrong. This solidifies the idea that you are out of place in the new role, which can cause your imposter syndrome to linger for much longer than necessary. That's a major reason why so many leaders who have risen to higher-level positions haven't mastered the competencies of executive presence that will allow them to thrive in their new role.

For women, imposter syndrome can be especially consequential: In an internal study, Hewlett-Packard found that women only apply for a job if they feel they fit 100% of the requirements, whereas men apply if they have 60% of the expected competencies.[iv] That suggests women are far more likely to feel unprepared for their leadership roles than men, even if in reality they have at least as strong a skill set. Further, in *Cracking the Code: Executive Presence and Multicultural Professionals*, Sylvia Ann Hewlett found that multicultural leaders are less likely to have support from their superiors in developing their leadership competencies, which places them at a disadvantage.[v] Intentionally working to cultivate executive presence therefore holds particular importance for women, people of color, and anyone else who doesn't fit the stereotypical mold of a leader! As you grow your executive presence, you'll increase your sense of belonging in every context and trust yourself to step into higher-level roles with grace and skill.

Do you have imposter syndrome?

Dr. Clance came up with a scale called the Imposter Test for assessing whether you have imposter syndrome.[vi] A positive response to statements like the following would support the presence of IS.

+ "When I've succeeded at something and received recognition for my accomplishments, I have doubts that I can keep repeating that success."
+ "I often compare myself to those around me and think they may be more intelligent than I am."
+ "If I receive a great deal of praise and recognition for something I've accomplished, I tend to discount the importance of what I've done."
+ "I'm afraid people important to me may find out that I'm not as capable as they think I am."

Do these statements resonate with you? If so, it's time to address your imposter syndrome so it doesn't hold back your development of executive presence.

Orla Overcomes Imposter Syndrome

Problem:

Orla had been a powerhouse in her previous role as a manager. Driven and capable, she fired up her team to achieve more than they believed possible. But when she received a promotion to a prestigious position, Orla felt shaken.

Even though she'd proven her strong leadership skills, she began to doubt her ability to handle the new responsibilities. It involved a lot of strategic planning and collaboration with high-level people. Could she really demonstrate the high-level visionary thinking needed for the new role?

As she stepped into the position of director, Orla felt out of place. The transition had destabilized her nascent executive presence, causing her to show up as self-doubting and indecisive as well as quieter and less bold than normal. She was good at managing her team, but she felt deeply anxious about the idea of having to eloquently present a strategy to the CEO. Maybe they'd jumped the gun in promoting her, she thought. At meetings with other high-level leaders, she still felt like a subordinate. She second-guessed her thoughts, causing her to rarely speak up.

Action:

One of the other directors invited her to lunch one day. "I know this position is a big leap from your previous role," he said. "It felt pretty daunting for me when I stepped into this role myself. Just know that we've all been there, and we understand. But you were chosen for a reason. I'm here to support you in learning this new role, and I know you're going to master it sooner than you might think."

Orla realized that she had imposter syndrome—and that it was totally normal. But she didn't have to stay in that mentality. She began to embrace the idea that she would soon feel comfortable in the new role, and until then, she could trust her new mentors to give her advice and guidance. She began to voice her ideas in strategic discussions and to weigh in on others' proposals. After a few weeks, she was excitedly debating ideas and finding it easier to trust her intuition on big decisions. She followed the lead of her fellow leaders, emulating their positive attributes like big-picture thinking and listening to their gut reaction—and it paid off.

Results:

Orla now felt like she belonged in the position of director. She knew others appreciated her presence, and she'd begun exuding executive presence no matter who was at the table. She'd also learned that it was okay to be vulnerable by talking about what she was going through with her peers, because they'd all been there before.

As this story shows, being comfortable in some contexts doesn't always translate into being comfortable in new contexts where the stakes are higher. You must work to gradually increase your confidence in the new environment—hopefully with support from a colleague or mentor. Remember that imposter syndrome is completely normal, and everyone in your new peer group probably felt that way at one point or another. Imposter syndrome is not logical—like yourself, each of those people was promoted for a reason and was probably quite capable of doing the job. In fact, imposter syndrome can appear despite abundant evidence of high achievement. It can appear despite excellent performance reviews, strong credibility and respect, and a high-level title. Despite all of this evidence, it keeps you stuck in an *illogical* fixation on your insecurities.

Imposter syndrome can appear despite abundant evidence of high achievement.

If you find yourself mentoring others with imposter syndrome, help them understand how normal it is, write W. Brad Johnson and David G. Smith in *Harvard Business Review*.[vii] "It's hard to encourage someone's glaring talent, achievement, and creativity when it doesn't jibe with the mentee's self-perceptions of potential and performance," they write. This individual's beliefs don't align with the reality. Learning to move beyond self-doubt by focusing on their positive qualities will help them to overcome imposter syndrome and show up as a leader with executive presence.

Do you find yourself doubting your own abilities despite abundant evidence of your competence? When you doubt your own experience, impact, or whether you deserve that promotion, you sabotage your own executive presence. It becomes hard to even see whether you have executive presence qualities. Through the lens of imposter syndrome, you'll think you don't have them. However, once you lift the veil of imposter syndrome, you'll see that you *do* have many of the qualities of executive presence. Look to your past performance, abilities, talents, and accomplishments. They will speak the truth to you.

When you doubt your own experience and impact,
you sabotage your own executive presence.

You may realize that you display executive presence in certain situations where you feel more comfortable, but not in newer situations that intimidate you. When you find yourself among others with more power, influence, and authority than you, your executive presence may decline. However, you still possess those qualities. So, where does your executive presence go when you're in front of that intimidating group? What veil do you place over it?

In these moments of self-doubt, you are filtering inward. You are listening to the fearful voice inside and reverting to a childlike mentality that urges you to hide who you are out of self-protection. Over time, imposter syndrome can be a self-fulfilling prophecy that causes you to act as though you're less capable than you truly are, unless you take initiative to work through it.

Conversely, leaders with high self-efficacy inspire others to have confidence in them. That's why overcoming your imposter syndrome is so critical. To truly radiate executive presence, you need to believe you deserve to be where you are today.

EP Confidence Model

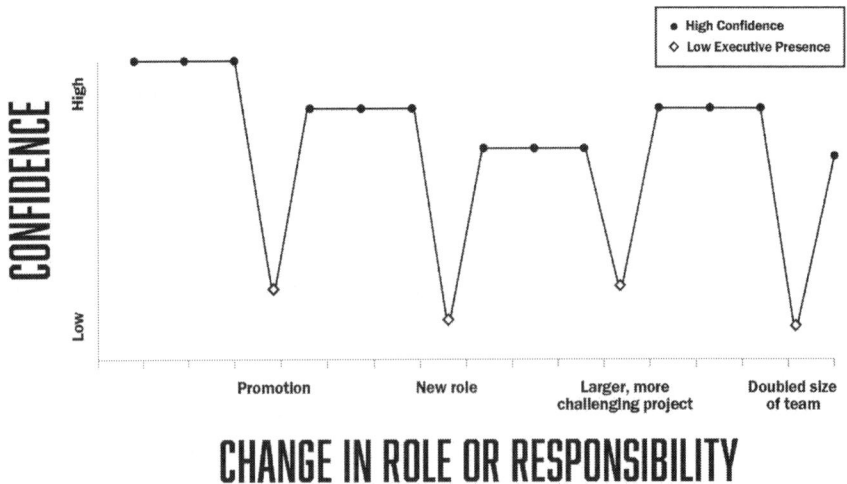

CHANGE IN ROLE OR RESPONSIBILITY

The above graph shows how executive presence can rise and fall in conjunction with career advancement. What's happening here? As soon as you master your current job, where you were feeling quite confident, a new opportunity arises. Imposter syndrome kicks in immediately, creating a tremendous amount of doubt and insecurity. With each change in role or responsibility, you lose confidence, and from that place of doubt, you are less inclined to utilize your executive presence competencies. You aren't as bold, decisive, and confident while working from this place of doubt. The doubt acts as a restraint that prevents you from using your EP qualities. You feel vulnerable and unprepared, so you shrink into a more timid version of yourself.

Here are examples of situations where this could happen:

+ You are promoted to a new level and feel intimidated about fully showing up with C-level executives. In turn, they perceive you as lacking EP.
+ You accept a new position and then feel unsure of yourself in this bigger and more challenging role. You become unassertive and soft-spoken, and coworkers view you as lacking EP.
+ You embark on a bigger, more challenging project and feel unable to carry it out well. You feel you've bitten off more than you can chew, and in turn, you come across as lacking EP.
+ You double the size of your team and feel you lack the competence to lead people, so your team sees you as lacking EP.

In any of these situations, you may feel like you don't deserve to be where you are today. You feel exposed, as if others can see how much you don't know, or you fear that they'll find out. In actuality, you possess all the skills needed to succeed—and the following action steps will help you start believing it.

Some of the world's most talented people have experienced imposter syndrome: Meryl Streep, David Bowie, Facebook's Sheryl Sandberg, and tennis star Serena Williams, to name just a few.[viii] Meryl Streep has said that she's thought, "Why would anyone want to see me again in a movie? And I don't know how to act anyway, so why am I doing this?"[ix] She's won 3 Academy Awards (nominated 21 times) and 8 Golden Globes (nominated

31 times), but higher-level accomplishments often leave people feeling flummoxed about how they ever made it that far. For many, it's hard to internalize the idea that they made it there with their own hard work and talent—not by luck.

Imposter syndrome often strikes people who don't fit the traditional mold of the corporate leader, such as women and people of color. They often have to work extra hard to overcome fears about how others will perceive them so their executive presence can truly shine. That's partly because they frequently lack mentors and advocates who can give them personalized guidance that helps them to fully cultivate their leadership presence and access new opportunities. Women of color are particularly likely to lack sponsors in the workplace.[x] Coupled with the fact that they don't fit into the stereotypical mold of a white male leader, they may doubt that others will ever actually perceive them as high-level leaders.

What to do when imposter syndrome strikes.

Don't let imposter syndrome control you. Start owning your abilities and embracing the chance to let your executive presence shine in a more challenging role. These tips will help you do just that.

+ **Remind yourself of the specific skills that got you to where you are today.** Your intelligence, strengths, and probably certain EP competencies brought you to where you are now. Before, while you were in the mastery-of-your-job stage, you didn't feel tentative, and you shouldn't act that way now.
+ **Adopt the attitude that *I deserve to be here*.** Let this realization in—there is no difference between who you were before and who you are today. The stakes are higher, the people around you are more powerful, the projects are bigger, but the work is not that different. The same goes for the people you manage— it's not that different than before, just larger and higher-profile.
+ **Know that your feelings are normal.** Remind yourself that the most talented people of every rank in the corporate world and elsewhere have experienced imposter syndrome. If you are

sitting at a meeting with 10 people, realize that at least 7 of them have experienced imposter syndrome.[xi]

+ **Learn to lean on your executive presence.** The further you go in your career, the more opportunities you'll encounter for imposter syndrome to emerge, *and* the more you'll need to have executive presence to leverage. You'll need to lean on a strong EP *especially* when your confidence is waning. Bring the 9 EP competencies into the new situation. Let them give you a foundation of confidence. If you were decisive before, why can't you be decisive now? If you were confident before, why can't you be confident now? Really, what is different? Remember that when you had achieved mastery of your prior role (before promotion), you weren't hesitant or unsure—and you shouldn't be now.

+ **Step outside of your comfort zone in smaller and then bigger ways.** Only by testing your own limits can you prove to yourself that you're fully capable of your new role. Ask yourself, "What's one step I can take today to increase my comfort zone?" As you start adopting bolder behaviors in this new context and witnessing your success, your confidence will grow—and soon the imposter syndrome will fade away.

+ **Project confidence even when you don't feel it.** The world doesn't need to know you're nervous. Use strategies for appearing confident despite your anxiety, like slowing the cadence of your speech so it doesn't sound hurried.

+ **Surround yourself with people who reflect your strengths back to you.** Even if you're not around them all the time, they'll have a positive effect on you. Go to lunch with a supportive mentor or colleague who will affirm your ability to handle your new role.

+ **Assemble a "board of directors" for your own career.** These should be experienced people with the wisdom to guide you in the right direction and clue you in about how you need to grow, says Tania Katan, author of *Creative Trespassing*.[xii]

+ **Challenge harmful self-talk with evidence of the truth,** as Johnson and Smith say.[xiii] Remind yourself that you at first lacked confidence in prior roles or opportunities, but confidence and competency always followed. Even though you feel as if you don't belong due to this new change in role or responsibility, eventually that will shift and you'll move from self-doubt to self-assurance.

Share the same advice with any direct reports who are struggling with imposter syndrome, and look out for self-deprecating statements. "Quite often, mentees struggling with imposter syndrome offer telltale blanket assessments of their capacity or performance," say Johnson and Smith. "Stay attuned to vague self-downing comments such as: 'I am so stupid!' 'I totally botched that presentation!' or 'I have no business being in this job!'" Then counteract them with evidence of your mentee's true capabilities. "In these moments, stick with the data, stay concrete, and work to create dissonance between the evidence and your mentee's self-statements," the authors urge.

Confident leaders have the conviction to advocate for their ideas even in new situations that might make them uncomfortable. They trust themselves enough to put their idea on the line even when someone with more authority could push back. Others might disagree with them, but these confident leaders will gain their respect. As you overcome the self-doubts that are holding you back, you'll become a candid and persuasive leader even when working with higher-level people. As you internalize your belief in your own executive presence competencies, they will become more fully a part of your identity. It won't matter who else is in the room—you're still *you*, radiating gravitas, authority, and expression. That's the power of executive presence when you've truly mastered it: You'll have it with you always, guiding you to present yourself as a powerful and influential leader.

Confident leaders have the conviction to advocate for their ideas even in new situations that might make them uncomfortable.

Now let's examine how behaviors that undermine your executive presence hold you back when executives are discussing the next promotion. We'll take a look at the kinds of conversations they have about leaders' self-sabotaging behavior so you can understand how this plays out in these critical moments.

Leaders often say, *"I wish I could promote you, BUT you lack executive presence."*

Imagine a talent review meeting where leaders are discussing who most deserves the next promotion. Your advocate speaks of several positive qualities you possess. Then someone else steps in, noting that while you do have some strong competencies, you lack executive presence. They may point out specific ways in which you fall short of what the role requires.

When working with clients, I refer to these as "BUT" behaviors. They're the specific behaviors that hold you back from that higher-level role by undermining your EP. To change how others view you, work on identifying them. These BUT behaviors shape others' perception of you as a person without executive presence. They're the behaviors that senior leaders mention at talent review meetings when they say, "I wish I could promote this person, BUT ..."

BUT behaviors shape others' perception of you as a person without executive presence.

Here are some extremely common "BUT" statements that many clients have heard:

1. Technically competent, **BUT** doesn't take command of a situation.
2. Excellent with customers and clients, **BUT** doesn't communicate clearly and succinctly with senior leaders.
3. Highly intelligent and smart, **BUT** is rigid, not poised, or hesitant when speaking.
4. Knows the business inside and out, **BUT** isn't willing to take charge when decisions need to be made.
5. Performs well, **BUT** won't make bold decisions or put a stake in the ground and own a position.

These clients needed to take action to overcome their BUT behaviors so they could move forward in their career. They successfully overcame them, and you can as well.

As you go through each of the nine chapters about the key competencies of executive presence, you'll learn about many "BUT" behaviors.

I'll outline many undesirable behaviors of leaders who lack each of those competencies—the "BUT" behaviors that sabotage career success. You'll have ample opportunity to reflect on your own as you read this book.

What are your "BUT" behaviors that limit your executive presence?

Write down the top 6 behaviors that undermine your EP.

_____

_____

_____

_____

_____

_____

_____

➜ Circle the top 2 that most limit your executive presence.

Write down an action step to take to improve one of these 2 behaviors:

_____

Consider action steps that can help you shift your self-perception in regard to this behavior. An action step should be achievable in the short-term—something you can do *now*, not something you might build up to doing in three months. These action steps can help you begin challenging the self-doubts that had led to your BUT behavior today. For example, if you have trouble feeling bold (and thus, presenting yourself as bold), vow to voice one bold idea in your next low-stakes meeting with your own team. Aim to make a bold statement at each weekly team meeting going forward, even if it's half-baked. Have fun with it! Practice making a declarative statement that voices your complete support for a controversial idea, or pitching an outside-of-the-box suggestion. As you hear yourself making statements like these in a low-pressure setting, you'll realize you have what it takes to be bold—and you'll get practice in delivering your message.

Remember, you'll remain undervalued and overlooked as long as you keep engaging in your BUT behaviors. Prioritize your action steps for overcoming them in your daily work. There is nothing more important to your career.

Shifting others' perception of you begins within yourself. "Your perception of yourself is critical—not the perception you project to others or the way you are perceived, but how you perceive you," writes Ellevate Network in *Forbes*. It all begins with conquering your imposter syndrome and insecurities.

You'll remain undervalued and overlooked
as long as you keep engaging in your BUT behaviors.

Laid-Back Lawrence Learns to Grow Charisma

Problem:

Lawrence, who had held a mid-level management position for the past five years, was intelligent and good at problem-solving. He'd quietly averted several crises in the past few months with his quick thinking and innovative mind. However, his laid-back personality didn't attract a lot of attention.

Lawrence rarely seemed very excited about a project. When he stepped into a room, people seldom approached him to ask for his input or discuss an idea, even though his wealth of knowledge and experience could really benefit them. He lacked charisma and a commanding presence that would make people want to hear his thoughts.

In meetings, Lawrence rarely pushed his own agenda or asserted his opinions. He tended to go with the flow, and he didn't recognize his own need to play a role in defining that "flow." Because he didn't appear to have a strong belief in his own ideas or enthusiasm for team projects, he lacked gravitas. In a crisis, his team wouldn't look to him for solutions with trust and confidence. And because he lacked decisiveness, boldness, and influence, he lacked authority.

Action:

Through executive coaching, Lawrence became aware of the specific BUT behaviors he was displaying. He also realized that he actually did have great insights. However, he needed to learn to recognize them and to give himself space to cultivate them. So, he took time for big-picture reflection every Friday afternoon. He then began to feel more confident in his own ideas, which gave him more excitement about his work. As Lawrence began sharing his ideas more vocally, it triggered a positive feedback loop. People responded positively to his assertions and insights, which made him feel more confident and enthusiastic about sharing them. Over the next six months, Lawrence worked to strengthen his competencies in each of the three EP domains.

Results:

The energy level and morale of Lawrence's whole team increased substantially. When he took part in a meeting, the atmosphere felt noticeably different, even though he did much more listening than talking. Not long ago, Lawrence never would have thought he could become a charismatic leader with executive presence, but he'd made great strides toward that goal—and now his boss was finally beginning to talk about advancement.

Consider your own fatal flaws. How are your own internal limiting beliefs undermining your executive presence? These self-sabotaging behaviors can put a halt to your career progression. They can deprive you of the opportunity for job fulfillment, leaving you stuck in a position that doesn't fully leverage your talents and allow you to enjoy your work. It's time to overcome them, and the solution is self-awareness.

Moving past doubt by deepening self-awareness.

Cultivating a high level of self-awareness plays a vital role in transcending your internal limiting beliefs. Self-awareness allows you to see yourself as you truly are, rather than in an overly positive or negative light. It lets you know when you have an overly critical thought or fall into an unhealthy thinking pattern that you've been working to step out of. Likewise, it allows you to see where you still have work to do.

There are four key dimensions of deepening your self-awareness. Work to become aware of how you project (or don't project) executive presence in each of these dimensions of your working life.

- The image you present.
- The opinions you share.
- The attitudes you convey.
- The actions you take.

The impression you make and the reputation you cultivate in each of these ways will show the world that you either possess or lack executive presence.

Spending time reflecting on your BUT behaviors and taking action to correct them will heighten your self-awareness over time. But don't only focus on the negative. Every day, give yourself positive reinforcement for the things you do well. Acknowledge them to yourself instead of letting them go by unnoticed. At the end of the day, think to yourself, "What were my three best moments today?" Do the same at the end of the week. Reflect on which moments stand out and why. When did you feel proud of your actions, or most courageous? Voice this to your partner, a close friend, or a family member. By recognizing these moments instead of letting them slip away, you'll affirm the idea that you can carry that courage with you from this point forward. As you recognize your small everyday wins, you'll internalize a stronger sense of pride and accomplishment, and in turn, you'll project that in the image you present to the world, the words you share, the attitudes you convey, and the actions you take.

We've now examined what executive presence is, why it's so important, and what you do to undermine it in specific ways. Hopefully you now are beginning to understand some specific ways in which you undermine your executive presence. In Part II of this book, you will deepen that understanding as we look at each of the nine competencies in the 3x3 Executive Presence Model. But first, it's time to assess whether others in your company, especially leaders, actually perceive you as someone who has executive presence. Their impressions of you override your actual performance, so no matter how much you accomplish in your daily work, you need to shape the perceptions of all those around you by projecting a strong executive presence. We'll take a look at how to guide the perceptions of even the most influential people by reflecting on how they view you, asking for feedback, and acting upon it to radiate executive presence wherever you go.

> No matter how much you accomplish in your daily work, you need to shape the perceptions of all those around you by projecting a strong executive presence.

Chapter 5

Know If Others Perceive You as Having Executive Presence

How do the people in your company perceive you?

Do they view you as having a low or high degree of executive presence?

To be anointed as a leader with executive presence, you first have to be perceived as one. Executive presence is not a title that you give yourself; it is an honorary title bestowed upon you by colleagues, peers, and senior leaders because you have gained professional credibility and earned their respect.

> To be anointed as a leader with executive presence, you first have to be perceived as one.

Your journey of growing executive presence begins with finding out how other people perceive you. Otherwise, you won't know where you need to focus your efforts. While every EP competency in the 3x3 Model is extremely important, you may already be stronger in some and weaker in others. By understanding how others perceive your level of executive presence, you'll equip yourself to make a plan of action that targets the right areas.

Let's take a deep dive now into the power of perception, which will help you evaluate whether other people in your company—especially influential leaders—perceive you as having executive presence.

Take a moment to consider how the specific leaders who make decisions about your career perceive YOU.

How do others in your company perceive you? Are you seen as someone with executive presence?

Write down the names of 8 people who will be sitting around the executive table discussing you at the next talent review meeting.

1. _____   5. _____
2. _____   6. _____
3. _____   7. _____
4. _____   8. _____

Imagine that YOU are being discussed for 10 minutes by these influential leaders. They review the 9 executive presence competencies and identify which ones you excel in and which ones you most need to improve.

Write down the 3 qualities that these influential leaders would choose as the ones that you most need to improve.

_____
_____
_____
_____

Write down the 1 competency they would choose that most needs improvement.

_____
_____
_____
_____

How does having a low degree of this competency limit your success at work?

_____
_____
_____
_____

Write down 1 commitment you'll make to improve this quality and infuse it into your work.

_____
_____
_____

Impressions override performance.

For most of your career, you've been rewarded for good performance. How you carry out your work has determined the level of success you experience in your company. You've been evaluated through the lens of your performance—the results, skills, abilities, and knowledge you bring. From day one of your career, you've embraced the mindset that says, "Let my work speak for itself. I'll just keep working hard and rely on my strong performance, and success will come." Up to a certain point in your career, this is 100% true. However, over time, a critical shift occurs: **Impressions override performance.** The impressions you make become *more important than your actual performance.* The success you achieve becomes directly tied to the impressions you make on others, which hinge on how others perceive you. The most successful leaders recognize that since they've already mastered performance, they now need to concentrate on making sure others perceive them as having a strong executive presence.

> The impressions you make become more
> important than your actual performance.

High Performance + Impression of Executive Presence = Most Successful Leaders

Why is perception important? Everything you do is being observed and documented inside the brains of others. People are constantly judging, evaluating, and observing you. What they see, notice, and observe matters. Your peers, bosses, subordinates, customers, clients, and vendors are all consciously and unconsciously forming opinions of you. Maybe you never thought of how you are perceived by all of these groups—or maybe you try to avoid thinking about it as much as possible.

The spotlight is on you, whether or not you desire it. You may not want the spotlight to be on you, and you may pretend that it's not. Many leaders don't appreciate the fact that they are always on camera and the higher their level, the more people are watching their every move. But if you don't embrace this reality, it will come at the cost of your career success.

"Perceptions of competence are just as important for success as actual competence," asserts Jack Nasher in HBR.[i] Perception matters because it's at the heart of many decisions that will be made about you. As you shape your executive presence, you are shaping the perceptions others have of you. As you display the nine EP competencies, you instill the perception that you have a strong executive presence. People will begin to perceive you as embodying these behaviors.

"Perceptions of competence are just as important for success as actual competence."
Jack Nasher

Making these competencies outwardly visible is key to allowing your executive presence to shine. Here are a few examples of how invisible competencies can be made more visible.

COMPETENCIES VS. PERCEPTION

LACKING EP	DISPLAYING EP
You're decisive in making choices within your personal projects. You take smart risks that usually pay off. In meetings, however, you go with the flow too much and often sound hesitant, so people don't *perceive* you as decisive.	You learn to be decisive in the points you make and ideas you advocate for during meetings. You don't give in so easily anymore; instead, you defend your position for as long as you can show evidence to back it up. Thus, others begin to actually *see you* as decisive.
You are eloquent and polished in all your written communications. Whether sending an email to your team or a report to senior leaders, you are clear and articulate, getting right to the point. When communicating face to face, however, you get nervous and ramble. You don't punctuate your important points to emphasize them, so they get lost in the muddle. People view you as inarticulate and unclear.	You learn to speak in the same way you write: clearly and succinctly. Writing your ideas down first helps you voice them in a more compelling way. You realize that you had convinced yourself you could never be an eloquent speaker, and you push past that belief. You organize your thoughts for a meeting the same way you organize an email—and others begin to view you as clear and insightful as a result.
In your new leadership position, you motivate and inspire your direct reports. They see you as charming and funny; you're good at radiating optimism within your team. Among your coworkers and superiors, you feel more intimidated because they all seem so poised and accomplished. As a result, they don't see those positive qualities in you. In fact, you seem closed-off and unapproachable.	You spend time getting to know your colleagues and superiors one on one over coffee or lunch, so you can be yourself around them. You come to see them as people who struggle with many of the same challenges that you do. Thus, you loosen up in group settings and unleash more of your natural enthusiasm, charm, and ability to make people laugh. They come to perceive you as witty and charismatic—which you are!

Others' *perceptions* of your competencies can differ greatly from your *actual* competencies. Making your competencies visible will help debunk and eradicate any false beliefs about your abilities that present you in a negative light. When you're not striving to make your competencies visible, others are consciously or unconsciously filling in the blank—and what they think may not be favorable.

What perception do the most powerful and impactful people have of you?

Let's consider for a moment how the senior leaders in your organization view your executive presence, and why this is so critical.

Imagine your boss, boss's boss, and other key executives in your company sitting around a table, behind closed doors. They are all discussing YOU. They are evaluating you. Talking about you. Judging you.

What are they saying about you? Is it positive? Is it negative?

Are you seen as confident, charismatic, and commanding? Do these important people find you decisive, articulate, and insightful? Or do you fly under the radar, remaining invisible to them?

Some might have a blank page inside their mind when they think of you because they don't know you. If they don't know you, that's because you haven't been speaking up in ways that they can hear. When you don't speak up, these important people don't have a sense of who you are. They don't understand what value you bring. They don't know your impact on the company—and they certainly don't view you as someone with executive presence. Instead, you are just a blank page.

As a blank page, you become just another "hidden leader" who gets overlooked for opportunities, advancement, and recognition. Upping your executive presence makes you more known and valued, rather than hidden. It highlights your ability to command a room and motivate people to action. Top leaders will then see you as someone they can depend on to take the reins and drive your team to success, rather than someone who will hang back and see if someone else will step up to the plate.

Before we go into what they are saying about you at this meeting, do realize that each of these top leaders often *prepares* for these meetings by getting input from others. They ask other people (both their peers and lower-level employees) for their opinion of people they are going to discuss. This aggregated data often shows up in talent review meetings. Thus, other people's opinions clearly matter a great deal to your career success—and not just top leaders' opinions, but everyone's.

These behind-closed-door meetings are important because they're where leaders share and debate their perceptions of you. "The biggest decisions about your career are often made when you're not in the room," says Davia Temin in *Forbes*.[ii] "Your professional fate is often determined in closed rooms where people are talking about—and evaluating—you, without the benefit of your input."

This is also where bias occurs. It's where senior leaders have a license to show favoritism. This is where the discussion about your peers can occur that results in their receiving the promotion you felt you deserved. These top execs are evaluating your capabilities and potential—often without having any concrete understanding of what you actually do and what you've achieved. You might imagine they carefully weigh the actual contributions of each person, but that's rarely the case. They come in with their own preconceptions, and if you're lucky, you have someone in your corner with whom you have a rapport. They'll quickly dismiss anyone who doesn't immediately catch their eye, relying heavily on "gut feel," as Temin says.

In these conversations, they're evaluating whether you're a leader with executive presence. This can be a turning point in your career, determining whether you'll step up to the next level or begin to falter. Seventy-eight percent of business leaders believe a lack of executive presence will hold a leader back from advancement, according to a survey by communications experts Sally Williamson & Associates.[iii]

To come out on top in these conversations, set a conscious intention to make your EP competencies visible. Again, you probably already embody some of them in at least certain contexts. However, you might move from good in one context to average or poor in another for any particular competency. In some contexts, you're in your power, while in others, you give your power away. It's time to make your EP competencies outwardly visible in every situation, not just a select few where you feel most comfortable.

In 360 reviews that I have conducted for a leader, one of their peers will often say, "I don't believe this, but people *think* this." The peers who know the leader best often see their best qualities—which others are missing.

They understand the difference between truth and perception. However, the leader needs to make these positive qualities visible to *everyone*, not just their closest colleagues.

Most people aren't going to study you closely in order to find out who the real *you* is. They take what they see at face value—and often, they don't see a lot of who you are. When you have a chance to interact with leaders, make the most of it. Your touchpoints with senior leaders are limited, so you have to make a great impression each time you interact with them. Each interaction gives you a chance to shape their perception of you, so use it wisely.

> "Research shows that people form impressions about a leader's competence in as little as half a minute."
> Carmine Gallo

People form their impressions of a leader quite quickly. "Research shows that people form impressions about a leader's competence in as little as half a minute," says Carmine Gallo in HBR. "This means, within seconds, listeners will decide whether you are trustworthy, and they will do it based on your body language and vocal attributes. What you say *and* how you say it are equally important."

As you build a reputation as a leader with executive presence, this is how influential people will see you:

+ **Credible:** You are consistently competent, effective, and accurate.
+ **Trustworthy:** Your words, deeds, and character are honest and authentic.
+ **Respected:** You are highly regarded; people admire and look up to you.
+ **Reliable:** You show people that they can depend on you to get the job done right and on time.

Others will know that when you're at the helm of a project or initiative, it's in capable hands. When you're leading the response to a crisis, they'll know you will steer the organization safely through stormy waters. Once you cultivate a strong executive presence, you'll establish yourself as one of the most dependable and competent people around.

Ask for feedback to learn how you are perceived.

You may not yet recognize the ways in which you are undermining your own EP, which is why gaining feedback from people at different levels is so crucial. Ask your direct reports, boss, coworkers, clients, and peers from other departments how they would characterize your strengths and weaknesses in regard to each of the executive presence competencies. Their insights will help you to truly understand where you need to improve.

You may have received feedback in various forms already—but does it expressly pertain to executive presence? Having recently gone through a 360-review process or performance review doesn't necessarily deliver insights on executive presence. Instead, you need to ask specific questions about the nine EP competencies.

> Proactively asking for feedback about your executive presence makes you appear stronger than if you were to shrink from it.

Asking for feedback can feel challenging. It requires you to make yourself vulnerable, as the truth can be hard to hear. However, it becomes a positive and enriching experience when you reframe how you view feedback. Proactively asking for feedback about your executive presence makes you appear stronger than if you were to shrink from it. And taking initiative to solicit feedback on your own feels much more empowering than having someone confront you about an issue. Most leaders find that when they ask for feedback, people appreciate the chance to voice their opinions. They also appreciate the concern those leaders are showing for their emotions and experiences. Relationships and trust grow stronger as a result.

People who feel a false sense of security and don't see the benefit of feedback will feel and act more defensive, resistant, and closed-off. They will grow more slowly, put limitations on their career success, and restrict the quality of the contributions they make to their organizations.

In contrast, when you commit to self-development and self-awareness, you'll understand the importance of seeking out feedback about your EP competencies, and you'll appreciate receiving it. You'll proactively seek out feedback rather than simply waiting for it. By making others around you feel comfortable sharing direct and candid feedback, you'll gain an accurate assessment of your strengths and areas for improvement. As you welcome feedback, you'll learn exactly how you need to continue fine-tuning your performance to establish yourself as a leader with executive presence. As a self-aware individual, you'll be a powerful asset to your organization because you'll make a conscious effort to grow. You'll look for opportunities to expand your abilities and provide support to those around you.

Everyone benefits when providing feedback becomes part of the company culture. A work environment that strongly supports and endorses a high degree of feedback will directly improve each person's effectiveness. Thus, all employees should pursue open and honest conversations regarding their performance and communication—especially leaders.

Asking for feedback takes courage. "Vulnerability is at the heart of the feedback process," says Brené Brown in *Daring Greatly*.[iv] "This is true whether we give, receive, or solicit feedback. And the vulnerability doesn't go away even if we're trained and experienced in offering and getting feedback. Experience does, however, give us the advantage of knowing that we can survive the exposure and uncertainty, and that it's worth the risk." Requesting others' honest opinions also shows courage. It would be easier to fly under the radar, but by asking for feedback and acting on it, you choose the bold course of moving past your comfort zone and tackling new challenges.

It would be easier to fly under the radar, but by asking for feedback and acting on it, you choose the bold course of moving past your comfort zone and tackling new challenges.

Self-developed and self-aware leaders have enough self-esteem and confidence not to be intimidated or fearful about what the feedback might reveal. They don't allow their egos to get in the way of receiving genuine feedback. As your EP grows, you'll feel less and less afraid of hearing feedback.

The higher you advance in an organization, the more people you'll have working for you. Your subordinates will work best and want to give you the most when they feel they can trust you and share their honest feelings with you. As a leader, you'll receive powerful feedback from them that directly informs how to best guide your employees to reach their full potential.

BETTER LEADERS ASK FOR MORE FEEDBACK

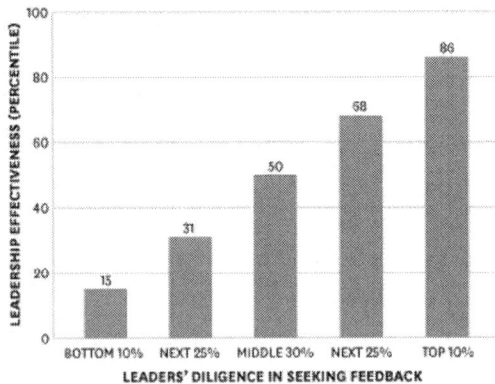

SOURCE ZENGER/FOLKMAN   HBR.ORG

In a study of nearly 52,000 executives, Zenger Folkman found that leaders who routinely ask for feedback achieve a far better performance than those who do not.[v] The top 10% who most effectively ask for feedback rank in the 86th percentile in terms of their leadership ability, the study found.

Moreover, the feedback you ask for is more effective than the feedback you *don't* ask for, Gallup has found.[vi] Asking, "Can you give me some feedback?" inspires feelings of good will, which allows for a more productive conversation, Gallup explains. "Those words can immediately create a trusting atmosphere in which feedback is exchanged and processed effectively," say the authors. Only 26% of employees say they get useful feedback from coworkers, the organization has found—and that's partly because they're not asking for it.

Brandy Rebrands Herself as a Leader

Problem:

Brandy had the sneaking suspicion that others didn't think as highly of her leadership skills as she had once believed. She knew she projected confidence in meetings and maintained strong communication with her team, so she felt at a loss about what the problem might be. So, we conducted a 360-degree feedback review that solicited input from direct reports, colleagues, and superiors.

Brandy acted completely oblivious to others' reactions in meetings, respondents said. Rather than glancing around the room to note people's body language, she droned on and on about her opinions. She talked over people and interrupted incessantly. Sometimes she would think aloud without having a real point to make. These behaviors undermined others' perception of her, making her seem less insightful than she actually was and minimizing the impact of her words.

Further, Brandy often lacked follow-through with projects. She fell short on taking full accountability and often dropped the ball, undermining her gravitas. Because she didn't follow through, she didn't project the persona of a confident and commanding leader.

Action:

Alongside those negative qualities, we pinpointed some positive ones as well. Brandy had a fairly high comfort level in terms of speaking up in meetings. She was a highly verbal, communicative person who did in fact check in on her direct reports every day, giving them clear (albeit overly verbose) feedback. She tended to make a much better impression in one-on-ones than in meetings; coworkers felt more comfortable interrupting her in a discussion over coffee than in a group setting.

Brandy felt discouraged at first when hearing the 360 feedback about her performance in meetings, but we immediately set about creating a plan for growth. We determined that she fell short on accountability because she became overwhelmed with the number of meetings and mundane tasks on her schedule. We restructured her workload with priority on high-importance projects. When checking in with her direct reports, she focused on more succinctly reminding them of project workflow requirements. She learned to listen as much as she talked, too, which meant she could clarify areas of confusion to ensure tasks got done on time. She also began learning to let others speak more in meetings, which allowed her to speak with more clarity and precision when she did voice her thoughts.

Results:

These changes greatly enhanced Brandy's gravitas and expression. Her coworkers, direct reports, and boss all noticed improvements within weeks. Her peers and subordinates found her far more approachable and much more effective as a leader, and she proved herself to be someone whom senior leaders could count on to get the job done.

How to get feedback on your executive presence.

To get beneficial feedback on your EP, you need to ask specific questions. Don't just ask whether you do well in meetings—ask *what* you do well and what you need to improve. Don't settle for general answers, either. Instead, ask follow-up questions that provide clarification.

Begin by writing down the names of five people you will contact to get their perspectives in a feedback conversation—your boss, a senior leader, your boss's boss, a peer. Email them right now to set up a meeting for this week or next.

1. _____
2. _____
3. _____
4. _____
5. _____

Then, consider how to approach the conversation for best results. Prepare thoughtful questions on the following topics so you'll get the information you're seeking.

Questions on your overall level of EP

The following questions will help you gauge your level of executive presence and where you most need to focus your efforts to change.

- "Am I perceived as having executive presence?"
- "In what ways do I show that I have executive presence?"
- "What do I do to undermine my executive presence?"
- "How can I improve my executive presence?"

+ "What would you be willing to do to help me improve my executive presence?"

Before asking the questions, you may need to share the nine competencies outlined in the 3x3 Executive Presence Model with the person you're asking for feedback. This will ensure you'll be working with a shared understanding of what executive presence means.

You may want to ask more specific questions as well, like those that follow.

Questions on the nine competencies

Ask for feedback on how well you display particular executive presence competencies. After all, not everyone understands what executive presence is, but they can still give you invaluable feedback on your EP attributes. Ask questions like the following:

+ "How confident do I sound in meetings? What could I do to improve in this regard?"
+ "How clear am I when I'm giving instructions? In what ways could I improve?"
+ "How could I come across as more decisive? Are there specific times when I really need to sound more decisive?"
+ "When I'm presenting, what are my greatest strengths and my greatest weaknesses?"
+ "How could I participate more effectively in meetings? What do I do well?"

Some of these questions ask for an assessment of strengths and weaknesses in a certain context. Others delve into specific EP competencies. By giving the other person a specific quality or context to focus on, you can gain more detailed and relevant input. If you're working to hone in on particular areas for growth, check in on your progress with various people. Use the above questions as a template for gaining feedback on any of the nine EP competencies.

How to approach the conversation

Set the right tone when asking for feedback, so you'll get a candid and constructive response. Follow these pointers to get high-quality feedback whenever you ask for it.

- **Avoid "yes-or-no" questions, or questions that beg the listener to give a positive reply.** Phrasing a question as, "Do you think I'm good at delivering presentations?" almost requires the listener to respond positively. Instead, say, "I'd like your honest feedback on how I deliver presentations. Please clue me in on any areas that I could strengthen for next time." Use open-ended questions that don't guide the reader toward a particularly positive response, which is many people's default reaction.

- **Relax your body language and expression.** If you appear tense, the listener may feel compelled to assuage your uneasiness rather than being as candid as possible.

- **Ask for *feedforward*.** This frames the feedback discussion around what you could do better in the future rather than what you've done poorly in the past. It may seem like a subtle distinction, but it can frame the conversation in a more positive and motivational light. Moreover, it results in actionable suggestions about specific behaviors you could adopt in the future. You can guide the conversation in this direction with questions like, "How could I show more confidence in the next meeting?" or "How could I be a better project manager for our next initiative?"

- **Ask follow-up questions when people don't fully illustrate their points.** Detailed, nuanced feedback wins out over vague statements every time.

Let's delve into the concept of *feedforward* a bit more, because I've seen it result in powerful insights for countless clients. Acclaimed executive coach Marshall Goldsmith offers up a nine-step process for asking for feedforward:[vii]

1. Choose a behavior you wish to change.
2. Describe the behavior to the people whose input you're seeking.
3. Ask for feedforward, requesting two suggestions you can use in the future to model the desired behavior.
4. Listen closely and take notes on their responses. Don't comment on their responses, even in a positive way!
5. Thank them for their input.
6. Ask them what they would like to change about themselves.
7. Provide two feedforward-focused suggestions.
8. Say "you're welcome" when they thank you.
9. Repeat the process with someone else.

These feedforward conversations will play a vital role in your development, and they'll show influential people that you're serious about self-improvement. Have these conversations with a broad range of people, which will give you a more well-rounded perspective of your executive presence attributes. Although it may feel daunting to ask for input at first, having a couple of good conversations about your performance will ease your anxiety. Remember, others already think and believe the feedback you're asking for. You are simply unlocking it so you will know the truth. As I often say to my coaching clients, "They already think it; you might as well know it."

> They already think it;
> you might as well know it.

As you gain this valuable feedback, you'll be able to detect themes within the data. These patterns will tell you where you need to focus your energy to improve your executive presence.

Scott Gets Strategic about Seeking Feedback

Problem:

Scott decided to strategically ask 10 influential leaders in his company about how they perceived him. He wanted to make a plan for how to improve his executive presence, and this was step #1. So, he carefully crafted a list of questions. He emailed those 10 leaders and set up a series of phone and in-person meetings with them. He brought the 3x3 Executive Presence Model with him to the meetings so he could ask them which of the nine competencies he most needed to improve in.

The leaders were impressed with how Scott cut right to the chase and asked the tough questions that would bring real insights. Scott realized this also provided an excellent chance to build a rapport with these leaders. They had great conversations that enlightened him about how others viewed him, and he took careful notes.

Scott learned that he needed to speak up more in meetings and be more forthright in his speech. He also needed to expand his network of influence and inform others of the impressive work his team was accomplishing. Multiple leaders told him that they'd only recently learned of the importance and impact of the team to the company's success. Too often he flew under the radar and important decisions were made without his team's input. He needed to build his rapport with many more influential leaders throughout the company.

Action:

Scott entered all of these suggestions into a spreadsheet under the appropriate leader's name, so he could keep track of his progress in follow-ups with them. He took clear notes that he could easily refer back to over time.

Results:

Through their advice, Scott learned how to have more confidence and presence at work, especially when interacting with senior leadership. He took action to present himself as more confident and grow his influence. After a couple of months had gone by, two of the leaders reached out to him to let him know they admired his progress.

The #1 way to increase your self-awareness is to ask others for feedback. They are the eyes you do not see with, perceiving things that you cannot. Have others rate you on your executive presence. How are your actions and behaviors being experienced by others? When you gather this feedback, you'll learn much more about the gaps between others' perceptions and your actual intentions. You may want to ask someone who is frequently in the same meetings as you to observe your behavior and share feedback on your EP later.

Create a spreadsheet to keep the information you receive organized and to track your progress over time. You can easily refer to it to remember who said what, so you can follow up with them to find out how you're progressing. Here's an example of what this might look like:

Feedback-Tracking Spreadsheet

	Sarah	Travis	Mateo	Lois
Meeting #1	COMMANDING: Need to take charge more readily. In tough situations, your team needs to depend on you for leadership. Show them you're able to steer the ship through choppy waters.	COMMANDING: Focus on handling stress more effectively. You seem too easily rattled. DECISIVE: You waver too much in meetings. Show that you trust your gut and follow your instincts.	DECISIVE: You seem to trust everyone's judgment but your own. Learn to listen to yourself first, and don't try to get consensus. You often take too long to make a time-sensitive choice.	COMMANDING: I want to see you taking command of the room more. Show conviction when sharing your opinions. DECISIVE: Don't try to get 100% of the information before making a decision. Show you believe in your ideas.
Meeting #2	COMMANDING: I saw a positive shift as we went through a recent change. You had a stronger leadership presence as you navigated the transition. You've started taking more initiative to provide guidance and reassurance.	COMMANDING: You've definitely begun to handle stress better, but keep working at this. You have some room to grow. DECISIVE: You are taking a more decisive stance in meetings, but your confidence still seems shaky.	DECISIVE: You recently had to make a tough decision, and I believe you trusted your gut more than you had in the past. I was glad to see that you asked a few people for their input but not everyone. That is progress!	COMMANDING: You are starting to build a stronger presence. This is a longer-term process, so stick with it. I still want to see you showing a lot more conviction in your ideas.

	Sarah	Travis	Mateo	Lois
Meeting #3	COMMANDING: I'm impressed at how far you've come so quickly. Your team is naturally looking to you as a capable leader in every situation, including the tough ones.	COMMANDING: You voice your ideas with more confidence. I can hear your conviction, so I'm more inclined to trust you myself. DECISIVE: I've seen you boldly make several decisions now. Keep practicing this and it will feel more natural.	DECISIVE: I get the sense that making a decision doesn't feel so hard for you anymore. You've clearly been practicing trusting your gut while getting input from a well-chosen circle of people.	COMMANDING: I witnessed you in a meeting with other leaders last week, and the difference was astounding. You really rallied support for an idea you believed in, and the influence you had on others was clear.

This is a simplified example; you can and should include much more detail in your own spreadsheet. You can certainly track your progress over more than three meetings, too.

By asking these leaders for feedback, you'll also be prompting them to watch you more closely. These influential players will place extra focus on you as a result. They'll notice the changes you're making and the effort you're putting in. In other words, you'll bring attention to yourself by asking them to observe you. They'll witness your executive presence flourishing through your dedication to self-improvement, seeing you as a proactive leader who follows through on your commitments and achieves your goals.

You'll bring attention to yourself by
asking them to observe you.

Carlos Becomes More Commanding

Problem:

During a 360 review on a client named Carlos, three senior leaders and two peers all said, "He lacks executive presence." When asked what they meant by that, this is how they replied.

"He needs to be more assertive," one leader said. "He comes across as being too laid-back. I wonder if he has enough strength to stand up for what he believes in."

"I would like him to portray a sense of command in difficult situations," said another. "He needs to have the strength to stand up to authority and hold a line in the sand when dealing with peers or subordinates."

"He needs to hold people accountable when they aren't doing their job," said a peer. "When people aren't delivering, he needs to not be afraid to have those tough conversations, or to get rid of people who aren't working out."

Action:

Carlos had no idea they all perceived him in this way. He began working to strengthen these qualities, and after two weeks, he began approaching people for feedback. "Where could I be more assertive?" he asked his colleague Marie. "And have you noticed any changes in my level of assertiveness?" Marie affirmed that she had been surprised to hear him making bolder, more decisive statements in recent meetings. She gave him a few pointers on where he could still bring in more assertiveness as well.

Results:

Carlos left their discussion with a smile on his face, feeling uplifted. Whereas feedback had once felt intimidating, he now felt empowered to continue taking action to strengthen his EP.

Now you have an excellent understanding of how to enhance your executive presence by shaping others' perceptions of you. Remember that you have the power to shift the perceptions of colleagues, leaders, clients, and everyone else around you. Changing their perceptions begins with making your executive presence qualities visible by using them in contexts where all of those people can see them. As you practice using your growing executive presence competencies in all of those circumstances, you'll see their perceptions of you transforming. Any limitations will be removed, and in their place, they'll see your full potential to blossom into a high-level leader who radiates executive presence in every situation.

You have the power to shift the perceptions
of colleagues, leaders, clients, and everyone else around you.

Part 2

Gravitas
Authority
Expression

Introduction

To become a leader with executive presence, you need to develop a balanced set of EP competencies. When a person has a great deal of one quality but not complementary ones, it can undermine their overall executive presence. For instance, a leader who comes across as always in command, but who hasn't cultivated charisma, probably won't seem approachable. Such people tend to intimidate others and seem domineering, which negatively affects their ability to lead. Similarly, leaders who are extremely decisive but can't vocalize the reason behind their decisions will have trouble gaining buy-in. To have executive presence, you need to develop the overall package, not just a few select characteristics.

The 3x3 Executive Presence (EP) Model will help you overcome each of those undesirable behaviors and replace them with a solid foundation of strengths. It delivers a comprehensive overview of the most important facets of executive presence. This allows you to see where your strengths lie as a leader—and where you could devote more energy and focus to enhance others' perception of your leadership. This model acts as a blueprint for becoming a leader with executive presence.

The core qualities of executive presence fall into three key areas—gravitas, authority, and expression—the 3x3 EP Model illustrates. To achieve a balanced set of executive presence competencies, you must cultivate the nine skills that together make up those domains. To be perceived as a leader who has executive presence, you need to build, develop, and fine-tune these nine competencies.

This book serves as a guide to using the 3x3 EP Model, helping you take action to build those nine core qualities. As you cultivate each of these areas, you'll become a leader with gravitas, authority, and exceptional expressive capabilities—and thus, executive presence.

To be perceived as a leader who has executive presence,
you need to build, develop, and fine-tune these nine competencies.

Understanding the 3x3 Executive Presence Model.

Let's first examine each of the three domains of the 3x3 Model. By understanding the end goal that you're driving toward, you'll better comprehend how cultivating each of the nine core competencies will help you get there.

THE 3 DOMAINS OF EXECUTIVE PRESENCE:

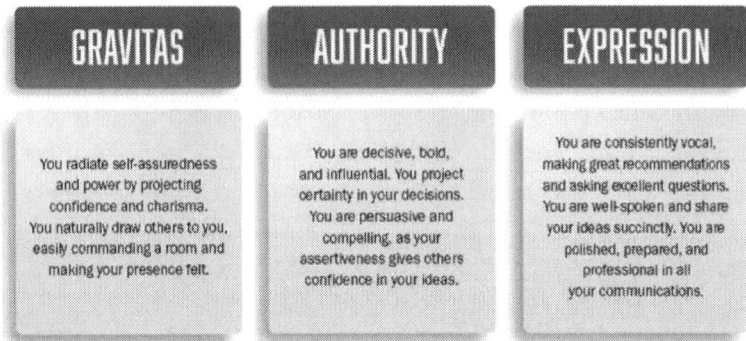

GRAVITAS	AUTHORITY	EXPRESSION
You radiate self-assuredness and power by projecting confidence and charisma. You naturally draw others to you, easily commanding a room and making your presence felt.	You are decisive, bold, and influential. You project certainty in your decisions. You are persuasive and compelling, as your assertiveness gives others confidence in your ideas.	You are consistently vocal, making great recommendations and asking excellent questions. You are well-spoken and share your ideas succinctly. You are polished, prepared, and professional in all your communications.

Gravitas is the powerful presence that leaders with executive presence exude, regardless of whom they're interacting with. Authority stems from the ability to act decisively and boldly while building influence throughout the organizational ranks. Expression involves conveying ideas clearly, consistently, and effectively. Each domain holds equal importance, and mastering the qualities of one will enhance the way a leader shows up in the other domains. For instance, a leader with a commanding presence will more effectively introduce bold decisions.

To distill this idea down to its essence, gravitas is who you *are*, authority is what you *do*, and expression is what you *say*. Each is a key component of a leader's daily practice.

HOW EACH DOMAIN LOOKS IN PRACTICE:

GRAVITAS IS:	AUTHORITY IS:	EXPRESSION IS:
Who You Are	What You Do	What You Say
How You SHOW UP	How You ACT	How You COMMUNICATE
Exuding Confidence	Making an Impact	Becoming Known

Now we're ready to get into the meat of each domain. As mentioned, each of the three domains within the 3x3 Model comprises three core qualities. Cultivating gravitas means becoming confident, commanding, and charismatic. Authority arises from being decisive, bold, and influential. And expression depends on your ability to be vocal, insightful, and clear in your communications.

9 COMPETENCIES OF EXECUTIVE PRESENCE

RADIATE GRAVITAS	ACT WITH AUTHORITY	EXPRESS YOURSELF FULLY
GRAVITAS	AUTHORITY	EXPRESSION
Confident	Decisive	Vocal
Commanding	Bold	Insightful
Charismatic	Influential	Clear

Throughout the next several sections of this book, we'll explore each of these qualities one chapter at a time. By the end of each chapter, you'll understand not only how each quality looks in practice, but how to develop it step by step. You'll learn the specific behaviors that demonstrate each quality, and I'll share advice that has helped many clients cultivate them in their leadership practice.

First, though, let's take a bird's-eye view of each of the nine EP competencies. This will give you a basic "lay of the land" so you can more fully understand what executive presence looks like in practice.

THE 3X3 EXECUTIVE PRESENCE MODEL

GRAVITAS	AUTHORITY	EXPRESSION
CONFIDENT You lead with the assuredness that you can do it. You're assertive, decisive, and willing to take risks. You state your opinions strongly. You believe in what you know and who you are.	**DECISIVE** You take initiative and move things forward. You act with conviction. You make up your mind quickly and arrive at a clear decision with certainty. You don't waver or hesitate.	**VOCAL** You share your thoughts and ideas without hesitation. You're forthcoming with your opinions. Your voice and presence are visible to others. You make your expertise, competence, and talents known.
COMMANDING You take charge, driving toward outcomes. People look to you for leadership. They defer to you. When you speak, people pay attention. Others perceive your presence and power.	**BOLD** You are willing to make bold decisions—then put a stake in the ground and own your position. You stand by your beliefs and convictions. You are willing to challenge and push back.	**INSIGHTFUL** You make great recommendations. You ask excellent questions and share ideas precisely, confidently, and with conviction. You are known for smart thinking and critical analysis.
CHARISMATIC You radiate enthusiasm, personal charm, and an optimistic attitude. You motivate and inspire others. People are drawn to you. You feel approachable.	**INFLUENTIAL** You are convincing, compelling, and forceful. You incite and encourage others toward action. Your articulate and assertive points of view persuade others. You can effectively counter-argue.	**CLEAR** When you communicate, you are succinct and to the point. Your message is clear and crisp; you are straightforward and direct. You're polished and express yourself without qualifier or filler words.

Now that you have a basic understanding of the nine competencies, it's time to determine where you stand on the EP spectrum. After all, if you can't measure it, you can't improve it.

Evaluate your executive presence.

Many leadership assessments measure the skills, traits, or qualities that make a great leader. However, most of them don't measure the specific qualities of executive presence. The following assessment will help you measure your current level of EP, giving you an accurate perception of your competencies. You'll find out how well you are doing in each of the nine key areas, and where you may be self-sabotaging your own leadership potential.

GRAVITAS

TOTAL: _____

CONFIDENT

You lead with the assuredness that you can do it. You're assertive, decisive, and willing to take risks. You state your opinions strongly. You believe in what you know and who you are.

HOW WELL DO YOU EMBODY THIS COMPETENCY? (RATE YOURSELF FROM 1–10)

1	2	3	4	5	6	7	8	9	10

COMMANDING

You take charge, driving toward outcomes. People look to you for leadership. They defer to you. When you speak, people pay attention. Others perceive your presence and power.

HOW WELL DO YOU EMBODY THIS COMPETENCY? (RATE YOURSELF FROM 1–10)

1	2	3	4	5	6	7	8	9	10

CHARISMATIC

You radiate enthusiasm, personal charm, and an optimistic attitude. You motivate and inspire others. People are drawn to you. You feel approachable.

HOW WELL DO YOU EMBODY THIS COMPETENCY? (RATE YOURSELF FROM 1–10)

1	2	3	4	5	6	7	8	9	10

Add up your total for each of the three competencies above to get your total Gravitas score: _____

AUTHORITY

TOTAL: _____

DECISIVE

You take initiative and move things forward. You act with conviction.
You make up your mind quickly and arrive at a clear decision with certainty.
You don't waver or hesitate.

HOW WELL DO YOU EMBODY THIS COMPETENCY? (RATE YOURSELF FROM 1–10)

1	2	3	4	5	6	7	8	9	10

BOLD

You are willing to make bold decisions—then put a stake in the ground
and own your position. You stand by your beliefs and convictions.
You are willing to challenge and push back.

HOW WELL DO YOU EMBODY THIS COMPETENCY? (RATE YOURSELF FROM 1–10)

1	2	3	4	5	6	7	8	9	10

INFLUENTIAL

You are convincing, compelling, and forceful. You incite and encourage
others toward action. Your articulate and assertive points of view
persuade others. You can effectively counter-argue.

HOW WELL DO YOU EMBODY THIS COMPETENCY? (RATE YOURSELF FROM 1–10)

1	2	3	4	5	6	7	8	9	10

*Add up your total for each of the three competencies above
to get your total Authority score:* _____

EXPRESSION

TOTAL: _____

VOCAL

You share your thoughts and ideas without hesitation. You're forthcoming with your opinions. Your voice and presence are visible to others. You make your expertise, competence, and talents known.

HOW WELL DO YOU EMBODY THIS COMPETENCY? (RATE YOURSELF FROM 1–10)

1	2	3	4	5	6	7	8	9	10

INSIGHTFUL

You make great recommendations. You ask excellent questions and share ideas precisely, confidently, and with conviction. You are known for smart thinking and critical analysis.

HOW WELL DO YOU EMBODY THIS COMPETENCY? (RATE YOURSELF FROM 1–10)

1	2	3	4	5	6	7	8	9	10

CLEAR

When you communicate, you are succinct and to the point. You present a clear, crisp message in a straightforward and direct manner. You're polished and express yourself without qualifier or filler words.

HOW WELL DO YOU EMBODY THIS COMPETENCY? (RATE YOURSELF FROM 1–10)

1	2	3	4	5	6	7	8	9	10

Add up your total for each of the three competencies above to get your total Expression score: _____

EVALUATING YOUR RESULTS

GRAVITAS

Refer to your total Gravitas score and find the corresponding number below.

Gravitas Total Score:

24 – 30: If your total Gravitas score falls between 24 and 30, you radiate an impressive presence and display a high degree of confidence.

People look to you for leadership. They trust you to guide them through any challenges that arise.

18 – 24: If your score falls between 18 and 24, you're above average in terms of your ability to command a room and inspire others. You fall short of exceptional in certain areas, but you will get there soon with consistent effort.

12 – 18: If your score falls between 12 and 18, you may sometimes show confidence and charisma, but not always. You may take charge and drive toward outcomes in certain contexts, like small group settings. Keep working on those competencies so you can reach the next level.

Below 12: If your score falls below 12, you probably aren't perceived as being very assertive or in command. You may shy away from the spotlight. But as you dedicate yourself to implementing the strategies shared in this book, you'll begin seeing an upward trend in your ability to show executive presence.

AUTHORITY

Refer to your total Authority score and find the corresponding number below.

Authority Total Score:

24 – 30: If your Authority score falls between 24 and 30, you are exceptional at making bold decisions, acting with certainty, and influencing outcomes. Others seek out your opinions, which you deliver assertively. You stand by your beliefs and communicate forcefully.

18 – 24: If your score falls between 18 and 24, you are above average and demonstrate authority fairly well. You can be extremely persuasive, strong, and resolute. However, sometimes you struggle with decision-making and being assertive with people more senior than you. You are doing well in this area, but a little extra effort will help you reach the next level.

12 – 18: If your score falls between 12 and 18, you have substantial room to grow, but you probably do have some nascent strengths to work with. You are decisive at times, but not assertive enough. You have difficulty convincing others to adopt your perspectives. Try to pinpoint whether you show authority in certain moments, and where you really need to demonstrate more of it.

Below 12: If your score falls below 12, you aren't demonstrating a lot of authority. You are perceived by others as being tentative and hesitant. You're uncertain and indecisive about making decisions. Work hard to build your competence in this domain so you can reap the rewards of having greater impact and influence.

EXPRESSION

Refer to your total Expression score and find the corresponding number below.

Expression Total Score:

24 – 30: If your Expression score falls between 24 and 30, you are extremely good at speaking up, making your insights known, and communicating in a clear, succinct way. When you open your mouth, others tune in.

18 – 24: If your score falls between 18 and 24, you are an above-average communicator. You may struggle a bit in one area while excelling in many others. For instance, you may candidly share your ideas and ask smart questions in meetings, though you need to become more concise and to the point when communicating.

12 – 18: If your score falls between 12 and 18, you need to hone your communication skills and work on cultivating more expression. To rise above average, you will need to be more forthright with your opinions, making your insights and knowledge known. Strive to become more articulate and condensed in your communication.

Below 12: If your score falls below 12, your communication skills sorely need strengthening. Notice when you aren't contributing in meetings and immediately begin finding ways to be vocal. Every day at work is filled with communications and thus provides numerous opportunities to improve your expression. Apply what you learn from this book within your work environment to become a strong communicator.

OVERALL SCORE

Tally up your total for Gravitas, Authority, and Expression and find the corresponding number below.

Overall Total Score:

80 – 90: The maximum possible score for this evaluation is 90, although few people will get a perfect score. (In fact, if you gave yourself a perfect score, you should find out if others would score you in the same way!) If your total falls between 80 and 90, you're doing exceptionally well. You have room to fine-tune your EP or may have one or two competencies that need more strengthening, but all in all, you are exuding EP on a daily basis.

70 – 80: If your score falls between 70 and 80, your executive presence is above average. Now it's time to work on strengthening particular areas that you haven't quite mastered, so you'll shine in each of these competencies across the board.

50 – 70: If you have a score of 50–70, while you are not always showing up as a leader with executive presence, in certain situations you may shine. Your EP is showing up in subtle ways or in particular contexts. With steady practice, you can allow it to shine *all* of the time.

40 – 50: If your score falls from 40–50, you probably show some nascent signs of executive presence. However, you haven't developed and leveraged these areas of strength. Through proactive work, you can quickly move up to the above-average zone.

Below 40: If your score falls below 40, don't fret. Through daily practice, you can build your EP skillset. Get comfortable simply practicing the skills you'll learn about in this book, and eventually they will become a natural part of how you interact with the world.

Now that you have a stronger idea of where you stand, let's delve into each of these domains in more detail, beginning with Gravitas. We are going to embark on a detailed exploration of these three domains and the three core competencies that make up each of them. As you make your way through the next nine chapters of this book, you'll gain a thorough understanding of exactly how your executive presence needs to grow.

Section 1:

GRAVITAS

Domain 1 of 3

Introduction

Understanding Gravitas

"When we feel powerful, even our voices spread out and take up more space than they do when we feel powerless. … We don't rush our words. We're not afraid to pause. We feel deserving of the time we're using," writes Amy Cuddy in her book *Presence*.[i] What she's describing here is gravitas—the quality that makes others instinctively feel a leader's great credibility, capability, and overall presence.

If you have gravitas, your thoughts, ideas, and actions carry a weight.

Gravitas defined.

The origin of the word *gravitas* lends insight into what it signifies. Its root, the Latin word *gravis,* means "heavy." We speak of the *gravity* of a situation when referring to something serious or critical. If you have gravitas, your thoughts, ideas, and actions carry a weight. People can feel your presence immediately. You have a powerful effect on another person. You hold the room or that person's attention. People take note of your opinions and insights.

Possessing gravitas leads others to see you as confident, commanding, and charismatic—the three core competencies that make up this quality. When you fully embody gravitas, people perceive you this way at all times, not just in certain situations.

In *Cracking the Code,* Sylvia Ann Hewlett asserts that 67% of the senior leaders she interviewed for the book said gravitas is seminal to executive presence.[ii] They cited qualities such as showing grace under fire and radiating vision and charisma as being central to strong executive leadership. Your company's C-suite are looking out for this quality—and even if you're already among their ranks, continuing to hone your gravitas will have a tremendous influence on your ability to get the most from your team.

GRAVITAS
Confident
Commanding
Charismatic

Your gravitas inspires confidence in others. First, it helps subordinates to feel their own potential to *do* more, *be* more, and *achieve* more than they thought possible. They know you are capably guiding them to reach the next level. Second, your peers are impressed by you, they respect the quality of your work, and they find you trustworthy—one of the top five most crucial qualities in a leader.[iii] They know they are on a winning team, and that your self-assuredness and abilities will buoy everyone else up. Third, superiors rely on you to produce excellent work, expand your influence, and go above and beyond what is asked of you. They know your confidence and powerful leadership will drive results.

Gravitas is the commanding presence that great leaders hold, radiating charisma and confidence to all those around them.

Sophia Masters the Art of Gravitas

Problem:

A GEC client named Sophia, a leader at a large software company, received the following feedback from her boss: "You have a great communication style. You're conversational, and you share ideas in an engaging way. However, your most powerful ideas can be too easily brushed off because you present them too casually."

Sophia's voice and level of conviction didn't change to accentuate important points, so they went unnoticed. "If you speak in a more passionate tone when you're describing your most critical ideas, others will respond," her boss said. "Speak with firmness and strength in those moments. Make sure your voice carries a heavier weight. Then people will feel the power of your best ideas."

Action:

In our next sessions, we practiced how Sophia could voice her ideas with the gravitas required to drive her points home. She learned to master the art of speaking with conviction. We also practiced how she could advocate for her own ideas persuasively when challenged, so she wouldn't lose footing in the moment.

Results:

As she put these lessons into practice, Sophia started getting noticed for her great ideas and steadily increasing her sphere of influence. Many people were blown away by the value of her ideas and shocked that they had been flying under the radar all that time!

Whenever you are presenting your ideas to an audience, you need to be prepared to address pointed questions and diverse points of view. You need to be standing on a foundation of gravitas. Don't lose your composure. Be calm. Hold your ground. Show that you can take a few blows and not waver or become submissive. Don't lose your confidence, and don't cause others to lose their confidence in you. People, especially top-level leaders, need to see that you remain in command with a solid sense of authority, even when called to question. When your superiors are discussing or questioning your ideas, speak to them as if they are your equals.

Let's explore the main components of gravitas now in a bit more depth, so you can more fully understand this EP domain.

The most essential qualities of gravitas.

GEC Research Center asked 1,400 U.S. employees, middle managers, senior leaders, and executives what they view as the top qualities of gravitas. Here's what they said.

THE MOST IMPORTANT QUALITIES OF GRAVITAS
% saying it is absolutely essential for a leader to be ...

Quality	%
CONFIDENT	93%
COMMANDING	80%
POISED	76%
CHARISMATIC	74%
INSPIRING	68%

Source: GEC Research Center Survey, Poll of 1,400 U.S. Workers.

As you can see, "confident" rose to the top as the most important leadership quality within this survey. "Commanding" followed closely behind. Further analysis determined that charisma is one of the three most important components of gravitas as well.[1] These findings led us to create the following definition of gravitas within the 3x3 Executive Presence Model. If you have gravitas, this describes how you show up in every situation.

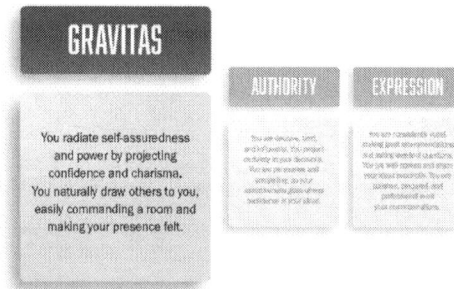

GRAVITAS

AUTHORITY **EXPRESSION**

You radiate self-assuredness and power by projecting confidence and charisma. You naturally draw others to you, easily commanding a room and making your presence felt.

Gravitas is the commanding presence that great leaders hold, radiating charisma and confidence to all those around them. Everyone can feel the powerful presence of a leader with gravitas, from subordinates to senior

---

1   As the GEC Research Center team analyzed the results of our survey, we found that "poised" strongly related to being in command and "inspiring" was a component of charisma. Thus, we arrived at "confident," "commanding," and "charismatic" as the three most essential qualities of gravitas.

executives. Such leaders have fully developed the three most essential competencies of gravitas: confidence, command, and charisma.

Gravitas is who you *are* and how you show up. Leaders who possess gravitas carry themselves in this way with *everyone*, not just certain people. It has become part of them, not a switch they can turn on and off.

GRAVITAS IS:
Who You Are
How You **SHOW UP**
Exuding Confidence

As you become a more confident, commanding, and charismatic leader, you'll exude a powerful presence in all of your meetings and interactions. Even if others can't describe exactly what has changed about you, they'll notice the shift, and it will shape their perception of you as a leader with executive presence.

Which behaviors show a lack of gravitas?

Sometimes it's easier to notice the qualities that harm your chances of success than the ones that could help you succeed. In the GEC survey, respondents asserted that the following qualities have the most negative effect on gravitas.

WHICH BEHAVIORS MOST UNDERMINE GRAVITAS?
% who say these behaviors show a lack of gravitas …

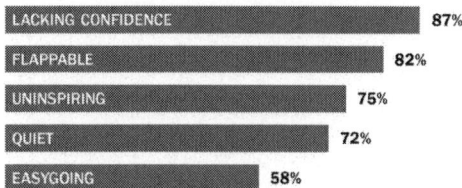

Behavior	Percentage
LACKING CONFIDENCE	87%
FLAPPABLE	82%
UNINSPIRING	75%
QUIET	72%
EASYGOING	58%

Source: GEC Research Center Survey, Poll of 1,400 U.S. Workers.

Since confidence is the most important quality of gravitas, it follows that *lack* of confidence would most heavily undermine gravitas. Being flappable undermines one's ability to be commanding, while being uninspiring undermines charisma. Let's take a more detailed look at each of these qualities, both positive and negative.

Comparison of qualities that cultivate or undermine gravitas.

The following chart will help you understand which qualities cultivate gravitas and which behaviors diminish it. If you're trying to develop one of the traits in column A, you need to know whether you're engaging in the behaviors in column B. If so, you need to work on changing those behaviors so you can truly exude gravitas—and executive presence.

15 WAYS TO BUILD OR UNDERMINE GRAVITAS

QUALITIES THAT CULTIVATE GRAVITAS	QUALITIES THAT UNDERMINE GRAVITAS
CONFIDENT • Self-assured • Grounded • Impressive • Certain • Composed	**LACKING CONFIDENCE** • Insecure • Self-doubting • Unassuming • Hesitant • Flustered
COMMANDING • Strong • Powerful • Filled with conviction • In charge • Poised	**EASYGOING** • Relaxed • Too casual • Laid-back • Despondent • Flappable
CHARISMATIC • Charming • Engaging • Passionate • Inspiring • Empowering	**DULL** • Reserved • Unexciting • Dispassionate • Unaffecting • Disempowering

If you want to see an example of gravitas in action, just look to Oprah. She radiates a natural confidence with her grounded, self-assured demeanor. She instantly commands a room with her powerful, poised presence. When she speaks, you know she's saying something important—you can feel it in the conviction in her voice. "She has a magnetic energy that pulls you in and keeps you captivated, under her spell. She owns her presence, the space around her, and she projects gravitas that easily pierces any screen," writes Stephanie Denning in *Forbes*. Oprah doesn't seek to intimidate others with this presence—quite the opposite.[iv] Her charisma draws people in, leading them to show up as their most authentic selves. She seeks to empower and inspire; anyone listening to her can see that. Her empathy makes her incredibly relatable despite her power and prestige. At the same time, she has no problem speaking up when she disagrees with something. Finally, her mastery of communicating her vision to others has propelled her up the ladder of success one rung after another, igniting passion in her team.[v] Oprah has mastered the domains of Authority and Expression as well, making her an excellent example of someone with exceptional executive presence.

Hopefully you are beginning to develop a clearer picture of what gravitas looks like—and whether you have it. Now we'll explore each of the three key competencies of gravitas, beginning with confidence. You'll gain a clearer picture of what a leader with each of these qualities looks like, behaviors that can undermine each quality, and how to cultivate these competencies within yourself and your employees.

Chapter 6

Confident

Gravitas Competency #1

"Self-confidence is a super power.
Once you start believing in yourself, magic starts happening."
— Anonymous

Your company needs leaders who are confident in their own abilities, and who let that confidence shine. Confidence is a key cornerstone of executive presence, affecting every aspect of leadership. Research has demonstrated that increased self-confidence correlates with stronger leadership performance, especially in the following key areas:[i]

+ Being persuasive
+ Embracing change
+ Radiating energy and enthusiasm
+ Trying out innovative approaches
+ Inspiring and motivating others
+ Representing the group positively

How can you master this key executive presence quality? Let's begin with exploring what having confidence means.

Your company needs leaders who are confident in their own abilities, and who let that confidence shine.

Behaviors of confident leaders.

As you develop a healthy level of confidence, you'll lead with assurance. You'll be assertive, self-possessed, and willing to take risks, feeling certain that you can learn from failure and ultimately persevere. Thus, you won't just play it safe. You'll state your opinions strongly and believe in what you know and who you are.

As a confident leader, you'll share your opinions often and powerfully. You won't hold back on sharing your ideas, because you'll know your insights are critical. Nor will you hesitate to challenge others when you disagree. By speaking up with conviction at meetings, you'll grow your influence, which will also broaden your team's pool of ideas.

Because you'll know you're equipped to handle any challenge, you won't shy away from new things—and you'll pursue your goals to fruition. You won't give up just because you hit a hurdle or two. Thus, you'll never stop learning and growing your competencies. You'll also take ownership of your actions, listening to feedback and working to remediate your behavior and the situation. You won't fear criticism.

As you become a more confident leader, you'll see the major rewards you can reap from testing what is possible rather than abiding by the status quo. Thus, you'll reach greater heights of success that wouldn't be possible without a high level of self-trust.

In the following chart, the column on the left shows the set of behaviors you need to develop to radiate confidence. In the column on the right, you'll see the behaviors that inhibit confidence, which can make you appear a weaker version of yourself. Master the competencies on the left to shine as a confident leader!

CONFIDENT QUALITIES	QUALITIES THAT UNDERMINE CONFIDENCE
Self-assured	Insecure
Grounded	Self-doubting
Impressive	Unassuming
Certain	Hesitant
Composed	Flappable

Confidence remains sorely in demand in most workplaces. A recent survey by Gartner, Inc. found that only half of all leaders feel equipped to succeed in a leadership role.[ii] That means a large proportion of leaders aren't coming close to fulfilling their own potential!

When leaders lack confidence, it reverberates throughout the organization. Their own people begin to second-guess them rather than boldly standing behind them. Thus, lack of confidence undermines their ability to guide their team to success.

As you become a leader with executive presence, you'll act with confidence no matter who is in the room. You'll believe in your ideas enough to tell hard truths at times, even to superiors. By doing this in respectful ways, you'll maintain the respect of others when sharing an unpopular or unexpected idea. You won't worry about skepticism from others, although you will be prepared to handle it. When others push back against your idea, you'll share evidence backing it up.

Confident leaders boldly influence others and gain their loyalty because they believe in the value of their own input. People trust leaders with genuine self-confidence and want to go the extra mile for them. Thus, your commitment to building your own self-confidence will bring enhanced success for the entire group. From your example, others will learn how to boldly accept new challenges, focusing on the desired results rather than any lingering fears. As colleagues, leaders, and direct reports feel your confidence, they'll become more confident in your whole team in turn.

Further, your abundance of confidence will lead you to make an excellent first impression. Because our brains are hard-wired to quickly form a perception of someone else, we unconsciously feel a greater sense of respect and admiration for a confident person.[iii] As your confidence grows, others will enjoy being in your presence more and gravitate toward you. Your self-assuredness will make you engaging and easy to talk to, drawing others out as well. You'll also inspire clients' confidence in your organization, since you'll radiate an inner belief in what you are doing.

Confident leaders boldly influence others and gain their loyalty because they believe in the value of their own input.

Self-evaluation: Assess your level of confidence.

You may still be having a hard time imagining exactly how to model confidence in your day-to-day work. Read through the following list of confident behaviors, placing a checkmark beside each one that describes you. This will help you assess your current level of confidence and which specific behaviors you need to improve.

I demonstrate confidence by ...

1. Sharing opinions with conviction, expecting them to be well-received.

2. Speaking in a calm, steady tone that shows my belief in myself is firmly rooted.

3. Reaching out to those who are senior to me to share my ideas.

4. Being direct and clear when speaking to higher-level leaders, and not hesitating to voice my thoughts.

5. Acting equal to those who are more senior than me, and feeling equal to people at all levels of leadership.

6. Taking on challenges with enthusiasm, since I have lots of practice with stepping outside of my comfort zone.

7. Backing up ideas self-assuredly if someone challenges them.

8. Questioning anyone else's ideas if I disagree with them.

9. Showing a clear rationale for the ideas I share, giving me immense credibility.

10. Announcing decisions with certainty rather than trepidation, and believing in their ability to drive change.

11. Not being afraid to take risks, knowing that taking strategic risks (and sometimes failing) is the only way to reach the next level.

12. Remaining poised even if I have to step outside of my comfort zone. While I might feel nervous at times, it doesn't show on my face or in my voice.

13. Not constantly second-guessing myself when I have an idea or hesitating to voice it.

14. Preparing ahead of time for meetings and presentations, so I'll be articulate and clear when speaking.

15. Always looking "put together," which helps me to feel like a leader in every situation.

16. If I need to have a difficult conversation, being able to guide it in a positive, productive direction.

17. Giving others a sense of reassurance during challenging times.

18. Showing vulnerability at times, but not erupting with anger, frustration, or fear.

19. Using body language that conveys I am centered and balanced—shoulders back, chin up, back straight.

20. Making strong eye contact, establishing a direct connection with people.

Now tally up the total points you checked. If you scored above 17, you have an impressive level of confidence, although you may have room to grow in certain areas. If your score falls below 14, you struggle with confidence, and if it falls below 8, you have an especially critical need to grow this competency.

Look at the confident behaviors you *haven't* checked. Does one or more of these points stand out as an area where you need to grow? Focus on shifting your behavior in these areas over the next several weeks by projecting self-assurance and stepping outside of your comfort zone. If you've left many of these behaviors unchecked, start with three to five areas of focus. We'll discuss action steps for improving them later in this chapter.

Isabel Improves Her Confidence with Careful Preparation

Problem:

Isabel had been working as a mid-level manager for several years, and she'd just received a promotion. She found herself giving report-backs to a table of leaders one level above her on a weekly basis.

Isabel didn't know most of these leaders well, and she felt far outside of her comfort zone. Her voice sounded anxious when she delivered her project updates. Since she just wanted to get it over with, she rushed through her words, which made her sound even more nervous. After this happened a couple of times, her boss pulled her aside and urged her to make improving her confidence in speaking her number-one priority.

Action:

That's when Isabel turned to executive coaching. We discussed several strategies she could use to both look and feel more confident. She began rehearsing her words in the morning before she went in to work, and creating notecards with the key deliverables she needed to mention. She also began doing a mini-meditation at her desk shortly before a meeting, so she'd feel more centered.

Results:

When Isabel didn't have to fear that she'd forget what to say, her cadence became more relaxed. After she pulled off a confident delivery a couple of times, she actually began looking forward to these weekly meetings, knowing she'd receive appreciation and praise for her great work.

> Displaying confidence starts from within.
> You'll exude more confidence when you trust your own ability and give yourself positive affirmations. Remind yourself of where you've excelled in the past.

Behaviors that undermine confidence.

Now let's take a look at some behaviors that can inhibit your efforts to show confidence. These potential derailers of success keep you from feeling and appearing like a poised and confident leader. Put a checkmark next to any of the following behaviors you engage in.

I undermine my confidence by ...

- Acquiescing to another person's opinion during a disagreement to avoid conflict.
- Feeling afraid to speak up in meetings and share my opinions.
- Deferring to others instead of sharing my own point of view.
- Feeling indecisive and doubtful when trying to make decisions.
- Seeking validation from others by trying to please everyone.

- Getting easily rattled when something stressful or unexpected occurs.
- Second-guessing myself rather than trusting myself.
- Feeling hesitant to take on challenges or new projects because I might fail.
- Overanalyzing what I am going to say (often resulting in saying nothing).
- Apologizing for my behaviors regularly.
- Speaking in a quiet or soft voice.
- Rarely (or never) asking for feedback.
- Slumping in my chair and looking disinterested rather than fully present.
- Not making eye contact with people I'm speaking with.
- Sitting in the back of the room or outside the table where the discussion is happening.
- Seeming overcome with anger, frustration, or fear about a stressful situation.
- Laughing nervously or speaking in a shaky voice.
- In Zoom meetings, keeping my camera off or not looking at the camera when speaking (which comes across as making poor eye contact).

If you lack confidence, you may notice yourself engaging in these behaviors. Others will *definitely* notice. To inspire others to have confidence in you, show your superiors that you believe in yourself. They need to see that you have self-confidence before they'll begin to trust you with greater responsibilities. Showing a high level of self-trust will naturally inspire others to feel more confident in you—and it will also show them what you can do. As you grow your confidence, you'll start reaching for more ambitious goals and proving what you're capable of, which will lead your boss to entrust you with higher-level projects.

When leaders lack confidence,
it reverberates throughout the
organization.

Gary Gains Confidence and Credibility

Problem:

A GEC client named Gary *did* have things to say and contribute, but it seemed like he always held himself back. Due to the amount of experience he had, one would expect him to be more confident in sharing his opinions.

His tentativeness was keeping his boss from seeing him as leadership material. He needed to show that he could take charge and handle situations when people needed his guidance. Gary also lacked confidence among his coworkers. When his boss asked him to mentor a colleague in a particular area, he felt daunted—what did he really have to offer? Surely there was a better person for the job, he thought.

Action:

We encouraged Gary to push through his self-doubts by organizing his thoughts before each of their peer-mentoring sessions and before meetings. Taking a few moments to do this reminded Gary of how much he actually knew and how much experience he had. We discussed how much Gary's boss depended on his input, too. Gary began pushing himself to insert his opinions into the conversation.

Results:

Gary felt surprised at first at the gratitude his colleague expressed for the knowledge he shared. The experience helped to affirm his own value. In fact, serving as a peer mentor reinforced his confidence so much that he found it easier to share his opinions in meetings, knowing he had an important perspective. As a result, his credibility and reputation grew among both colleagues and leaders. Gary's boss commended him for his efforts and said he'd witnessed a significant change.

Do others perceive you as confident?

This exercise will help you to better understand how others perceive you. While you'll need to directly ask people for feedback in order to truly gauge how they view you, this rating scale will give you a cursory sense of how confident you appear. Assign yourself a score of 1 to 10 for each of these statements, with 1 being the lowest and 10 being the highest:

+ Others feel more confident in their own abilities with me at the helm.
+ My boss regularly asks me to take on high-level responsibilities.
+ People ask me to take charge in high-stakes situations.
+ Colleagues rarely second-guess my judgment.
+ When I reach out to senior leaders, they're eager to hear what I have to say.

If you scored above 43, you're likely projecting a healthy level of confidence. Otherwise, leverage the exercises and action steps in this chapter to develop your confidence.

Action steps to become a more confident leader.

These action steps will help you cultivate a reputation as a confident leader. As others come to see you this way, you'll either be perceived as a leader with executive presence or someone who's on the road to that destination.

1. Schedule time to explore what holds you back from having confidence at work.

As you take this courageous step forward and begin learning more about yourself, the obstacles will become less restricting and you'll open up to possibilities previously unknown. In your reflection time, answer these questions:

+ Why am I not showing up with confidence?
+ What excuses am I making to not be confident?
+ What obstacles are keeping me from being confident?
+ What fears are stopping me from feeling confident?
+ Do I have certain limiting beliefs about myself that prevent me from being confident?

Once you identify the obstacles, you can counteract them with positive self-talk and lean into your fears through the following steps.

2. Get comfortable being uncomfortable.

If you want to keep growing, you'll continually be feeling uncomfortable, so get used to that idea now. As a leader, you'll experience more than your share of criticism, uncertainty, tough choices, and sometimes public failures. However, you can learn to cope with these challenges head-on so they don't overburden you with stress. And the more you step outside of your comfort zone, the wider your comfort zone will grow.

How can you learn to feel comfortable with discomfort? Instead of avoiding uncomfortable situations, practice saying "yes" to them. Accept and embrace them. Say to yourself, "I am capable of handling this situation." By doing so, you'll learn to operate from a place of self-confidence rather than a place of stress as you negotiate difficult circumstances. And every time you do so, you'll increase your sense of being ready to tackle any challenge.

3. Volunteer for new types of projects.

Step outside of your comfort zone by signing up for a project that forces you to stretch your skillset. Choose something achievable but ambitious. Take the lead on a team project for the first time or pitch an innovative idea to your boss.

4. Surround yourself with advocates and supporters.

When you spend time with people who truly believe in you, you'll find it easier to believe in yourself. They'll remind you of your strengths and the times you've overcome your weaknesses. Cultivate relationships with people at different levels of the organization, as well as colleagues from outside of it, who share encouragement and help you see yourself in a positive light.

Where to find these advocates? Ask your boss or mentor for an introduction to leaders you admire. Or, learn about the projects these leaders are doing and consider how you can help troubleshoot issues. Offer to problem-solve or take certain tasks off their plate. Showing that you've been studying their work will emphasize that you're someone they want on their team.

When you spend time with people who truly believe in you, you'll find it easier to believe in yourself.

5.   Do things that make you feel confident.

Even though you should be doing things on a daily basis that stretch your comfort zone, you should also pinpoint the things that make you feel supported and capable. They'll help you navigate new terrain with grace and skill, giving you a boost of confidence that will keep you motivated. For example, do you think best in writing or while brainstorming with a friend? Use that strategy to come up with ideas to share at a meeting. Do you feel tongue-tied when interacting with new people? Think of some conversation starters for that lunch with your boss's boss in advance. Do you get a quick burst of confidence from showing people how to do something that's easy for you, but new to them? The positive feedback you gain will help keep you motivated throughout the day.

6.   Look for evidence of your abilities.

Most of the time, we look for evidence that our abilities *aren't* good enough (i.e., *what we are lacking*). Confident people look for evidence that their abilities *are* good enough. They expect to find that evidence most of the time. Prove to yourself what you are capable of doing. Gather data that show you are smart and talented. Be a lawyer arguing your own case.

7.   Practice positive self-talk.

We all fall into negative patterns of self-talk, which hinder our chances of success unless we actively work to correct them. According to one researcher, we speak to ourselves at a rate of up to 4,000 words per minute![iv] That's a lot of negative self-talk, if we don't correct course. Notice the types of things you say to yourself about your abilities and efforts. When you catch yourself saying negative things, give yourself the advice you would give a friend or coworker instead. Practice using positive, motivational language, since it's sure to bring better results than negative statements.

8.   Make sure your voice sounds relaxed yet energized when speaking.

Instead of rushing your delivery in a meeting, vary your pacing to emphasize key points.

9.   Accept your own vulnerability.

Feeling vulnerable is an innate part of the human experience, not a weakness. If you repress your sense of vulnerability, you'll only become more afraid of feeling vulnerable. That increases fear and insecurity, rather than decreasing it! Instead, acknowledge what makes you feel vulnerable. In an interview with Brené Brown, Oprah recognized vulnerability as "the cornerstone of confidence" because it shows that you're self-assured enough to take risks that ultimately allow you to identify with others around you.[v] "Vulnerability sounds like truth and feels like courage," Brown says in *Daring Greatly*.[vi] "Truth and courage aren't always comfortable, but they're never weakness."

10.   Embrace the opportunity to fail.

If you're taking risks that have the potential to take you to greater heights in your career—as you should be—there's always a chance that you'll fail. Embrace the possibility of failure, and then you'll no longer feel so afraid of it. Do everything you can to set yourself up for success, and then take the leap.

Switching from those low-confidence to high-confidence behaviors is an easy and quick way to start appearing more confident now. You'll feel more confident as you present yourself with confidence, allowing you to speak and act with more conviction in turn.

As you adopt these behaviors, you'll make the shift to modeling confidence in your daily work—and others will take note. Most importantly, know that displaying confidence starts from within. You'll exude more confidence when you trust your own ability and give yourself positive affirmations. Remind yourself of where you've excelled in the past. When making a choice, you'll then trust your own judgment and intellect to guide you in the right direction.

Alicia Grows Her Rapport with Senior Leaders

Problem:

Whenever Alicia, a GEC client, had a chance interaction with a higher-level leader, she'd get tongue-tied and fail to make a strong impression. A very introverted person, Alicia assumed she simply didn't have what it takes to come across as a leader in those situations. When she saw her more outgoing colleagues interacting with senior leaders, she couldn't imagine herself sounding so gregarious. She unconsciously thought to herself, *Why even try?*

Action:

In order to act confident, Alicia first needed to *feel* confident. She needed to truly believe in her own value. Of course, that's easier said than done. We discussed how she didn't have to project the exact same persona that her peers projected. Everyone wears confidence differently. Alicia learned to remind herself of what made her truly proud of her work and the results she was achieving. She crafted a short but compelling elevator pitch based on these strengths.

Results:

The next time Alicia ran into a high-level leader, they had a great conversation that helped them develop a rapport. This leader remembered her and asked her how her work was going in their next interaction. By mustering up her confidence in that first chance meeting, Alicia had created a positive feedback loop that kept her confidence growing.

Help your employees grow their confidence.

"Good leaders inspire people to have confidence in their leader. Great leaders inspire people to have confidence in themselves."
— Eleanor Roosevelt

As a leader, you're responsible for helping your people grow their confidence. It won't just benefit them at some future point in time when they land a promotion to a leadership position. Rather, it will help them reach a new level of excellence in their work right now.

How will enhancing employees' confidence build a stronger team?

Here are some key benefits you'll see in your whole team as employee confidence grows.

- They'll address issues as they arise, rather than letting them fester. The team will therefore function more harmoniously rather than being plagued by disruption.
- Others will listen to them when they speak, and they'll listen to others in turn, improving group communication.
- They'll push themselves to tackle new types of projects, setting stretch goals that grow their capabilities.
- They'll foster a culture of positivity within their team because they won't feel threatened by new or contradictory ideas, creating an atmosphere of open communication.
- They'll motivate others because their enthusiasm for their work is contagious, and they'll serve as excellent peer role models who bring out the best in each other.

For all of these reasons, confident employees are valuable contributors who are well-positioned to become future leaders.

How to help your employees grow their confidence.

Your subordinates can grow their confidence with encouragement and repeated practice. Here are some action steps you can take to help them expand their confidence.

- Tell them how much their opinions matter. Often people forget that others are actually depending on them when they avoid speaking up.
- Ask for their feedback and opinions, so they know you view them as intelligent and capable.
- Challenge them to take risks. Create a culture of celebrating failure as long as they took a calculated risk.
- Assign them to projects that take them outside of their comfort zone in appropriate ways. Don't push them too hard too fast, but make sure they're tackling new challenges.
- Coach them rather than micromanaging them as they try new things. They need to know you trust them to carry out their responsibilities, but that you're also there to provide guidance when they need it.

- Praise their efforts often in genuine ways, so they know the full value they bring.

Each success your employees achieve will make them less preoccupied with the potential for failure and more certain of themselves. As their leader, work to model confidence yourself, and you'll take your people far beyond what they thought possible.

Confident employees are valuable contributors
who are well-positioned to become future leaders.

Chapter 7

Commanding

Gravitas Competency #2

"When placed in command, take charge."
— Norman Schwarzkopf

Leaders with executive presence are commanding. When people look at them, there's no doubt that they're in charge. Superiors gladly hand them the reins when they offer to take a leading role in a project, knowing they'll get things done. Others innately know they can trust these leaders to guide the team to success.

"Leaders lead *with* the authority of leadership ... or without it. The authority is largely irrelevant—if you are a leader, you will lead when you are needed," says pastor and motivational speaker Clay Scroggins in *How to Lead When You're Not in Charge*.[i] That's exactly what commanding leaders do. They take charge and drive their team toward a clear goal with a laser focus. Others respond to their determination and conviction by springing into action.

Your company needs leaders with a commanding presence who will move people toward a strategic vision. Let's take a closer look at what this competency is, and then how to cultivate and master it.

Leaders with executive presence are commanding. When people look at them, there's no doubt that they're in charge.

Behaviors of commanding leaders.

Commanding leaders are *socially brave*, as Gallup says; they seem to take control of situations effortlessly, without wavering.[ii] It's not hard to spot the commanding leaders in your workplace; you probably intuitively know who they are. In times of crisis or transformation, these commanding leaders will help their team stay the course and navigate change successfully. They're the people you want steering the ship through stormy waters.

In contrast, passive leadership has detrimental effects on the whole team, researchers have found.[iii] It leads to role overload and ambiguity among employees, mental fatigue, and ultimately even mental health impacts.

People can quickly sense a leader's commanding nature even without knowing him well. As they witness the leader's power and presence in action, they only become more convinced of his strength and immense capability.

As you become a commanding leader, you'll learn to take charge and drive outcomes. People will naturally look to you for leadership, regardless of your title. They'll defer to your judgment. When you speak, people will pay attention. Others will perceive your presence and power.

Here's what a commanding leader looks like, in contrast to a leader who does not embody this competency.

COMMANDING QUALITIES	QUALITIES THAT UNDERMINE YOUR ABILITY TO BE IN COMMAND
Strong	Relaxed
Powerful	Too casual
Filled with conviction	Laid-back
In charge	Despondent
Poised	Flappable

Others never wonder what a commanding leader thinks—and these leaders' ability to be direct improves the flow of communication throughout the workplace. As you become more commanding, you won't shy away from the difficult conversations that lead to real progress when people's behavior needs to change. And when you have these conversations, others will fully listen.

Further, you'll prove to others that you will get things done. Others will instinctively defer to you as you step up to the plate, allowing you to take the reins on a difficult project or in a tough situation. People will trust you to guide the team through turbulent times, knowing you will stay the course.

Importantly, having a commanding presence doesn't mean being a bully. Great leaders are adept at balancing their commanding presence with their nurturing qualities. Having a strong emotional IQ will help you act in ways that benefit those around you and rely on their strengths. Rather than being a dictator, you can use your aura of authority to rally people for a productive brainstorming session, strategic discussion, or implementation of a new idea. You can build comradery with employees rather than being domineering, helping the team feel like a cohesive unit. Instead of railroading people into going along with your ideas, you'll naturally inspire others' confidence in them. But no one would call you laid-back, as they'll know that you're firmly committed to ensuring the success of your projects—and your initiative will propel the team forward. Since you readily spring into action with gumption, you'll help the whole team accomplish much more than a passive leader does.

As you learn to be in command, you'll gain others' full respect. Your subordinates won't second-guess your ideas, and they'll seek out your valuable feedback and guidance, which will help them advance in their own careers. They'll have a manager who actively coaches them to success. And by modeling courageous leadership, you'll help others to find courage within themselves as well. Further, you'll inspire more confidence in your client base and guide your clients persuasively. All stakeholders will have more trust in your organization as a result.

Winston Churchill provides an excellent example of someone who wasn't born a commanding leader, but who rose to that stature nonetheless. "When Churchill was 29-years old, he stood up to give a speech in the House of Commons as a newly elected representative and literally froze for three whole minutes," writes Carmine Gallo in *Forbes*.[iv] "He managed to say a few words, but returned to his seat in despair and covered his head with his hands. He vowed it would never happen again."

Churchill honed his delivery until he became one of the world's most gifted orators. On June 4, 1940, when Belgium had just surrendered to

Nazi Germany, Churchill faced pressure to do the same. But instead, he masterfully stood up and told the House of Commons that he would never capitulate to Hitler's forces. And by doing so, he changed the course of history. "We shall go on to the end ... we shall defend our island, whatever the cost may be, we shall fight on the beaches, we shall fight on the landing grounds, we shall fight in the fields and in the streets, we shall fight in the hills; we shall never surrender," he asserted with firm resolve.[v] Through ongoing practice in taking a commanding stance, Churchill became the powerful leader the nation and world needed. It didn't come naturally, but it became who he was—and by following his example, you'll become a commanding leader in your own right.

Self-evaluation: How commanding are you?

Are you struggling to understand exactly how you can become more commanding in your daily work? As you read through the following list of commanding behaviors, place a checkmark by each one that describes you.

I demonstrate that I am in command by ...

1. Taking charge and moving toward results rather than waiting to see what happens.
2. Being direct and clear with instructions and expectations, rather than beating around the bush.
3. Taking control of situations where leadership is lacking, even if I'm not the official leader.
4. Motivating my team toward more ambitious goals, driving projects and outcomes.
5. Letting my expertise and enthusiasm for my projects shine.
6. Expecting others to act upon my instructions quickly and enthusiastically—which they do.
7. Making unpopular decisions when I believe they're the best course of action.
8. Not fearing how others will react to my assertions or decisions.

9. Challenging others to assume more responsibility and take risks.

10. Prompting others to share their expertise and opinions in group settings.

11. Leaning into my fear so I can have a greater impact, confronting situations that feel difficult.

12. Presenting my opinions and ideas boldly and being willing to speak the truth, even if it's uncomfortable for others.

13. Standing up to authority when the situation calls for it.

14. Drawing a line in the sand when I need to hold a position with peers or subordinates.

15. Compelling people to believe in my vision by showing my own implicit belief in it.

16. Not allowing myself to get exasperated, as I believe in my ability to manage a challenge.

17. Radiating calm and a steady hand, especially under pressure, so I can manage any tough situation with grace and skill.

18. Cultivating a practice that helps me remain level-headed in difficult scenarios (e.g., taking a walk, meditating, exercising regularly).

19. Making sure my appearance radiates professionalism, including when I'm around senior leaders. I dress as though I'm at their level.

20. Reassuring the group that we will find a way to surmount any challenge together.

If you scored above 17, you have an impressive ability to be in command, although you may still have room to grow in some ways. If your score falls below 14, you struggle with being commanding. If it falls below 8, you have an urgent need to grow this competency.

Review the behaviors you haven't checked. Which ones stand out as your key areas for growth? Choose up to five behaviors to develop over the next few weeks. We'll discuss action steps for improving them later in this chapter. As you focus on remaining poised in all situations, radiating calm, and taking charge in group settings, you'll grow your commanding presence.

Now let's review the behaviors that sabotage your ability to be commanding, so you can work to eliminate them.

Behaviors that undermine your ability to be commanding.

Let's look at some behaviors that can derail your ability to come across as a commanding leader. Place a checkmark by any that describe you. These behaviors directly undermine a leader's executive presence, so if you engage in them, work to break these habits!

I demonstrate a lack of command by ...

- + Deferring too often to others instead of taking the lead.
- + Not holding my team accountable for results.
- + Being tentative in decision-making, presenting myself as uncertain and insecure in my judgment.
- + Making decisions based on the desire to appease people rather than based on what I know will drive results.
- + Going with the flow, being laid-back and too casual.
- + Avoiding giving constructive feedback that could help people and processes to improve.
- + Being passive rather than taking action.
- + Saying yes to most requests, even if I don't have the capacity to handle them.
- + Being too nice and accommodating rather than pushing back when I disagree.
- + Failing to confront a challenging situation directly.
- + Apologizing too often, including for minor things that were out of my control.
- + Being unclear about my directives or expectations for others.

You may notice yourself engaging in some of these behaviors, or you may receive feedback from others that you're engaging in them. Either way, this is a red flag that you are undermining your EP. These behaviors all present you as a more passive, ineffective leader rather than someone who is in command.

You may not present yourself as commanding because you have a people-pleasing nature. Being assertive and holding others accountable may not come naturally to you. Like many people—leaders included—you may find it more comfortable to defer to others, while feeling anxious about the idea of putting a stake in the ground. However, even if being commanding is not an innate part of your personality, you can learn to become a commanding leader.

Angela Learns to Stop Giving Her Power Away

Problem:

Angela too quickly gave her power away and let others direct. She needed to be the one who gave direction and took control of situations. Her strengths included being nice, approachable, likeable, collaborative, and inclusive. However, these strengths are a double-edged sword—they can have unintended negative consequences.

For instance, because Angela cared too much about what others thought, she could be indecisive. She would default to consensus-building instead of flexing more of her leadership muscle. She needed to become more commanding by learning how to present herself as composed, grounded, and strong.

Action:

When Angela pursued executive coaching with GEC, we urged her to tap into what she truly thought about a situation rather than deferring to the wisdom of the group, and then advocate for that position. This felt uncomfortable to her, because it pushed her outside of her comfort zone.

Results:

Angela feared that others would see her as unlikeable and bossy. However, once she started asserting her opinions and maintaining her position, she saw that she actually gained more respect and admiration from others. They appreciated her strong leadership, because it helped everyone to feel more certain of their team's ability to succeed.

Do others perceive you as commanding?

How commanding are you? Assign yourself a score of 1 to 10 for each of these statements, with 1 being the lowest and 10 being the highest:

+ People feel more comfortable when I'm in charge.
+ When I speak, all eyes look to me. People stop what they're doing and listen.
+ When I give directives, people take action immediately.
+ People ask me to take the lead when a challenging situation arises.
+ When I voice a contrary opinion, others take it seriously. They may accept, debate, or discuss my idea, but they never ignore it.

If you scored above 43, others likely view you as a commanding leader. Otherwise, focus on the action steps and exercises in this chapter to develop this competency.

Action steps to become a more commanding leader

What can you do to become a more in-command leader? Here are some action steps that you can start taking now. As you make your ability to take the reins more visible, people will start seeing you as a commanding leader.

1.   Schedule time to explore what is holding you back from being more commanding at work.

Becoming conscious of your fears and perceived limitations is the first step to overcoming them. As you take this courageous step forward, those so-called obstacles will become less relevant and you'll open the door to possibilities previously unknown. In your reflection time, answer these questions:

+ Why am I not being more commanding at work?
+ What excuses am I making to not be commanding?
+ What obstacles are keeping me from being commanding?
+ What fears are stopping me from being commanding?
+ Do I have certain limiting beliefs about myself that stop me from being more commanding?

2. Own your areas of expertise rather than deferring to others.

When you know a lot about a topic, take an authoritative stance.

3. Present your ideas with conviction, emphasizing your main points.

Your credibility will increase as you learn to drive your points home.

4. Show that you're a big-picture thinker by engaging in strategic planning, both for your own team and with other leaders.

Devote time to visionary thinking at the team level and seek out opportunities to shape your department or organization's direction.

5. Speak with power by projecting your voice in meetings and other interactions.

Eliminate minimizing language like the following words and phrases:

1. "Not sure about this idea, but …"
2. "I don't really know, but …"
3. "I'm no expert, but …"
4. "I could be way off base, but …"
5. "This might be a dumb idea, but …"
6. "Sorry, but I just want to say …"
7. "This is just my opinion …"
8. "I think"
9. "Sort of"
10. "Kind of"
11. "Almost"
12. "Maybe"

6. Avoid uptalk: Ending declarative statements with an upward inflection.

Ending on a higher note makes it sound as though you are asking a question when you're really trying to make a definitive statement.

7. Make yourself known as a visionary by bringing innovative big-picture solutions to the table.

Claim space for yourself even among higher-level leaders, showing you know you deserve to voice your excellent ideas.

8.   Own your role as a leader, showing up to meetings as someone who is ready to take charge and take initiative.

If you're not the formal leader of a project, but leadership is lacking, step up to the plate by guiding discussion, structuring the workflow, or doing whatever else is needed.

9.   Understand the scope of your authority.

Know where you have leverage, both officially (in terms of your job description) and unofficially (your influence), and use it.

10.   Don't worry too much about being liked or having popular opinions.

Being authentic by speaking your truth and holding your ground will garner genuine respect and admiration. And that means far more than being seen as "a nice person" or "a people-pleaser," who is unlikely to fire up a team and incite action.

11.   Focus on giving yourself approval and appreciation, rather than needing it from others.

Remind yourself every day of what you bring to the table.

12.   If an employee isn't pulling his weight, isn't following your instructions, or is contributing to a negative workplace culture, have a tough conversation without delay.

Don't put up with any dead weight, gossip, or inappropriate comments. The other employees will appreciate knowing that such things aren't tolerated.

13.   Set the right example, modeling the behaviors you want to see in your employees.

If you want them to stop working after hours and feeling frazzled, don't answer emails in the evening yourself. They're emulating your example, whether they realize it or not.

14.   Expect others to follow your instructions.

When you make an important decision, you're not asking for their permission to implement it. You may at times seek their input, but when you share guidelines, expect them to be followed. Sounding sure of yourself rather than hesitant or apologetic will lead others to automatically get on board.

15. Dress as though you're one level above your position.

You'll project that you're in command by radiating the appearance of professionalism. This works in both virtual settings and in person, by the way!

As you become a more in-command leader, your executive presence will grow immensely. When you speak, even without raising your voice, everyone will listen. You will command attention, and in turn, the full respect of everyone around you.

Help your employees become more commanding.

> People at all levels of the organization will appreciate having strong, commanding leaders.

Maybe you're hoping to prepare some of your direct reports for future leadership positions—or maybe they already manage other people. Either way, developing the qualities of a commanding leader will allow them to truly inspire others and drive toward results.

> Own your role as a leader, showing up to meetings as someone who is ready to take charge and take initiative.

How will helping employees become commanding build a stronger team?

Here are some key ways in which helping your employees strengthen this competency will benefit the entire team.

+ They'll inspire a strong sense of purpose in others, instilling a belief in your mission and vision among the whole team.
+ They'll bolster engagement and productivity among the whole team by showing others that their work has meaning.
+ You'll know you can trust them with any project they take on,

as they won't take responsibility lightly. Their direct reports and peers will trust them as well, inspiring loyalty and dedication.

+ Others will seek them out when they need direction, meaning less weight falls on your shoulders. They'll solve problems on their own rather than always deferring to you.

+ You'll know you're not missing out on vital input from your people because they're not afraid to share their perspectives with you.

People at all levels of the organization will appreciate having strong, commanding leaders. Subordinates will progress in their careers with the support of a capable leader, coworkers will thrive on teams that reach higher goals, and superiors will know their managers are getting the most from their people.

How to help your employees become more commanding.

How can you support your aspiring leaders' development of this competency?

+ Instill a sense of *psychological safety*. Inclusive leadership tends to promote psychological safety, the authors of a recent study assert.[vi] When employees feel safe to test their own limits and try a new approach—and encouraged to do so—they'll become bolder leaders.

+ Give them consistent mentorship and coaching as they work to assert themselves with conviction. They're likely to have some self-doubts, wondering if they're coming on too strong or remaining too passive, so let them know how you perceive them.

+ Give them a nudge when you believe they should volunteer for a leadership role. Before a meeting where you announce a project, suggest they step up to take the lead.

+ Make sure they feel a strong sense of purpose in the work they're doing, and a belief in their team's vision. That's a prerequisite for taking charge and driving toward change.

+ Share positive feedback whenever they demonstrate the ability to be in command, even in small ways. Instead of second-guessing whether they're being too bossy or presumptuous, they'll start feeling more secure in those behaviors.

As you model what being commanding looks like in action, employees will have a strong example to follow. Giving them frequent feedback will help them strike a balance between being assertive and nurturing in their leadership. As a result, you'll have a more balanced, capable, and effective team.

Chapter 8

Charismatic

Gravitas Competency #3

"Charisma is the intangible that makes people want to follow you, to be around you, to be influenced by you."

— Roger Dawson

Leaders with executive presence radiate charisma. Whether you realize it or not, your senior management is looking for leaders with the charisma to rally their team around an idea and keep them driven to pursue it to fruition. These leaders exude a contagious passion for their work that more deeply engages everyone around them.

A recent survey of over 300,000 leaders found that the ability to inspire and motivate others is the most pivotal leadership quality[i]—and charismatic leaders have it in spades. By becoming a charismatic leader, you'll infuse your team with a passion for their work.

Charismatic leaders also make others feel good about themselves. Just being in these leaders' presence puts people in a good mood. Thus, they do wonders to create a positive and inspiring workplace culture.

By becoming a charismatic leader,
you'll infuse your team with a passion for their work.

Behaviors of charismatic leaders.

Charismatic leaders radiate personal charm, optimism, and enthusiasm. They're often described as having a magnetic personality because they naturally draw people to them. Their social nature makes them highly approachable and engaging, and they often ignite rousing debates about ideas that result in productive brainstorming sessions. Charismatic people understand what moves their audience, and they speak to it. They are emotionally intelligent people who tune in to others' feelings. They may tell witty stories or have a poignant sense of humor, since they feel relaxed and self-assured in the presence of others. They feel comfortable in their own skin, and that makes them come across as more dynamic and enjoyable to interact with.

As you become a charismatic leader, you'll also make yourself approachable to people at all levels, rather than being aloof and standoffish. People will find you highly likeable, but not a pushover. They'll take you seriously, respecting your insights. Colleagues and superiors will look forward to talking over ideas with you. Because you naturally facilitate open conversation, you'll spark fascinating discussions that often result in innovative developments. Others will find you deeply inspiring, and these conversations will empower you to keep stepping into your own potential.

Take a look at this comparison of behaviors that cultivate or undermine charisma:

CHARISMATIC QUALITIES	QUALITIES THAT UNDERMINE CHARISMA
Charming	Reserved
Engaging	Unexciting
Passionate	Dispassionate
Inspiring	Unaffecting
Empowering	Disempowering

As an inspirational leader who conveys a deep sense of passion for your work, you'll ramp up employee engagement and loyalty. You'll draw promising talent into big-picture discussions, showing how much you value their contributions. And you'll let people know they matter. Thus, your team will feel more excited about coming in to work every day, knowing they can accomplish big things. Moreover, they'll feel confident in their ability to achieve them, knowing you believe in their abilities. You'll empower them to voice their own ideas and take on greater responsibility as a result.

By drawing people to you and establishing a strong rapport, you'll build unity and cohesion among your team.

Further, with your high level of emotional intelligence, you'll have a people-centered approach that focuses on nurturing their development. People will implicitly trust you, instilling a sense of psychological safety that encourages others to be their authentic selves. By drawing people to you and establishing a strong rapport, you'll also build unity and cohesion among your team. You'll have strong relationships with your direct reports and other colleagues, so you'll know what motivates and inspires them. And your people-oriented approach will foster a harmonious culture, encouraging strong relationships between all team members. You'll naturally bring people together to focus on common goals. For all of these reasons, charisma will enhance your executive presence.

Marillyn Hewson, whom *Forbes* characterizes as "the most powerful executive that the modern defense industry has produced," serves as an excellent example of a charismatic leader.[ii] Named the most powerful woman in business by *Fortune*,[iii] she also placed a priority on interpersonal relationships throughout her time at Lockheed Martin. She made sure that other leaders treated their subordinates as teammates, focused on being a good listener, and modeled how to be a defense industry dynamo who affirms others' strengths and value.

"Leaders must exemplify integrity and earn the trust of their teams through their everyday actions," writes Hewson in *Fortune*.[iv] "When you do this, you set high standards for everyone at your company. And when you do so with positive energy and enthusiasm for shared goals and purpose, you can deeply connect with your team and customers." Master these qualities and you'll become deeply charismatic by fostering genuine human connections with everyone you interact with, regardless of their position or status.

"Leaders must exemplify integrity and earn the trust of their teams through their everyday actions."
Marillyn Hewson

Self-evaluation: Assess your level of charisma.

What does charisma look like in action? We often think of charisma as something you either have or you don't, but you can actually work to grow it within yourself. By adopting certain behaviors, you'll be embodying the quality of charisma in your own leadership. Read through the following list of charismatic behaviors and put a checkmark beside each one that describes you.

I demonstrate charisma by …

1.   Exuding joy, excitement, and passion for what I do. (This means letting myself be visible to my team on a daily basis, rather than hiding in my office all the time.)
2.   Being authentic and true to myself, showing I make decisions that align with my values.
3.   Fully showing up for every meeting and interaction.
4.   Finding ways to stay energized so I can maintain a healthy level of enthusiasm.
5.   Communicating what I value, my beliefs, and my convictions with others, so they understand who I am—making me a more authentic leader.
6.   Driving toward a common cause or greater good, which makes my team's work feel more meaningful to everyone.
7.   Making others feel special and important by pointing out their positive qualities and achievements.
8.   Telling stories that inspire and move people toward action, since they often illustrate a point better than facts and data.
9.   Being optimistic by seeing the best in people and situations.
10. Using humor to maintain an upbeat attitude.

11. Inviting open-ended conversations and debates with a wide variety of people, including those who are both above and below me in seniority.

12. Influencing people across the organization by sharing my ideas in compelling ways.

13. Guiding people toward my team's strategic vision, keeping them focused on why it's important.

14. Building a strong rapport with people across the workplace, remembering important details about their lives and what they care about.

15. Igniting conversations about new ideas—and truly wanting to hear diverse perspectives.

16. Appealing to the emotions of the audience, using pathos to influence their response to my ideas.

17. Allowing my enthusiasm to show in my voice.

18. Being approachable and pleasant to be around, so people will want to share their thoughts with me and seek out my opinions.

19. Sharing gratitude with people frequently.

20. Creating a positive, energized atmosphere in every team meeting to build camaraderie.

If you scored above 17, your charisma truly shines, even though you may have room to grow it even further. If your score falls below 14, you have substantial room to hone your charisma, and if it falls below 8, you have an urgent need to grow this competency.

Look at the behaviors you *haven't* checked off here—which ones seem like your biggest weaknesses? Choose up to five to strengthen over the next several weeks. The action steps in this chapter will help you grow your charisma by connecting more with colleagues, developing a genuine rapport with people, and radiating excitement for your work. By adopting or strengthening these behaviors, you'll mark yourself as a charismatic leader.

Now, let's look at some self-sabotaging behaviors that can make leaders less charismatic, so you can avoid them.

Charismatic people understand what moves their audience, and they speak to it.
They are emotionally intelligent people who tune in to others' feelings.

Behaviors that undermine charisma.

The following behaviors decrease a leader's charisma, and thus, executive presence. They're very common derailers of success, so reflect on whether you're engaging in any of them unintentionally. Place a checkmark by any of these behaviors that describe you.

I demonstrate a lack of charisma by ...

+ Coming across as low in energy and enthusiasm.
+ Not striving to inspire and invigorate others.
+ Showing little personality rather than showing up as my full self.
+ Staying quiet and not contributing at meetings.
+ Seeming disinterested or disengaged from projects.
+ Being reluctant to take risks.
+ Constantly stating why things won't work, marking myself as a pessimist or a naysayer.
+ Resisting new ideas rather than embracing possibilities, and fearing change.
+ Not showing appreciation for others or praising them often.
+ Acting disengaged toward others rather than sparking conversations.
+ Staying immersed in tedious tasks and constantly busy.
+ Presenting facts without conveying why they matter and establishing a human connection.
+ Speaking in a monotone, with little enthusiasm for the words I'm expressing.
+ Settling for projects and responsibilities that don't truly feel meaningful to me.
+ Not defining and expressing my values and how they connect to my projects and vision.

If you come across as lethargic, boring, and dull, you lack charisma. The same holds true if you always have a negative attitude rather than focusing on what is possible. To become charismatic, you need to show that you care deeply about your work. If you've lost your passion for what you do—or never had it to begin with—it's time to rediscover it, or to find something else that you feel more driven to pursue.

Similarly, losing sight of the big picture can undermine charisma. Do you get bogged down by mundane tasks most of the time? If so, you might seem very busy, but you're focused on things that you should be delegating or eliminating from your workload. You've lost sight of the need for strategic direction and idea-sharing that could lead to exciting innovations. You've gotten into a rut, and to build your charisma, you need to get out of it. Again, begin by rediscovering what excited you about your work in the first place.

Yes, introverts can be charismatic too!

If you're an introvert, you may find yourself wondering if you have what it takes to become charismatic. When you picture a charismatic person, you may fall into the trap of imaging that bubbly, gregarious extrovert who always dominates the room. But that's not the only way to be charismatic. Let's recap on the key qualities of charismatic people, because when you really take a look at them up close, you'll realize they're not out of your reach at all. In fact, you probably already embody many of them to some degree.

First, introverts can be masters of sparking great discussions. With their propensity for reflection, they know how to bring great ideas to the table and ignite discussions. They can guide the conversation without dominating it. They're also just as good as extroverts at radiating enthusiasm, joy, and optimism for their work, since they're equally passionate about it! With their thoughtfulness, they can conceptualize exactly how to motivate their team to move toward a strategic vision. If you haven't fully cultivated all of these qualities yet, know that you probably hold these latent strengths within you.

Further, as an introvert, you probably know yourself well. Your high level of self-awareness makes you an authentic, genuine person who remains true to your values and brings your full self to your work. As you cultivate your executive presence, you can learn to become more expressive of your personal beliefs and opinions, but you already have an excellent foundation.

Finally, introverts tend to excel at making others feel good about themselves. You probably know what it feels like to be an outsider looking in, so you may be especially attuned to opportunities to draw in anyone who may feel left out. By honing these natural strengths, you will find yourself cultivating a subtle but powerful magnetism that many great introverted leaders possess. In fact, the CEO Genome Project found that introverts tend to make better CEOs than extroverts (probably for all of these reasons!).[v]

Jennifer Holmgren, CEO of the biotech company LanzaTech, spoke to CNBC about how being an introvert has made her a better leader. ""The advantage, I think, of being an introvert is you listen more. You think before you speak, often, which means that you're listening," she asserts.[vi] "I have found that by listening more you enable more people and more ideas. You get a diversity of input because you aren't just hearing one voice (usually the loudest one!) or worse, just listening to yourself speak." In other words, introverts tend to be great at synthesizing the full brainpower of the group, rather than just focusing on their own ideas.

In a nutshell, there are different ways of being a quieter person, just as there are different ways of being loud. A quieter person who is truly engaged in what others think and feel can exude charisma as well as (or better than) the boisterous person who loudly tells jokes to the group. Find your own personal brand of charisma, knowing it will look different for every person.

Do others perceive you as charismatic?

This exercise will give you a better sense of how others view you. Assign yourself a score of 1 to 10 for each of these statements, with 1 being the lowest and 10 being the highest:

+ My team believes in a shared vision that I've rallied them behind.
+ I have an excellent rapport with everyone I work with.
+ People know who I am and what I care about.
+ My team has a great sense of camaraderie.

- My direct reports bring a great deal of enthusiasm to their work, seeming energized as they start their day.

If you scored above 43, others likely view you as a charismatic leader. Otherwise, focus on the action steps and exercises in this chapter to develop this quality.

A New Approach Boosts Phil's Charisma

Problem:

Phil came across as low in energy and a bit lethargic. He couldn't seem to arouse enthusiasm for his ideas within his team. While he was extremely competent, worked hard, and completed tasks on schedule, this wasn't enough for someone in a leadership position. They needed him to show interest in them and excitement for their projects. His disengagement created low morale.

Action:

Phil was naturally reserved and hadn't had any leadership training over the past year, so he decided to turn to an executive coach. We worked to unpack what he could do differently in some of his daily interactions to generate more enthusiasm. A role-playing exercise revealed that Phil was making a lot of negative statements and communicating a subtle disregard for people and projects. He learned to make changes to his language and tone so he would sound more upbeat and energized.

Phil also began devoting time to big-picture strategic thinking, blocking out time for it on his schedule. He realized he'd been devaluing himself by neglecting to prioritize higher-level thinking.

Results:

After making these changes, Phil soon became more enthusiastic about his own work, knowing his strategic contributions could make a real impact. Over the next couple of months, he began to see much more excitement and engagement among his team. Instead of plodding through the day, people animatedly talked about ideas, feeling empowered to explore new possibilities. One day, his boss's boss commented on the dramatic difference in motivation she noticed among Phil's team!

Now let's delve into how to fully cultivate your charisma as a leader, so you can motivate and inspire your team, peers, and senior management.

Action steps to increase your charisma.

"Charisma is the transference of enthusiasm," says speaker and actor Ralph Archbold.[vii] It's how you convey your passion for what you do. Take these steps to begin dramatically boosting your charisma right away!

1.   Spend time exploring what holds you back from being charismatic at work.

As you dig deeper into these supposed obstacles, you'll find they'll become less restricting and you will open up to new possibilities. Answer these questions:

- ✦   Why am I not being more charismatic at work?
- ✦   What excuses am I making to not be charismatic?
- ✦   What obstacles are holding me back from being charismatic?
- ✦   What fears are stopping me from being charismatic?
- ✦   Do I have certain limiting beliefs about myself that stop me from being more charismatic?

2.   Encourage idea-sharing by facilitating brainstorming sessions and discussions.

Be supportive of outside-of-the-box ideas rather than shooting them down just because they seem unrealistic.

3.   Show your passion for what you do.

By exuding enthusiasm, you'll inspire your team to pursue their work with the same vigor. Charismatic leaders motivate their teams to act.

4. Listen actively.

Show others that they matter by listening intently to their words and asking follow-up questions. Be fully present rather than focused on what you're going to say next.

5. Pay attention to people's body language as well as the words they're saying.

Make sure your own body language shows that you're interested and paying close attention.

6. Vary your pacing and tone in your speech.

When you speak in an animated voice, you signal that your ideas are interesting to you and should therefore be interesting to others. You automatically become more compelling, persuasive, and charismatic.

7. Nurture your people's growth.

Spend time getting to know them through one-on-one conversations about their goals and aspirations. Strive to make them feel important by showing genuine interest in their life and ambitions. Help them to map out a path toward professional success, connecting them with learning resources and mentoring.

8. Give out plenty of praise and appreciation (as long as it's authentic).

Notice the small and big things people do. When you make people feel good about themselves through genuine praise, they'll enjoy being around you more.

9. Enhance your emotional intelligence.

Practice focusing on how particular situations make other people feel. Ask how they feel about certain projects or circumstances often. Tune into what their body language and tone of voice reveal about their emotional state. Simply thinking about their emotions more frequently will help you grow more attuned to them.

10. Seek out their input.

Proactively invite them to share their insights about ideas and current projects. Truly successful leaders aren't trying to outshine their people by being the source of all great ideas; rather, they're developing a team of innovators. Ask for feedback about your own performance as well.

11. Become an advocate for others.

Speak about the small successes and big wins of your direct reports, coworkers, and others. Highlight them at meetings and in front of superiors. By illuminating their victories, you'll become a champion of their success, and your charisma will grow in turn. Allow and encourage them to lead at times, while remaining on hand for support.

12. Encourage people to push their own boundaries.

A leader who challenges them to boldly take a strategic risk will increase their self-confidence and be remembered as a wise, insightful, and committed mentor.

13. Tell stories to drive your ideas home.

Charismatic people are often great at telling stories. Share stories based on your own life experience that instill lessons you want your people to learn, like how to persevere against the odds. The more you do this, the more naturally you'll tell such stories, and you might find moments of humor or suspense arising as well!

As a charismatic leader, you'll understand what moves your audience and speak to it. By cultivating your charisma, you'll also instill a positive, supportive culture. Your team will see you as someone who wants them to succeed, and they will strive to continue fulfilling your expectations. You'll radiate positivity and optimism because you believe in your team's ability to navigate any situation.

Charisma doesn't grow overnight, but by taking these steps on a regular basis, you'll find yourself becoming a charismatic leader sooner than you may think. There's no mystery to how this transition happens—it's all about establishing yourself as someone who cares about the people around you, works to connect with them strongly, and takes steps to nurture their growth.

Help your employees grow their charisma.

As a leader, you need to help your employees build up their charisma as well. Here's why that is so important and how to go about it.

How will helping your employees grow their charisma build a stronger team?

Truly successful leaders aren't trying to outshine their people by being the source of all great ideas; rather, they're developing a team of innovators.

Charismatic leadership plays a major role in a company's overall success. Here are some of the key reasons why.

+ Charismatic people readily influence others, which means they'll get people on board with organizational changes. When negotiating a challenging transformation, they'll easily rally people around them to navigate it together.
+ They'll persuade all of their people to believe in the company's vision and mission, creating a sense of cohesion and unity among their team.
+ They'll draw out everyone's insights and experience by engaging them in productive conversation. They'll coax out their more reserved colleagues and direct reports so the team can leverage their input.
+ They'll raise productivity by inspiring others to believe in and love their work. Others will follow their example of giving it their all every day, so their team will continue raising the bar.
+ They'll catalyze growth in their own people, serving as inspirational mentors.

Emotions are contagious; just as being around a negative coworker can make you feel more pessimistic, having a boss who is highly motivated and driven will make employees feel passionate about their work.[viii] This is true in both the short-term (the mood their boss is in on Tuesday) and the long-term (ongoing office morale).[ix]

How to help your employees grow their charisma.

Just as you can grow charisma within yourself, you can help others grow it too. Here are some tactics for doing that effectively.

- ♦ Guide them through developing a vision for their own career—or at least for the next several years. This will help them feel more excited and energized about their work.
- ♦ Invite them into higher-level discussions when they show promise as future leaders.
- ♦ When they share their beliefs and personality authentically, give them positive affirmation. Let them know you appreciate how they're showing up as their full selves, as a reserved person may feel self-conscious about it.
- ♦ Encourage them to speak their mind more. Give them tips on how to get the creative juices flowing if they find themselves stumped in social situations. For example, journaling or one-on-one brainstorming could help.
- ♦ Share advice on how to deliver captivating presentations. Stay positive and upbeat, reassuring them that most people can use tips on this subject.
- ♦ Give in-the-moment feedback when possible, so they can understand exactly what they could do differently. Share examples of how they could frame something in a more positive light, inspire others, and radiate enthusiasm.

As you help your employees cultivate their charisma, your own charisma will grow as well. Within this positive feedback loop, your efforts to motivate and encourage them will reveal your own charisma. As each individual's charisma grows, your team will develop exceptional interpersonal dynamics and work will become exponentially more rewarding. And of course, your organization will gain access to a wealth of new ideas from people who no longer feel afraid to share their authentic thoughts.

We've now thoroughly covered Gravitas, the first key domain of executive presence. You've gained an in-depth understanding of the three competencies that make up this domain. Next, we'll explore the second domain, Authority, and the three competencies it entails. Read on to learn how to master these strengths in order to act as a powerful leader in your daily work.

Section 2:

AUTHORITY

Domain 2 of 3

Introduction:

Understanding Authority

To convey executive presence, you must learn to exude authority. As you begin projecting an aura of authority in every situation, you'll rise up in the ranks of leadership or expand your impact where you are right now.

Having authority means being decisive, bold, and influential—the three core competencies that make up this domain. Every time you act with decisiveness, boldness, and influence, you earn another notch in your leadership foundation of authority.

The key word is *act*. While gravitas encompasses how you present yourself, authority deals with how you act and the impact it has on others.

Authority defined.

Here's how authority looks in practice:

- Making clear decisions and sticking to them.
- Taking strategic risks.
- Persuading others to action.

> Authority isn't something that's bestowed on you just because of your position or title. Rather, it's earned.

Authority isn't something that's bestowed on you just because of your position or title. Rather, it's earned. Even if you step into the most prestigious leadership position in your company, you still need to earn your authority. You gain it when you've successfully modeled the ability to be decisive, bold, and influential.

Here's what authority is *not:*

+ Trying to intimidate others.
+ Leading through fear.
+ Striving to appear superior to others.

You don't gain authority by demonstrating power, control, dominance, or supremacy over others. And you don't build authority by acting as a dictator who uses a command-and-control style of leadership. True authority doesn't result from fear and domination. Rather, you gain real authority when people instinctively *want* to follow you and strive to emulate your example.

AUTHORITY
Decisive
Bold
Influential

In fact, those leaders whose approach relies on dominating others through intimidation tend to limit their team and organization's potential, as Jon Maner writes in an article published in *Current Directions in Psychological Science.*[i] Some dominant leaders in his study chose to work with less talented rather than more talented people—probably because they posed less of a threat to their egos. And some even "isolated their subordinates and prevented them from bonding with one another, because alliances among subordinates were viewed as posing potential threats." As Maner's study shows, leaders who use a dominant approach undermine their organization's potential.

It follows, then, that the competencies of authority discussed in this book will absolutely benefit people following a servant leadership approach.

Servant leaders need to empower their workforce, inspire people to trust them, and incite people to believe in their ability to accomplish a shared vision. The three core qualities of authority will help them achieve these goals.

Authority takes time to establish, but you can begin taking steps now. Eventually, you will gain a reputation as someone who makes things happen by being decisive, bold, and influential. Your credibility will increase, along with others' respect for you. You'll begin projecting an aura of authority as you take these steps to act more assertively. You won't be tentative about making decisions, and you won't hesitate to put your ideas out there for all to see. When introducing a plan, you'll give clear direction to others, providing clarity on ideas, needs, and expectations.

Importantly, to become a decisive and bold leader, you can't just sit back and wait for the confidence to arrive. In this in-between place of waiting, you may hope for the right time to come along, or for a situation in which you'll have enough conviction or self-assurance to take a big step forward. While you are waiting for the confidence to come, you'll grow more indecisive, unsure, and hesitant. Why? You're essentially telling yourself that you don't have what it takes, and you can only get there if the right moment magically happens upon you. The solution is not to wait, but to just make the leap—and make decisions. As you make decisions without being 100% secure in your choices, your confidence will grow exponentially. Each time you step out of your comfort zone by acting boldly, your confidence will dramatically increase. The key to being a decisive, bold, and influential leader is to dive in without knowing how cold the water is.

> To be a decisive and bold leader, you can't just sit back and wait for the confidence to arrive.

Sarah Learns to Put a Stake in the Ground

Problem:

When she first stepped into a leadership position, Sarah worried about offending people by expressing unpopular opinions or changing the way her team did things. Her trepidation prevented her from truly leading.

Sarah's boss approached her one day. "You seem like you're just trying to maintain the status quo," he said. "You need to stop being afraid of making waves. It minimizes your ability to project authority."

Action:

Sarah pursued executive coaching at her boss's urging. She learned that a leader *must* take a bold stand for what she believes in, and the more she did just that, the more respect she gained from her team. We mapped out specific ways in which she could act decisive, show boldness, and grow her influence, like taking a stand for ideas she believed in. Sarah bravely took action, stepping a bit further out of her comfort zone week after week.

Results:

Six months later, Sarah's manager said the following about her: "Of all the director-level employees, Sarah is the only leader. The rest are managers. Sarah will put a stake in the ground and own a position when others are afraid to do so. She holds her ground, showing she's willing to challenge and push back when needed. Others are afraid to make decisions and instead spend too much time building consensus and agreement, not making any choices at all." As Sarah's example shows, authority is something that can and must be grown—not something a leader is born with.

Others are afraid to make decisions and instead spend too much time building consensus and agreement.

Let's delve into the main components of authority in a bit more depth, so you can fully understand this EP domain.

What qualities are most essential for authority?

GEC Research Center asked a sample of 1,400 U.S. workers, middle managers, senior leaders, and executives what they believe are the most central qualities of authority. Here's what they said.

THE MOST IMPORTANT QUALITIES OF AUTHORITY

% saying it is absolutely essential for a leader to be ...

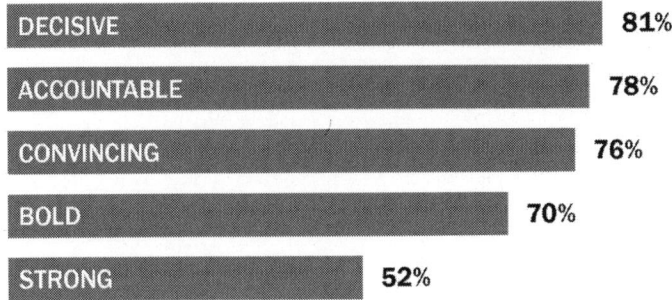

DECISIVE	**81%**
ACCOUNTABLE	**78%**
CONVINCING	**76%**
BOLD	**70%**
STRONG	**52%**

Source: GEC Research Center Survey, Poll of 1,400 U.S. Workers.

"Decisive" had a clear lead, which was no surprise, as the ability to make decisions is a vital skill that many leaders struggle with. As the GEC Research team processed the data, we distilled the results into three main competencies: decisive, bold, and influential.[1] We then crafted the following definition of authority within the 3x3 Executive Presence Model, based on our findings.

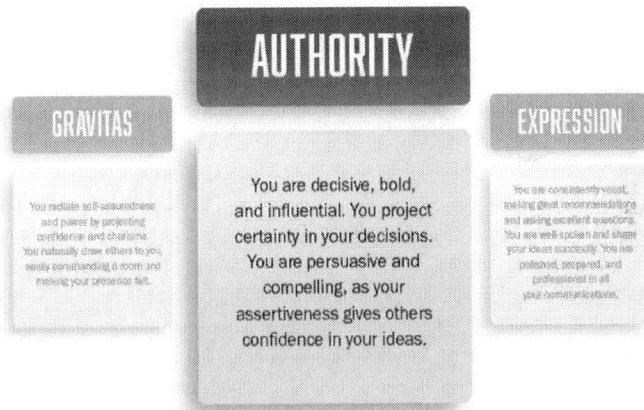

AUTHORITY

GRAVITAS

You radiate self-assuredness and power by projecting confidence and charisma. You naturally draw others to you, easily commanding a room and making your presence felt.

You are decisive, bold, and influential. You project certainty in your decisions. You are persuasive and compelling, as your assertiveness gives others confidence in your ideas.

EXPRESSION

You are consistently vocal, making great recommendations and asking excellent questions. You are well-spoken and share your ideas succinctly. You are polished, prepared, and professional in all your communications.

---

1   As the GEC Research team examined the survey results, we found "strong" closely related to being bold and "convincing" and "accountable" closely pertained to being influential. Thus, we arrived at "decisive," "bold," and "influential" as the three cornerstones of authority.

By acting with decisiveness, boldness, and influence, you'll solidify your authority. As you master these competencies, you'll seem to exercise authority effortlessly. Others will instinctively look to you for direction and want you at the decision-making table.

Again, while gravitas is about *who you are*, authority deals with *how you take action*. Your authority shows up in the actions you take and the ways you make an impact.

AUTHORITY IS:

What You Do

How You ACT

Making an Impact

Which behaviors show a lack of authority?

In the same poll, we asked participants which behaviors most negatively affect a leader's authority. Here's what they had to say.

WHICH BEHAVIORS MOST UNDERMINE AUTHORITY?

% who say these behaviors show a lack of authority ...

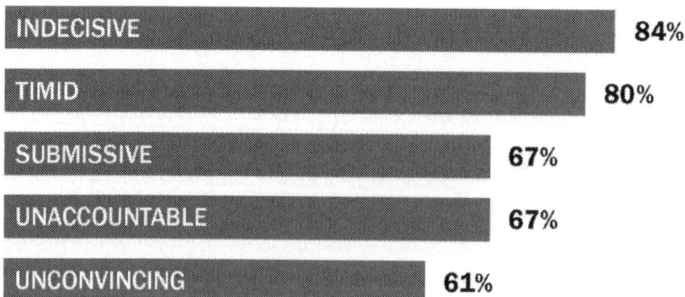

Behavior	%
INDECISIVE	84%
TIMID	80%
SUBMISSIVE	67%
UNACCOUNTABLE	67%
UNCONVINCING	61%

Source: GEC Research Center Survey, Poll of 1,400 U.S. Workers.

Since "decisive" ranked first among the top competencies of authority in our survey, it follows that being *indecisive* would most undermine authority. Further, since "bold" is one of the three core competencies, being timid would naturally have a detrimental effect on authority. And a leader who is submissive, unaccountable, and unconvincing would have a hard time being influential.

Comparison of qualities that cultivate or undermine authority.

The following chart outlines each of the top qualities of authority in more detail. The ones on the left enhance a leader's authority, while the ones on the right diminish it. For each line in the table, ask yourself whether you tend to project the quality on the left or right side.

15 WAYS TO BUILD OR UNDERMINE YOUR AUTHORITY	
QUALITIES THAT CULTIVATE AUTHORITY	QUALITIES THAT UNDERMINE AUTHORITY
DECISIVE • Certain • Unwavering • Resolute • Determined • Forceful	**INDECISIVE** • Tentative • Unsure • Uncertain • Overanalyzing • Submissive
BOLD • Courageous • Risk-taking • Assertive • Gutsy • Taking ownership	**TIMID** • Hesitant • Shy • Afraid • Meek • Complacent
INFLUENTIAL • Convincing • Making change • Persuasive • Believable • Inciting action	**UNINFLUENTIAL** • Uncompelling • Ineffective • Inconsequential • Uncredible • Passive

For an example of authority in action, look to Richard Branson. He exemplifies decisiveness, boldness, and influence. Known for his adventurous stunts that build publicity for his brand, like crossing the English Channel in an amphibious vehicle, Branson genuinely revels in testing the untested and exploring the unknown. No one would ever accuse the man who attempted to fly around the world in a hot air balloon (and was the first to cross both the Atlantic and Pacific in one[ii]) of flying under the radar, and his exploits have forged a vast array of social connections that brought new opportunities. "If you allow the fear of failure to become a barrier you're already putting road blocks in your way. ... Entrepreneurs take risks by attempting to change the status quo," he says in *Forbes*.[iii] "No one ever reached for the stars from the comfort of their couch!" In the Audacious Project, he funds other revolutionary ideas with the power to transform society,[iv] and with Virgin Galactic, he's also working to make space tourism possible.[v]

You now have a good sense of what authority means. Next, we'll dive into each of the three key competencies that make up authority in more depth, beginning with decisiveness. Even if you don't yet possess these qualities, you can absolutely develop a high level of authority as you move through the lessons in this book. As with gravitas, we'll examine what each quality looks like in practice, along with key ways to cultivate it within yourself and each person on your team!

Chapter 9

Decisive

Authority Competency #1

"Be decisive. A wrong decision is generally less disastrous than indecision."

– Bernhard Lange

Decisive leaders take initiative and move things forward. They act with conviction. Believing deeply in the choices they make, these leaders take a stand and follow through. They mobilize their team around a promising course of action, even if they don't have 100% certainty about whether it's the best choice.

Decisiveness takes courage, but it's also the wiser approach—and an important building block of executive presence. The ability to make a decision is even more important than the ability to make the *best* decision, as the alternative is inaction. "High-performing CEOs do not necessarily stand out for making great decisions all the time; rather, they stand out for being more decisive," say Elena Lytkina Botelho and fellow researchers from the Genome Project.[i] "They make decisions earlier, faster, and with greater conviction. They do so consistently—even amid ambiguity, with incomplete information, and in unfamiliar domains. In our data, people who were described as 'decisive' were 12 times more likely to be high-performing CEOs." That's why decisiveness is a cornerstone of executive presence—and why your senior management is looking for decisive leaders.

> Decisive leaders take initiative and move things
> forward.
> They act with conviction.

Behaviors of decisive leaders.

Think of the effective leaders you've seen in action. They probably all have one thing in common: They know how to take action with certainty. Because they know themselves and trust their own judgment, they know how to make choices. While many people wait and weigh the options indefinitely, these leaders know that they will never have perfect information. Rather, they must listen to their own intuition and their trusted advisors, and then determine the best course of action.

As you become a decisive leader, you'll make up your mind quickly and arrive at a clear decision with certainty, rather than wavering or hesitating. When the situation demands urgency, you'll know how to quickly make a choice. You'll provide your team with prompt direction toward a well-defined objective rather than endlessly debating the options.

Once you make a decision, you'll see it through rather than losing focus or getting discouraged and giving up. Even when confronting hurdles, you'll remain resolute. Further, you'll hold yourself accountable for the results of your choices, striving to learn from mistakes so you can make better decisions.

Here's an at-a-glance comparison of behaviors that cultivate decisiveness vs. those that undermine it. For each line in the table, ask yourself whether you tend to embody the quality on the left or on the right.

DECISIVE QUALITIES	QUALITIES THAT UNDERMINE DECISIVENESS
Certain	Tentative
Unwavering	Unsure
Resolute	Uncertain
Determined	Overanalyzing
Forceful	Submissive

Delaying decision-making due to uncertainty and hesitance to commit to a course of action has real impact. "Fretting excessively over the quality of our decisions unfortunately hurts our confidence, exacerbating our decision paralysis," explains Harrison Monarth in *Personal Excellence*.[ii] "While contemplating a decision, we are in a state of uncertainty, which can make us feel out of control and even pessimistic. Not only can these feelings make it harder for us to make choices, but the feelings may also be perceived by others, which can make us seem weaker than we are when we are in control and optimistic."

In contrast, decisive people inspire and invigorate their team. As a decisive leader, you'll effectively guide your people through times of transition, changing initial uncertainty into transformation. People will trust you implicitly and form a united front pursuing the chosen plan. You'll even be able to turn a crisis into an opportunity by inspiring everyone to take cohesive action. Ultimately this leads everyone to feel more committed to and satisfied with their work. You'll gain the confidence of your direct reports, coworkers, and leaders because everyone tends to trust decisive people more than those who don't trust their own judgment.

Jeff Bezos speaks of the value of "high-velocity decision making," asserting that "most decisions should probably be made with somewhere around 70 percent of the information you wish you had. If you wait for 90 percent, in most cases, you're probably being slow."[iii] He continues, "If you're good at course correcting, being wrong may be less costly than you think, whereas being slow is going to be expensive for sure." Similarly, Colin Powell has laid out the 40/70 rule: the idea that you should make a decision after you have 40% of the total information but before you reach 70%.[iv]

The ability to make a decision is even more important
than the ability to make the best decision.

Why does decision-making prove so challenging for many of us? The brain has two different decision-making systems, and many of us tend to rely more on one or the other. We have a faster, instinct-based system, as well as a slower, more deliberate one based on careful thought.[v] The latter, located in our prefrontal cortex, evolved later than the instinct-based system. Fortunately, we can use a combination of these systems by checking in with our gut and confirming whether logic points us in the same direction.

Higher-IQ people often struggle the most with decision-making, say Botelho and coauthors.[vi] They may tend to have a strong awareness of all the potential considerations or repercussions, and their brain goes on overdrive to analyze them. Meanwhile, they could miss out on opportunities and fail to carry out appropriate damage control when needed.[vii]

Not making decisions quickly brings a heavy cost: The time wasted agonizing over every option, rather than putting a plan into action. Not trusting your own judgment and intuition also brings a hefty cost: It causes you to relinquish decision-making responsibility to others who quite often are actually less competent. For instance, you may hand over power to a coworker who has less experience in that area, simply because the coworker projects more confidence. It's time to start owning your experience and expertise, so you can show up in the way your senior leadership needs and expects you to!

Self-evaluation: Assess your level of decisiveness.

You may now be able to point to some decisive leaders that you've worked with. But evaluating this quality within yourself can prove more difficult. Taking this self-evaluation will help. As you read through the following list of decisive behaviors, place a checkmark beside each one that reflects you.

I demonstrate decisiveness by ...

1. Making decisions and standing by them rather than second-guessing my choices.
2. Quickly coming to a conclusion, making up my mind swiftly and firmly.
3. Making things happen by taking action rather than delaying my response.
4. Courageously making a decision, even if it's a hard one.
5. Having conviction in the decisions I make, knowing I did my best with the available information.

6. Stating my decision clearly, projecting my voice and speaking firmly.

7. Boldly making decisions, even if they could lead to conflict or friction.

8. Making decisions despite imperfect information and uncertainty, knowing that leaders rarely have all the facts before taking action.

9. Trusting and relying on my gut instincts to make decisions.

10. Speaking up and sharing my ideas, without hesitation, at a meeting.

11. Taking charge of the situation when action is required, even if I'm not the official group leader.

12. Not wavering, hesitating, or displaying ambiguity in my decision-making.

13. Bringing data to back up my decision, elaborating on how it will benefit people.

14. Knowing when I've gathered enough data to make an informed choice.

15. Taking responsibility for decision-making rather than assuming that somebody else will.

16. Assuming ultimate responsibility for my actions, holding myself accountable for my choices.

17. Making the right decision, even if others won't approve.

18. Having a clear plan for how to act on my decision.

19. Urging my team to immediately take action on the decision I've made.

20. Following through by measuring progress with clear benchmarks of success.

If you scored above 17, you have an impressive ability to be decisive, although you may have room to grow in certain areas. If your score falls below 14, you struggle with acting decisively, and if it falls below 8, you have a critical need to grow this competency.

Reflect on the behaviors you *haven't* checked off here. Which ones represent your biggest weaknesses within this area? Choose up to five to work on over the next few weeks. Through the action steps shared later in this chapter, you'll learn to believe in your decisions, stand by them, and move your team to act swiftly and effectively in any situation. As you adopt these behaviors, you'll prove yourself to be a decisive leader who relies on your own excellent judgment to guide the group in the right direction. Your influence will grow as others take note of your ability to make strong decisions and stand by them.

By relinquishing the focus on being perfect, you'll allow yourself to move forward rather than remaining paralyzed by fear of what could go wrong.

Behaviors that undermine decisiveness.

Now let's take a look at some potential derailers of your decisiveness. If you're engaging in any of these behaviors, they're directly undermining your executive presence. Place a checkmark by any of the following behaviors that describe you.

I demonstrate a lack of decisiveness by ...

- Appearing afraid to make decisions or be the decision-maker.
- Showing ambiguity during the decision-making process.
- Not projecting confidence when making decisions.
- Trying to gain complete alignment of everyone and everything before making a decision.
- Letting others with less knowledge, experience, and competence make decisions.
- Spending too much time trying to find common ground.
- Staying quiet instead of regularly voicing my insights and perspectives.
- Feeling consumed by all the reasons why something can't happen.
- Worrying that I've missed an important piece of the puzzle.
- Becoming bogged down with too much information, overanalyzing the situation.
- Wanting to debate and discuss ideas for an extended period of time.
- Not being willing to make decisions based on my gut.
- Constantly asking others for their opinions.

+ Holding back from sharing my opinions until more data is gathered.
+ Taking too much time to deliberate and think things through.
+ Hesitating to make a commitment due to fear of making mistakes.

Indecisiveness stems from fear of failure. It's as though you're saying, "There is one perfect decision to be made, and I must gather all the information that exists on this topic before making it." Even with the wealth of data that surrounds us today, we never operate with perfect information. Instead, you need to learn to use a mix of hard data and intuition, along with a healthy range of other perspectives when appropriate.

Have you received feedback from others that you're engaging in the behaviors listed above, or noticed them in yourself? If so, don't fret—we'll take a look at some action steps later in this chapter that will help you become a more decisive leader!

Manuel Learns to Trust His Gut

Problem:

Manuel felt afraid to be the decision-maker who is ultimately responsible for outcomes. Cautious and conservative, he spent a lot of time thinking about all the things that could go wrong, getting overwhelmed with too much information. He would sit on the fence, asking for everyone's opinion, when firm action was needed. When he did ultimately make a decision, it wasn't backed by a solid foundation of confidence. Thus, he would quickly acquiesce to others he deemed to have more expertise or better judgment than him. He constantly anguished over the options, going back and forth without actually taking a stance. Only after gaining agreement from everyone involved would he make a decision (which didn't require much actual decision-making at that point). Even then, he would be quick to change his view if others disagreed with it.

In a private conversation, a coworker gave him some sage advice. "You're too focused on what 'they' want to do—but there is no 'they.' *You* are the director, and your team needs to know what *you* want to do."

Action:

Manuel first needed to recognize that he was viewing others as being much more competent than they actually were—and devaluing his own judgment at the same time. He then started giving himself a time limit for reaching a decision, coupled with a new set of guidelines for how to make a choice. He would begin with his gut reaction, rather than other people's opinions. During that timeframe, he could collect input from a few trusted people, weigh the options, and do research if needed. But then he had to take a stand, voicing his decision boldly.

Results:

After using this process to make bold decisions several times, Manuel found himself less focused on consensus building and not afraid of making a choice. He received much acclaim for a few of his choices informed by his own intuition, and that bolstered his courage even more.

> "You're too focused on what 'they' want to do—but there is no 'they.' You are the director, and your team needs to know what you want to do."

Do others perceive you as decisive?

This exercise will help you understand how others view you. Assign yourself a score of 1 to 10 for each of these statements, with 1 being the lowest and 10 being the highest:

+ When a tough situation arises, others ask me what should be done.
+ My team is often focused on a clear course of action while others struggle to find direction.
+ In times of transition, my team enthusiastically drives the change.
+ Senior leaders and peers feel my choices are ambitious yet viable.
+ Superiors trust me to make important decisions in a timely manner.

If you scored above 43, others likely view you as a decisive leader. Otherwise, focus on the action steps and exercises in this chapter to develop this competency.

Colin Powell has laid out the 40/70 rule:
the idea that you should make a decision after you have
40% of the total information but before you reach 70%.

Action steps to become a decisive leader.

In a recent survey, researchers found that four key abilities help a leader to become more decisive: a deep level of knowledge, clear organizational direction, courage, and thorough implementation. In other words, those with expertise, courage, and a clear organizational vision are well-positioned to become great decision-makers.[viii] Following through with thorough implementation will help ensure success while also enhancing confidence. When people are above average in each of these areas, they reach the 82nd percentile for decision-making prowess, the researchers found.[ix]

Here are some key steps to take as you work to establish yourself as a decisive leader. Keep a record of your progress so you can accurately observe how you've grown as you implement these strategies.

1. Spend time exploring what holds you back from being decisive at work.

As you strive to learn what guides your behavior, you'll find the obstacles becoming less restricting. Answer each of these questions:

- *Why am I not being more decisive at work?*
- *What excuses am I making to not be decisive?*
- *What obstacles are holding me back from being decisive?*
- *What fears are stopping me from being decisive?*
- *Do I have certain limiting beliefs about myself that stop me from being more decisive?*

2. Set a clear vision and goals.

It will be easier to see which decisions support your long-term plans when they are based on a clear vision and predetermined goals. "It's much easier to make decisions when you're abundantly clear on what you're trying to achieve, why you're trying to achieve it and how you plan on achieving it," says Danae Ringelmann, founder of Indiegogo.[x] "Your mission (why), values and strategy (how), and metrics (what) serve as guidance, bumper lanes and filters to your decision making. With this foundation, many questions answer themselves, which is arguably faster than time spent engaged in exhaustive debate or mental wrangling. After building this foundation, I began making decisions many times faster."

3. Embrace the certainty of uncertainty.

You will never be 100% certain of any decision's outcome. No one is omniscient, and seeking absolute certainty is an exercise in futility. Only hindsight is 20/20—in the present, we only have our imperfect perspective.

> Embrace the certainty of uncertainty.
> You will never be 100% certain of any decision's
> outcome.

---

4. Communicate with power and conviction.

Assert a clear point of view that doesn't confuse your audience by wavering or focusing on nuances.

5. Block out time to make decisions.

It doesn't need to be a lot of time. Focusing your attention on the decision-making process can help you think with more clarity and arrive at a solution more quickly. If you're just devoting half your attention to the decision between (or during) other tasks, you're not using your time wisely.

6. Practice trusting your intuition with the small decisions.

You may have five smaller decisions that you can practice making more quickly today. When you catch yourself deliberating, prompt yourself to decide. (It doesn't really matter if you choose the strawberry or pistachio ice cream, so choose immediately and congratulate yourself on making the right choice!)

7.   Take the plunge.

Make a decision once you have close to 70% of the information. Within that window, you have enough info to make an educated decision, but you're not waiting so long that you're stalling.

8.   Own your choices.

Follow through on your plan, rallying your team to action. Stay the course to see it through.

9.   Remove qualifiers from your speech.

When you announce a decision, never use words like "just," "I think," or "kind of"—and *never* apologize! Likewise, don't devalue your own ideas with phrases like "I'm not the expert." Those words only weaken your speech and make you sound insecure. Practice how you'll announce your decision with conviction.

10.   Think of your decisions as stepping-stones rather than life-and-death matters, as Tony Robbins says.[xi]

That will take off a lot of the pressure, allowing you to think more clearly and take more risks.

11.   Rank the pros and cons of any potential options.

Determine how serious any potential pitfalls are, and how likely they are to happen. Assign them each a number based on potential severity. Then assign the "pros" a number based on their potential benefits. That will give you a better sense of your potential outcomes.

12.   Force yourself to act without hesitation, says Chris Plough, serial entrepreneur and advisor.

Accept a speaking engagement or a challenging project before you have time to think about it.[xii]

13.   Limit your choices to the most viable ones.

Overcomplicating the decision-making process is more likely to lead to inaction than a better choice.

Decisive leaders know that every decision won't be perfect. As they take action, they observe the results and adapt as needed. By relinquishing the focus on being perfect, you'll allow yourself to move forward rather than remaining paralyzed by fear of what could go wrong. Making decisions sooner allows you and your employees to begin *acting* as quickly as possible. In contrast, stalling on a decision means stalling on success.

Remember the value of timeliness. The best decision made too late won't achieve optimal results. Successful people learn how to identify when it's time to take action, and then they get moving. They avoid overanalyzing a situation, knowing there are an infinite number of rabbit holes that they could dive down. Making a less-than-optimal decision is better than opting for inaction. If you're moving forward, you're putting your decision to the test, and you can adapt as needed! If you're standing still, you're holding back progress. Whichever choice you make, you'll feel more satisfied and energized as you maintain momentum.

Making a less-than-optimal
decision is better than opting
for inaction.

Help your employees become more decisive.

Instilling decisiveness in yourself is just the beginning. The next step is to help your employees cultivate this quality as well. As a manager, coaching your employees on how to become more decisive will benefit not only these individuals, but also your whole organization.

How will increasing your employees' decisiveness build a stronger team?

You probably have more than one employee who needs to strengthen this quality. Here's how strengthening it will benefit the whole team.

+ Decisive employees are more self-directed, so the team will operate more efficiently. They won't need to ask permission for everything they do. Thus, they won't take up as much of your attention and they'll enhance their own productivity.

- They will have sound judgment. Rather than getting bogged down by worry and fear, they'll be able to synthesize the available information to the best of their ability and make stronger decisions.
- They'll know how to play a supporting role in group decision-making, since they'll understand that you can't gain complete consensus before taking action.
- They'll raise morale and effectiveness in times of uncertainty by making others feel more secure.
- They'll feel more optimistic and empowered, giving them and the people around them greater drive.

For all of these reasons, you'll be able to increasingly rely on decisive employees to take on higher-level responsibilities.

> If you don't affirm the value of quick decision-making, employees may assume that they should deliberate until they reach the absolute best decision.

How to help your direct reports become more decisive.

You can encourage your direct reports to become more decisive in the following ways.

- Commend them on making decisions swiftly, even minor ones. Then they'll see that this is a priority for you. If you don't affirm the value of quick decision-making, employees may assume that they should deliberate until they reach the absolute best decision.
- Share stories about how you've made decisions with imperfect information. Often a leader's decision-making process is invisible to direct reports, so illuminate how you deal with uncertainty. This can be a good time to share some vulnerability, too. Tell a story that shows you were able to triumph over uncertainty by trusting your judgment.
- Model strong decision-making for them. Allow them to be privy to the decision-making process at times. Choose a small

circle of people to invite to the table when making a decision of some importance, so they can see what information you've gathered and how the process unfolds.

- Talk with them about why they feel indecisive, and help them to strengthen their confidence in their own judgment.
- Work to eradicate fear of failure. Emphasize that there is rarely an absolutely correct decision, and that we are all using trial and error to arrive at solutions.

As you take these steps, you'll see individuals making better choices more quickly. You'll also see your team becoming stronger in its ability to make decisions collaboratively. People will waste less time worrying about making decisions and more time putting in the effort to bring their plans to fruition.

Chapter 10

Bold

Authority Competency #2

"Do not follow where the path may lead.
Go instead where there is no path and leave a trail."
— Ralph Waldo Emerson

Your senior management needs you to be a bold leader, because bold leaders drive great ideas forward. By embodying this key executive presence competency, you'll maximize your impact in your organization. Bold leaders have the courage to explore untested options that can take their companies to greater heights of success. Being consistently bold rather than playing it safe dramatically increases a leader's perceived effectiveness,[i] so you can no longer afford to be overly cautious.

Only 11% of companies are truly bold and courageous, according to Deloitte.[ii] In a study of Canadian businesses, Deloitte found that 69% of courageous companies saw their profits rise in the year of the study, and 67% of them expected to increase their investment in R&D activities in the coming year. Conversely, just 46% of fearful companies saw an increase in profits, 34% saw falling revenues, and just 22% planned to increase R&D investment. By becoming a bolder leader, you will be your company's competitive advantage.

Because they know their own worth and believe others value them highly, bold leaders don't feel they're putting themselves at risk by being forthright.

Behaviors of bold leaders.

Think of the leaders you know who act boldly. They set themselves apart from the crowd in the way they fearlessly introduce groundbreaking ideas and take action. Rather than maintaining the status quo and settling for incremental change, bold leaders bring in or champion the great ideas that catalyze real transformation.

As you become a bold leader, you'll think outside of the box. You'll always be looking for new ways of doing things, even if they break with tradition. You won't spend time worrying about what others might think, because you won't worry about pleasing everyone. And importantly, you won't think it's okay to challenge certain people's ideas but not others. You'll be willing to speak your mind to people at all levels of the organization. Because you'll know your own worth and believe others value you highly, you won't feel you're putting yourself at risk by being forthright.

By refusing to play it safe, you'll drive innovative solutions that transform your organization—or even your industry. Learning to follow your instincts will help you project boldness in all situations. By modeling boldness for others, you'll also inspire the people you lead to become more courageous themselves.

Here's a quick look at the core behaviors that project boldness, in contrast to those that undermine this quality.

BOLD QUALITIES	QUALITIES THAT UNDERMINE BOLDNESS
Courageous	Hesitant
Risk-taking	Shy
Assertive	Afraid
Gutsy	Meek
Taking ownership	Complacent

Importantly, boldness is not the same as arrogance—that quality has no place in this list, you'll note. Boldness doesn't involve having a superiority complex. Rather, bold leaders can be highly inclusive and work to empower others. They assertively advocate for their direct reports and others. They have the courage to do what their moral compass tells them is right and to look for new ways of collaborating effectively. In contrast, arrogant people are attempting to project a façade of extreme boldness over their deep insecurities. Believing that their authentic self is not up to par, they attempt to mask it with misguided efforts to establish superiority. In contrast, executive presence—and boldness itself—is all about authenticity and being comfortable with who you truly are.

Keep in mind, too, that most people will never be accused of being bold to the point of arrogance. Most of us need to become substantially braver and bolder in our work lives, getting into the game rather than standing on the sidelines. People are inherently risk-averse, research has found—when faced with high-stakes options, they gravitate toward the safer choice.[iii] Throughout much of human evolution, taking risks carried profound consequences—and like many other species, humans tend to avoid risks unless they are essential to survival.

"We all have an inherent bias against venturing into unknown territory," says Ed Harrington, co-author of *Outsmart Your Instincts: How the Behavioral Innovation Approach Drives Your Company Forward.*[iv] "We're descendants of risk-averse ancestors whose self-preservation instincts served them well in a time when potential danger lurked behind every boulder or bush. But in today's world, where innovation rules the day, our survival necessitates overcoming these ingrained behavioral biases that hinder new ideas and stifle creative solutions." Fortunately, most of the choices we make today are not life-or-death decisions, and we can teach ourselves to be less risk-averse—and more bold.

George Hu, CEO of Salesforce, describes his rise to the top in an interview with *The New York Times.*[v] Starting out as an intern with the company, he got ahead by making bold moves that no one expected. When he first began working there, the CEO sent out a note to employees telling them the company was having trouble in Europe. "I talked to 20 people, did an analysis and sent it to him," says Hu. "He called me to his office and said, 'I want you to tell me what's wrong with the company.'" Clearly, Hu's bold and unexpected move had earned him recognition and credibility.

Steve Jobs showed great boldness at a very young age in his own rise to the top. At twelve, he called up the CEO at home to ask for the parts he needed to build a frequency counter.[vi] That bold act landed him not only the parts, but a job as well. In 1997, when he returned to Apple, he found the company producing a dozen versions of the Macintosh computer. "'Stop!' he shouted. 'This is crazy,'" Walter Isaacson writes.[vii] "He grabbed a Magic Marker, padded in his bare feet to a whiteboard, and drew a two-by-two grid. 'Here's what we need,' he declared. Atop the two columns, he wrote 'Consumer' and 'Pro.' He labeled the two rows 'Desktop' and 'Portable.' Their job, he told his team members, was to focus on four great products, one for each quadrant. All other products should be canceled. There was a stunned silence. But by getting Apple to focus on making just four computers, he saved the company."[viii]

Trusting your intuition is key to true boldness. Consider how strongly Steve Jobs trusted his own gut when slashing production of most of the company's computers to focus on a critical few. Learning to trust your own instincts will dramatically expand your own impact.

Self-evaluation: Assess your level of boldness.

Now it's time for a quick self-assessment of your own boldness. You demonstrate boldness when you engage in any of the following behaviors, proving yourself to be a courageous leader. Place a checkmark by any that describe you.

I demonstrate boldness by ...

1. Taking action in the face of uncertainty and risk.
2. Challenging and improving current standards, practices, and processes rather than settling for the status quo.
3. Identifying areas that are ripe for transformation, even if it means implementing a major change.
4. Pushing toward unknown and uncharted directions.
5. Holding my ground when others challenge me.
6. Producing or embracing innovative or disruptive ideas that haven't yet been tested.
7. Pushing boundaries beyond what is safe and acceptable, even though I can't guarantee success.
8. Continuously seeking out opportunities for personal growth.

9. Courageously thinking big and striving to make huge leaps of progress rather than only incremental change.

10. Encouraging opposing viewpoints and welcoming robust debates.

11. Fearlessly taking on riskier projects, after determining the potential benefits are worth the risks.

12. Creating opportunities for growth, change, and improvement.

13. Trusting others to take on increased responsibilities when my intuition tells me they are ready.

14. Maintaining a contrary position and not backing down.

15. Being willing to make mistakes and be wrong.

16. Voicing my ideas forcefully so they get noticed.

17. Pushing back on senior leaders' ideas when I disagree.

18. Confronting challenging situations head-on without delay, so they don't fester.

19. Taking on ambitious and uncomfortable goals that stretch my capabilities.

20. Being disruptive and provocative when I spot a way to give my team a strategic advantage.

If you scored above 17, you display an impressive degree of boldness on a regular basis, although you may certainly have room to grow. If your score falls below 14, you probably struggle with boldness, and if it falls below 8, this is a critical weakness to address.

Of the behaviors you haven't checked, which ones do you feel represent your greatest weaknesses in terms of boldness? Choose up to five behaviors to strengthen over the next several weeks. The exercises and action steps in this chapter will help you project boldness by embracing novel ideas, taking strategic risks, and pushing your own growth edge. Through these bold actions, you can establish yourself as a leader who gets things done and isn't afraid to challenge the status quo.

Now let's take a look at behaviors that may be sabotaging your boldness, so you can work to eliminate them as you build up your strengths.

By refusing to play it safe, you'll drive innovative solutions that transform your organization—or even your industry.

Behaviors that undermine boldness.

If you're *not* bold, you stand out for all the wrong reasons. Rather than being viewed as courageous and impactful, you come across as insecure and ineffective. Check off any of the following behaviors that describe you.

I undermine my boldness by ...

- Wanting to leave things as they are rather than changing them.
- Pushing back on opportunities for growth, change, and improvement.
- Feeling comfortable with my daily routine, current progress, and job performance.
- Not being willing to tackle bigger issues.
- Resisting new and innovative ideas.
- Acquiescing to what others want or need.
- Not feeling comfortable or willing to take a risk.
- Giving in rather than holding a position I believe in.
- Focusing too much on why something can't be done or won't work.
- Worrying too much about what other people think.
- Being okay with easy, attainable, and incremental goals.
- Not challenging leadership when I disagree.
- Being complacent and content with where I am.
- Being timid and afraid of taking big steps.
- Waiting around for "the right opportunity" rather than creating it.

Look back over the last few weeks and ask yourself how often you engaged in the limiting behaviors that you have checked here. Were there many times when you could have been more courageous, taking big or small steps to assert yourself at work? Did you focus more on what others would think of you than on what you believe is right? If so, this is a red flag that you are undermining your executive presence. But don't worry—we'll discuss action steps for becoming a much bolder leader in a moment!

Maggie Learns to Shape Change Through Bold Thinking

Problem:

Maggie wanted to stay in her comfort zone and avoid doing anything that would rock the boat. Risk-averse by nature, she hesitated to take on any opportunities that involved lots of change. She rarely pushed back against others' ideas and would quickly acquiesce to what they wanted, especially if they held any seniority over her. "I can't help deferring to elders. It's just in my DNA," she said. The respect for elders in her culture caused her to automatically give their ideas more respect than her own. "If they have any authority or power over me, I see them as always being right," she added.

Maggie's unwillingness to challenge the status quo ensured that she'd never get noticed as a leader—unless she made some big changes. As she reviewed her annual goals with her boss, Tim, he pointed out that none of her proposed goals were truly pushing her limits.

Action:

Tim worked with Maggie to set some stretch goals that would help her step outside of her comfort zone. "The status quo is change and transformation, Maggie," he told her. Something clicked in her mind when he said that. She realized that if she failed to take risks, challenge existing beliefs, and try out new ideas, she'd be letting senior leadership down. So, with the help of ongoing coaching and mentoring, she got serious about learning to take chances and embrace uncertainty.

In our sessions, we discussed the kinds of communication that she'd held back from engaging in that week. The things she'd stopped herself from saying didn't actually sound disrespectful. In fact, quite the reverse—it would be much *more* respectful to trust the other person to hear her point of view. Her coworkers and superiors needed her to be willing to have a genuine conversation with them that had the power to shape change. Maggie recognized a clear pattern: She'd been giving her power away to others. She needed to embrace the mindset that she deserves to be there and have her say. Moreover, her company *needs* her to assert that right. Her need to show them respect was inhibiting her ability to share a conflicting or opposing point of view or express her ideas with clarity.

Results:

> With mindful practice over the next several months, Maggie became a more forthright leader who grew comfortable sharing her genuine thoughts—no matter how much seniority the other person held. In turn, others began to respect and seek out her opinions more and more.

Like Maggie, many women who are rising up in the leadership ranks have difficulty making their ideas known. Even if they know they have great ideas that need to be heard, they often have trouble getting them noticed. At the executive level, I've seen many big, strong personalities in male employees. Women leaders I am coaching have stated, "Men dominating meetings makes it difficult for me to share and be impactful. I feel like I'm getting run over by you guys." Honing in on the quality of boldness will empower women leaders—and *all* leaders who don't fit the mold of an extroverted male with a forceful personality—to make their ideas heard and recognized.

Do others perceive you as bold?

This exercise will give you a better sense of whether others view you as a bold leader. Assign yourself a score of 1 to 10 for each of these statements, with 1 being the lowest and 10 being the highest:

- When you announce a new project, people often seem blown away by its originality.
- Your direct reports are stretching their capabilities as they pursue ambitious team goals. They find their work challenging and mentally stimulating.
- Leaders a couple of levels up have reached out to you to comment on the potential impact of your ideas.
- In meetings, your ideas often surprise or even shock people (though others ultimately recognize their value).
- Your team has a culture of congratulating people for trying a novel idea, even if it fails.

If you scored above 43, others likely perceive you as a bold leader. Otherwise, focus on the action steps and exercises in this chapter to develop this competency.

Action steps to increase your boldness.

Here are some specific actions that you can take to increase your boldness. Every step you take will be nurturing boldness within yourself until it ultimately becomes a core trait that you exude naturally.

1. Schedule time to explore what holds you back from being bold at work.

As you dive into the task of learning more about yourself, you'll find those obstacles less restricting. (In fact, most of them may be all in your head!) Work to answer these questions:

- Why am I not being bolder at work?
- What excuses am I making to avoid being bold?
- What obstacles are keeping me from being bold?
- What fears are stopping me from being bold?
- Do I have certain limiting beliefs about myself that stop me from being bold?

2. Voice some of your ideas before they're fully baked.

Speak with confidence even if you don't have it all mapped out yet. Take a chance!

3. Challenge others when you believe you've spotted a problem or want to improve upon an idea.

A debate often enhances an existing idea by building upon it. Don't shy away from going against the grain, even if you think you have an unpopular idea.

4. Create a detailed vision of your future, populated by ambitious goals.

Excitement about your future will inspire you to take risks in the present and give you the energy to follow through.

5.   Look for challenges that can teach you.

Every problem you solve and hurdle you overcome should sharpen your experience and expertise, equipping you to handle other situations more effectively.

6.   Push yourself to voice your opinion in a variety of situations.

Speak up in meetings, in interactions with your boss, when talking with your peers, and with clients. Make suggestions, even if others haven't invited them explicitly. Know your input is valuable and needed.

7.   Think outside the box, continuously asking how things could be done in new and different ways.

8.   Seek out new perspectives so you can debate your ideas, putting them to the test.

Show you're not afraid of controversy.

9.   Choose a position and defend it.

Next time you find yourself trying to find neutral ground between different ideas, stop yourself.

10.   Pretend you're a bold role model or character you admire.

Strive to emulate how this person would handle challenges. As you follow their example, you may find yourself acting more boldly in situations where you'd normally recoil. And guess what—it was *you*, not them, making those choices!

11.   Take action before you have time to think of the reasons why you shouldn't.

Set up a chat with your boss's boss; tell your team you have an idea to pitch at your next meeting. Just take the plunge before you talk yourself out of it.

12.   Write a list of things you're giving yourself permission to do.

You probably have ideas brewing in your own mind that aren't as out of reach as you believe they are. Then do them without feeling 100% ready! Aim to dive in when you're about 80% ready—you'll continue learning and preparing as you implement your plan.[ix]

13. Build your momentum.

Set a plan that lets each success propel you toward a larger one. After you reach a goal, set your sights on the next one. Start small and work your way up.

14. Do something you think you're not capable of doing (or that others would never expect you to do).

Create a list of things you haven't yet dared to try, and choose one of them to try now. For example, train for a 10K, learn to tango dance, or deliver a presentation at the next company town hall.[x] You don't have to be great at it—you just have to take the plunge.

As you grow adept at taking these steps yourself, urge your direct reports to take them as well. Reward and praise innovation and risk-taking. "Pursue the path of excellence by defining expectations above and beyond what's easily attained to stretch the imagination of your team," urges leadership strategist Tameka Williamson.[xi] "By doing so, you will cultivate a tribe of leaders not afraid to go above and beyond, while overcoming fear."

Reward and praise innovation and risk-taking.

Help your employees become bold leaders.

As a manager, you have a duty to encourage your people to step into their potential by becoming bold leaders in their own right. If your company has reached a plateau in terms of its competitiveness, bold leaders can open new doors.

How will strengthening employees' boldness build a stronger team?

Boldness benefits not only individuals in their careers, but the entire organization as well, in these key ways.

- Bold employees often become thought leaders who provide strong guidance that influences your company's direction.
- They'll challenge their own people to go beyond what they believed they could do. Others will see that it's okay to make mistakes, and that taking risks brings great rewards.

- They'll find their work exponentially more rewarding and engaging as they provide creative direction to their organization.
- They'll tackle challenging issues head-on when they arise, rather than letting them fester.
- When the team refuses to maintain the status quo, your organization can become a disruptive force in your industry. Rather than following others' lead, you can guide the direction of change.

In all of these ways, having a team of bold employees brings tremendous advantages.

> If your company has reached a plateau in terms of its competitiveness, bold leaders can open new doors.

How to enhance your employees' boldness.

As a leader, take initiative to close the "courage gap," as Deloitte puts it.[xii] Here are some key ways to do that.

- Transform how your people view mistakes and failures. Show them that striving toward challenging goals creates opportunities beyond what they deemed possible. Failure is sometimes inevitable, especially when you keep trying to achieve something great that lies beyond your comfort zone. Failure and mistakes will teach you what doesn't work so you will be more successful next time.
- In one-on-one sessions, point out specific ways in which each person can become bolder. Do they need to make riskier choices to pursue more ambitious goals?
- Give immediate feedback on how they could have been bolder in recent meetings or decisions. Sharing just-in-time feedback can help them correct course in time to achieve different results.
- Emphasize the value of boldness. As with decisiveness, being bold can feel counterintuitive at first. Your people need to know you value boldness above perfection.

+ Share examples of how boldness has helped you and other leaders you respect to get ahead. Tell them how you pushed yourself to embrace your inner boldness, and describe how you felt in those moments.

You'll become more innovative and productive as you unleash your people's courage. Model how to embody boldness through the action steps outlined in this chapter, and you'll embolden your entire team.

Chapter 11

Influential

Authority Competency #3

"The key to successful leadership today is influence. Not authority."
– John C. Maxwell

Leaders with executive presence know how to influence others, shaping big-picture priorities and driving results. To grow your executive presence, you must learn how to influence others at all levels. Being intelligent, highly qualified, and talented can position you to become an influencer, but it takes more than that. Becoming an influencer means being able to motivate and inspire others to believe in your vision, goals, projects, and ideas.

If you have influence, you deliver a high level of value to your company. Leaders with influence accomplish more high-level achievements and guide their company's strategic direction. Senior management looks to them for solutions and trusts their ideas. Master the competency of influence to expand your executive presence.

If you have influence, you deliver a high level of value to your company.

Behaviors of influential leaders.

Think of the influential leaders you've known in your career. What qualities do they display? They are probably dynamic, engaged leaders who don't passively sit by and let things happen. Instead, influential people lead the charge toward change. They're comfortable being the louder voice driving an issue, process, or project forward. Further, they continuously strive to expand their scope of responsibility to a much wider and more impactful level, which keeps their influence growing.

Influence doesn't stem from a title; it comes from within. To become an influential leader, you don't need a promotion. Rather, you need to become convincing, compelling, and forceful. By exerting influence, you'll incite others toward action. People will follow you not because they're afraid of going against your judgment, but because they truly believe in your vision. By presenting your point of view articulately and assertively, you'll persuade others to believe in your ideas, and you'll effectively counter-argue when necessary.

Furthermore, you'll exert influence in all directions:

- Downward, among the people you manage.
- Horizontally, among your peers.
- Upward, among your superiors.

Rather than just influencing the people you supervise, you'll influence people at all levels of the organizational hierarchy. You'll know your ideas are worthy of being heard by whomever they can benefit. By developing a strong rapport with all those you interact with, you'll build social capital, making others eager to hear your ideas. And you'll demonstrate thought leadership, meaning you'll put forth innovative ideas that guide the direction of your company or even your entire field, which 88% of decision-makers believe is vital to the success of an organization.[i]

Consider this list of qualities that enhance or sabotage influence. Master the qualities on the left and work to eradicate those on the right.

INFLUENTIAL QUALITIES	QUALITIES THAT UNDERMINE INFLUENCE
Convincing	Uncompelling
Making change	Ineffective
Persuasive	Inconsequential
Believable	Uncredible
Inciting action	Passive

Through the qualities on the left, you'll drive your team to believe in and pursue a cohesive vision. This will dramatically improve organizational effectiveness. When teams and their organization have the same vision, commitment goes up by 32% and satisfaction by 46%—and they have 125% less burnout, reports McKinsey.[ii]

With a high level of influence, you'll also have more autonomy over the types of projects you pursue. Your work will become more and more rewarding as you gain the ability to shape more of your job responsibilities.

Influential people also have a high emotional IQ. They know how to read people and appeal to emotions as well as reason. "Focus on the emotional versus the rational," urge Rich Berens and Jim Haudan in *What Are Your Blind Spots? Conquering the 5 Misconceptions That Hold Leaders Back*.[iii] "When organizations manage change, they almost inevitably gather all the critical facts, prepare extensive communication plans to share those facts, and then are frustrated when nothing changes. We then often hear that 'our people don't get it' and 'they don't want to change.'" In contrast, influential leaders know how to use pathos to convey the importance of those facts and figures.

For all of these reasons, having more influence will allow you to accomplish more. It creates a positive feedback loop—as people respond enthusiastically to your ideas, you'll develop more confidence and drive, causing your influence to expand even further. Growing your influence will also have reverberating effects on the people around you. You'll inspire your colleagues and direct reports to innovate in particular areas, making the organization more competitive. By instilling a shared sense of purpose, you'll keep your team driven and engaged.

Take the example of Elon Musk, who was voted the most inspirational leader in the tech field in a survey of industry professionals.[iv] He has earned his status as an incredibly influential leader by putting forth a compelling vision of progress, even in terms of developments that no one else was seriously considering. He's a master of driving his team to pursue a goal that others had thought impossible—like creating a civilization on Mars, which takes some serious persuasion. "Through original thinking, technical precision and smart marketing, Elon is making space transport rise up to our biggest ambitions," writes *Time*.[v] "Along the way he has reinjected the most powerful fuel of all into the mission: public enthusiasm. For the first time since the

1960s, space once again feels like the greatest adventure." In other words, Musk influences not just the people in his organization but *all* stakeholders, convincing them to believe in the greatness of his vision and mission.

As psychologist Daniel Goleman says, "Remember, leadership is the art of getting work done well through other people. And influence is the most powerful way to do that. By the same token, influence is also crucial when you work with a division over which you have no direct authority, yet their work is necessary to your own success. You can't order them to do what you want, you must persuade or inspire them to put forth their best efforts toward the clear objective you have defined."[vi] This horizontal influence is growing more and more important as organizations develop increasingly flatter structures.[vii]

Self-evaluation: Assess your level of influence.

How can you become an influential leader—and do you exert influence already? As with every other EP quality, growing your influence requires consistent choices on a daily basis. Through the following behaviors, you can build influence day by day. Place a check next to the ones you're engaging in already.

I demonstrate influence by ...

1. Motivating others to achieve a goal.
2. Presenting ideas assertively and persuasively to my team or senior leaders.
3. Putting together arguments that incite action, convincing others to adopt my plan wholeheartedly.
4. Leveraging my expertise to back up my ideas, establishing credibility.
5. Pursuing broader initiatives that go beyond the scope of my role.
6. Offering my insights and perspectives to those who can benefit from them, including people in other functions.
7. Striving to expand the scope of my responsibility.
8. Promoting projects I believe in and gaining buy-in for them.

9. Focusing on the game-changing ideas that have the greatest impact, even when they take the organization in a new direction.

10. Building relationships with people across the organization and at all levels.

11. Mentoring others as they reach for more ambitious goals.

12. Offering guidance for projects I believe in, sharing consistent input.

13. Telling powerful stories that support my point of view.

14. Enrolling people in my vision for change.

15. Rallying the team to find solutions to challenges.

16. Advocating for controversial ideas and convincing others of their merit.

17. Securing the necessary resources to implement my ideas or the projects I support.

18. Engaging in strategic planning for my organization that helps set its future direction.

19. Getting key stakeholders on board before I finalize a decision, so I know it has widespread buy-in.

20. Providing ongoing support for my projects to make sure they succeed.

If you scored above 17, you exert broad influence in your organization, although you may still have room to improve. If your score falls below 14, you probably struggle with influence, although you do have some nascent strengths in this area. If your score is below 8, this represents a critical area for growth.

Don't wait until you're appointed to a certain position or level to start growing and leveraging your influence. In fact, influence is critical within relationships where you hold no formal authority. You need to start building influence *first*, and it will propel you to the next level.

Of the behaviors you didn't check off, which do you struggle with the most? Choose up to five to focus on strengthening over the next several weeks. The action steps in this chapter will help you grow your powers of persuasion, cultivate meaningful relationships, and establish yourself as a visionary leader to expand the scope of your influence.

Don't wait until you're appointed to a certain position or level to start growing and leveraging your influence.

Now, let's examine the behaviors that undermine influence, so you can work to eradicate them as you grow new strengths.

Behaviors that undermine influence.

Leaders who lack influence are minimizing the scope of their impact within their organization. They prevent others from truly knowing and leveraging their abilities, and they miss out on the satisfaction of driving transformation. Place a checkmark by any of the following behaviors that describe you, so you can take action to eliminate them.

I undermine my influence by ...

- ✦ Looking to someone else to take responsibility and ownership of projects, acting in a supporting role when I could be leading.
- ✦ Not sharing a compelling enough argument to persuade others.
- ✦ Delegating higher-level responsibilities to my peers or superiors.
- ✦ Staying quiet rather than pushing my ideas forward.
- ✦ Not taking action to expand my limited resources.
- ✦ Focusing too much on the tactical rather than the strategic; getting consumed by more mundane tasks.
- ✦ Pushing through shortsighted ideas with limited value.
- ✦ Keeping to myself rather than building relationships with people across functions and at all levels of the organization.
- ✦ Not spending time generating innovative ideas.
- ✦ Not taking risks or being willing to make change.
- ✦ Stepping back and withdrawing from ideas I believe in.
- ✦ Not offering direction to others who can benefit from it.
- ✦ Being too humble about my achievements, which prevents others from knowing the true impact of my work.
- ✦ Not leveraging my expertise to persuade others.

If you lack influence, you probably grow immersed in the weeds of your job rather than setting your sights on broader, more impactful initiatives.

You may act as though your own ideas aren't worth pursuing, rather than leveraging your experience, conviction, and relationships to push them through.

If you're engaging in some of these behaviors, it's a red flag that you're undermining your executive presence. It's time to correct course now! Make a note of these behaviors so you can address them once we cover the action steps for building influence.

Dominic Learns to Take Charge and Build Influence

Problem:

Dominic couldn't seem to motivate his team to take action or generate buy-in for ideas he believed in. He'd receive a lackluster response for his proposals at best, even among the people he managed. We sat down to unpack the reasons why he appeared to lack influence. First, it quickly became clear that Dominic felt most comfortable in a supportive role. If an opportunity to take charge arose, he would never volunteer, instead waiting to be asked. That prevented him from building credibility as a leader. Second, he didn't present his opinions in a compelling and persuasive way. He didn't masterfully show how his ideas fit into a broader strategic vision. He remained so focused on the tactical parts of his job that he didn't see, embrace, or advocate for the more important broader initiatives.

Action:

To become an influential leader, Dominic needed to concentrate on making bigger-picture contributions. He needed to reflect on his strategic priorities and discover his capacity to drive change. By offloading some of his lower-priority tasks, he made time to delve into strategic ideas. Through coaching, he learned how to make compelling arguments by appealing to both emotion and reason. He learned to pitch his ideas with authority. And by building relationships with peers, senior leaders, and direct reports, he created a network of connections who would advocate for his ideas.

Results:

After months of steady effort, Dominic looked back and could hardly believe the difference he saw in himself. He had a strong network of people who backed his ideas and believed in him, and he was focusing his energy on exciting higher-order issues. In turn, his job satisfaction and enthusiasm for his work steadily increased.

Do others perceive you as influential?

This exercise will help you better understand how others view you. Assign yourself a score of 1 to 10 for each of these statements, with 1 being the lowest and 10 being the highest:

- People want me on board with their projects, so they make an effort to sell their ideas to me.
- People seek my input before moving forward with an idea.
- Senior leaders reach out to me for input at times.
- Others are easily persuaded to get on board with my ideas.
- In meetings, people express enthusiasm about ideas that come from me.

If you scored above 43, others likely view you as an influential leader. Otherwise, focus on the action steps and exercises in this chapter to cultivate influence.

Action steps to build your influence.

Whether you're in a high-level leadership position or not, actively grow your influence across the organization so you can have a wider impact and drive greater change. These action steps will help you do exactly that.

1. Schedule time to explore what holds you back from being influential at work.

As you enhance your self-knowledge, the obstacles will become less restrictive and you'll open up to possibilities previously unknown. In your reflection time, answer these questions:

- Why am I not being more influential at work?
- What excuses am I making to not be influential?
- What obstacles are preventing me from being influential?
- What fears are stopping me from being influential?
- Do I have certain limiting beliefs about myself that prevent me from being more influential?

2. Be convincing when sharing your data.

You and your team can shape strategy. Present a convincing methodology, content, and data when standing in front of important stakeholders. Tell people exactly what needs to be done, and why. Using the boldness you've been cultivating, be direct. You need to be a shaper of strategy, not just a data sharer. Put yourself on the line, taking a stand with powerful and persuasive arguments.

3. Nurture early adopters of your ideas.

Promoting your ideas among a small group of supporters before introducing them to everyone else can facilitate successful adoption. If you want the group to use a new technology, for instance, cultivate a handful of advocates for that software first.

4. Listen to those with different perspectives.

People will gain more respect for you when they see you genuinely taking in all points of view. This strengthens your relationships with them, helping them to hear you better in turn. Good listeners practice *dynamic* rather than *defensive* listening.[viii] While defensive listening involves being constantly reactionary to what the other person is saying—and planning your next response—dynamic listeners truly strive to learn from the other person and understand what is being said.

5. Create an influence map, as Dorie Clark says in HBR.[ix]

"Draw a *power map*, using circles that show who has the most influence over your career—and, in turn, the people who have the most influence over them," she advises. "Figure out what you can offer the influential people—expertise, assistance on a project, help with networking—and ways to cultivate unique knowledge or skills they'd find valuable." If you don't yet know some of these people, figure out whether you can influence them through your relationships with others whom they respect and admire.

6.   Build relationships based on trust throughout your organization.

Show you genuinely care about your coworkers, leaders, subordinates, and clients, and that you remember important details about their lives. Ask them how their new hobby or work project is going. By doing so, you'll establish authentic relationships with people who truly like and appreciate you.

7.   Remember the principal of reciprocity:

Giving something to others will predispose them to make a concession or buy in to your idea.[x] It doesn't need to be anything major—praising their idea will make them more likely to get on board with your endeavor. Make this part of your routine interactions, not just something you do when you want agreement on a specific initiative.

8.   Cultivate first followers who will advocate strongly for your ideas.

Choose people in positions of authority who will influence those in their social circles to support your plan.

9.   Acknowledge potential counterarguments.

Prepare for how to address them in advance. Briefly explain why they are not a cause for concern, showing you've carefully considered the situation.

10.   Study what moves the people you're trying to influence to action.

What do they care most about? Appeal to what they believe in, showing how it connects to your initiative. Emphasize your common ground in these areas.

11.   Give others a seat at the table.

Though everyone doesn't need to be involved in every aspect of a project, you can gain a great deal of buy-in from asking for others' input. They'll feel more invested when they've played a role in designing the project.

Invite high-profile people to share their insights, as well as a range of other people from other levels of the organizational hierarchy.

12. Listen to feedback.

Show you're genuinely interested in listening and responding to concerns so your project can move forward as smoothly as possible.

13. Welcome collaboration with others.

Look for areas where your interests overlap, and propose mutually beneficial strategic partnerships with them.

The more you grow your influence, the more support you'll garner for your initiatives, and the more effective you'll be as a result. You'll also shape the direction of others' endeavors and growth, guiding peers as well as direct reports to fulfill their potential as leaders. And as you step into your own potential as a master influencer, you'll guide organizational strategy and vision. By doing so, you'll mark yourself as a leader who knows how to steer the group toward transformative solutions that reconceptualize what is possible.

Help your employees expand their influence.

By now it should be clear how growing your own influence will benefit your career. But as a leader, you need to go a step further by helping your employees cultivate their own influence as well.

How will growing your employees' influence build a stronger team?

Here's how taking the time to help your employees cultivate their influence will benefit your whole team and organization.

- Their ideas will be heard and utilized, so you'll take advantage of all the ingenuity that exists within your team to generate stronger solutions.
- Everyone will be driving toward a shared vision. Employees with influence will guide others to get behind that vision, and they'll come up with strategies to support it.

- Collaboration will soar as people compellingly share their ideas and feel empowered to take action. People will increasingly connect across functions to leverage all the available talent, rather than remaining in their silos.
- They'll persuade clients to adopt the best solutions for them by making a strong case for the ideas they believe in.
- Work will flow more smoothly because your team will be staffed with highly communicative people.

In a nutshell, influential people give their team a clear sense of direction. Even if your employees don't hold formal leadership positions, they'll motivate and inspire their peers as they expand their influence.

How to help your employees grow their influence.

If you're someone who naturally has a lot of influence, it can be easy to overlook employees' need for growth in this area. You may unconsciously think of it as something you either have or you don't. Or you might simply lack self-awareness in this area, since it's something you effortlessly excel at. But with perseverance, anyone can grow their influence.

- Identify employees who especially lack influence. Consider how each individual employee could bolster their influence over others. Why do they lack it? Are they consumed by tasks rather than strategies, or do they avoid championing new ideas due to a lack of confidence?
- Talk with each employee about how they could exercise more influence. Affirm the importance of strategic thinking and urge them to block out time for it regularly.
- Help them to pinpoint three situations in which they can exert more influence over the next two weeks. Challenge them to take initiative to do that.
- Give them feedback on how they craft a pitch when sharing a new idea. Share tips on how to present their idea more persuasively.
- Ask them to identify five people they could be networking with to grow their influence, at various levels of the organization.

By mentoring your employees to success with these tips, you can help them become more effective leaders in their own right. As a result, your team will become a driving force for change within your organization or even beyond.

Now you have a thorough understanding of the components of authority as well as gravitas. It's time to take a deep dive into the third domain of executive presence, expression. We'll explore how to master the three remaining competencies of executive presence so you can reach your full potential as a leader.

Section 3

EXPRESSION

Domain 3 of 3

Introduction

Understanding Expression

Leaders with executive presence have mastered the art of expression. They are eloquent communicators who know how to make themselves heard and understood.

The three competencies that make up the domain of expression are being vocal, insightful, and clear in your communication. Every time you speak up, share insights, and explain your ideas clearly, you increase your leadership foundation of expression.

Your speech is the vehicle that carries your authority and gravitas. Without speaking up regularly, you can't make those qualities known. In this section, we'll delve into the nuances of how to leverage expression to establish yourself as an articulate and powerful leader.

Every time you speak up, share insights, and explain your ideas clearly, you increase your leadership foundation of expression.

Expression defined.

Expression encompasses how you convey your thoughts, ideas, and insights. The first step of expression is actually speaking up to make your thoughts known—not just within your group, but throughout the organization. Second, when you communicate, what you say needs to be *insightful*, elevating the conversation. It's not just about taking up space; you actually have to have a point of view worth hearing. Third, you need to be clear and succinct when you communicate. The fewer words you use, the more confident you'll sound.

All leaders affect the spaces they inhabit, whether intentionally or not. When you actively express yourself, you fill more of this space with *you*. If you remain silent and expressionless, you impact the space by acting like a nonentity. Your boss and other leaders need you to voice your opinions. Your company needs to hear from you. If they don't, you become an underutilized leader who has less influence and contributes less than your potential.

EXPRESSION
Vocal
Insightful
Clear

Whenever you express yourself and voice your opinions, you need to make sure you own that message. Don't be quiet, passive, or timid in your delivery. Instead, be striking, distinct, clear, and impactful every time you speak up. If you don't, two things will happen: 1) your message will not be truly felt or understood by other participants, and 2) you'll leave the door open for someone else to voice the same idea in their own words. Then, people might jump on "their" idea instead of yours. This happens all the time. One person shares an idea and someone else says the same thing more forcefully five minutes later, and everyone gets on board without realizing where it originated. The first person who voiced it gets ignored because it was delivered in a forgettable way that didn't gain traction or hold the audience's attention, like a small pebble that barely makes a ripple when tossed into the water. When you own the idea by sharing it with confidence, command, and power, the pebble becomes a boulder and when dropped into the water, it makes a huge wave. Amplify your messages so they land with a splash when you speak up at meetings. People will then digest the ideas as your own and remember that you are the person behind them.

Own the fact that you're here for a reason. People in the company have assigned a value to your point of view. This is why you belong in the room and have a seat at the table. Speak up and make yourself heard. By doing so, you'll ensure your company fully leverages your value rather than squandering it.

Your presence needs to be felt in each space you step into. There is always room for you to express yourself. Your impact must be known. Others must observe your engagement and involvement, or you'll remain unknown and overlooked. As Rebecca Shambaugh writes in HBR, "Whether you are an associate manager or a senior executive, what you say, how you say it, when you say it, to whom you say it, and whether you say it in the proper context are critical components for tapping into your full strategic leadership potential."[i]

> People in the company have assigned a value to your point of view.
> This is why you belong in the room and have a seat at the table.

Tammy Makes Her Talents Known

Problem:

Tammy's manager commented on her lack of expression, saying, "I don't hear her speak up or share in meetings. She lacks visibility. I don't really know the things she's involved in. This really hurts her because she is then less influential and less relied on. She doesn't get opportunities to take the lead on projects because she's not seen as a driving force and go-to person. She needs to put herself out there more. I want to hear her opinions. How is anyone to know what's on her mind, if she doesn't tell us?"

Action:

Tammy was shaken when she heard this, but then she realized she'd been making a common mistake: Trying to let her work speak for itself. Instead, she needed to focus on cultivating expression so people would hear her thoughts and know what she was doing. At every meeting, she began speaking up at least three times. Soon she was regularly chiming in and making her presence felt. She shared expertise people hadn't even realized she possessed.

Results:

Soon Tammy's boss offered her an exciting project in one of her areas of expertise, realizing he'd been missing out on leveraging the full scope of her knowledge. More high-profile projects followed, making Tammy's job far more rewarding than it had ever been before.

When you aren't succinct, you will lose your audience.

Whether you're engaged in a presentation, a one-on-one discussion, or a team meeting, you need to be clear, crisp, and to the point in your communication. When you aren't succinct, you will lose your audience. They will begin tuning you out and questioning your competence and presence.

Let's delve into the main components of expression in a bit more depth, so you can more fully understand this EP domain.

Which qualities are most essential for expression?

In the survey that GEC Research Center conducted on the most critical executive presence competencies, we asked a wide spectrum of people what they considered the most pivotal qualities of expression. Here's what 1,400 U.S. employees, middle managers, senior leaders, and executives said:

THE MOST IMPORTANT QUALITIES OF EXPRESSION

% saying it is absolutely essential for a leader to be ...

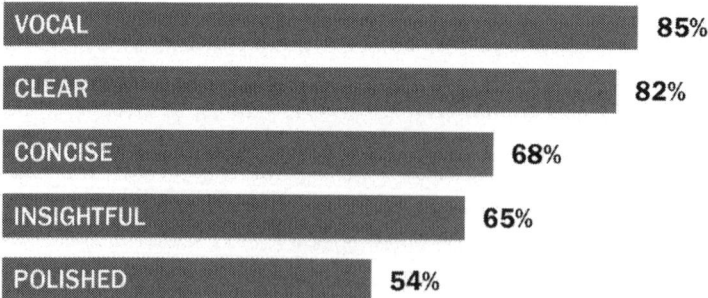

Quality	%
VOCAL	85%
CLEAR	82%
CONCISE	68%
INSIGHTFUL	65%
POLISHED	54%

Source: GEC Research Center Survey, Poll of 1,400 U.S. Workers.

In the survey, "vocal" clearly took the lead as the most crucial quality of expression. "Clear" followed closely behind. Through careful analysis,

UNDERSTANDING EXPRESSION | 225

we arrived at "vocal," "insightful," and "clear" as the three core qualities of expression.[1] We then crafted the following definition of expression within the 3x3 Executive Presence Model.

GRAVITAS	AUTHORITY	EXPRESSION
You radiate self-assuredness and power by projecting confidence and charisma. You naturally draw others to you, easily commanding a room and making your presence felt.	You are decisive, bold, and influential. You project certainty in your decisions. You are persuasive and compelling, so your assertiveness gives others confidence in your ideas.	You are consistently vocal, making great recommendations and asking excellent questions. You are well-spoken and share your ideas succinctly. You are polished, prepared, and professional in all your communications.

As you work to become vocal, insightful, and clear, you'll transform into a leader with exceptional powers of expression. You'll appear more professional and competent in every situation, and you'll brand yourself as a poised and capable leader.

At its core, expression is all about how you use your words to communicate like a leader in all your interactions.

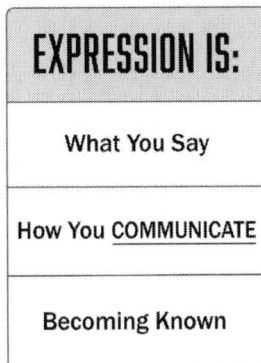

EXPRESSION IS:

What You Say
How You COMMUNICATE
Becoming Known

---

1   While analyzing the results of our survey, my team surmised that "concise" and "polished" both strongly pertained to "clear." Thus, how to build those two qualities will be addressed in the chapter on becoming clear.

The higher you advance in your organization, the more integral expression becomes. When you hold a position of leadership, the messages you communicate carry much more weight. People will attach extra importance or meaning to them. What you say gets amplified as if you were speaking into a megaphone. The higher up you are, the more amplified your message becomes. When you speak, your words carry greater impact. People are watching and observing what you say. They are listening extra carefully and reading more into what you say than you might have intended.

The higher up you are, the more amplified your message becomes. When you speak, your words carry greater impact.

Body language also subtly affects your executive presence by influencing how you express yourself. When you sit up straight at meetings as you present your ideas, your words take on more power. When you place yourself in a position of high visibility, like the front of the room rather than the back, you also communicate your own importance. Paying close attention and dressing one level above your own role shows that you take your work seriously, so you should be taken seriously in turn.

Lorraine Learns to Show Up Fully in Meetings

Problem:

Lorraine excelled in one-on-one meetings. She was open and conversational with both leaders and direct reports, inspiring trust and building a strong rapport. In fact, in our coaching sessions, she presented herself as very engaged and charismatic. In meetings, however, it was a different story. She completely lacked awareness of how her body language as well as her words (or lack thereof) were presenting her as disengaged and ineffective. She'd slouch in her seat and look down at the table as she listened to a coworker. She'd sit back and listen as others debated ideas. Lorraine needed to learn to bring her A-game to meetings as well as one-on-ones.

Action:

We came up with a list of five key body language changes Lorraine needed to prioritize immediately: Making strong eye contact, sitting up straight, placing herself in a prominent position in the room, showing interest with her facial expressions, and using open body language. She also needed to prepare detailed thoughts on the topics to be discussed, and then push herself to vocalize them.

Results:

Knowing she had thought through her ideas ahead of time gave Lorraine the confidence to voice them frequently. The changes she'd made impressed her boss, who commented on the value of her contributions.

Which behaviors show a lack of expression?

In the survey, the GEC Research team also asked participants which behaviors most undermine expression. Here's what they said.

WHICH BEHAVIORS MOST UNDERMINE EXPRESSION?

% who say these behaviors show a lack of expression ...

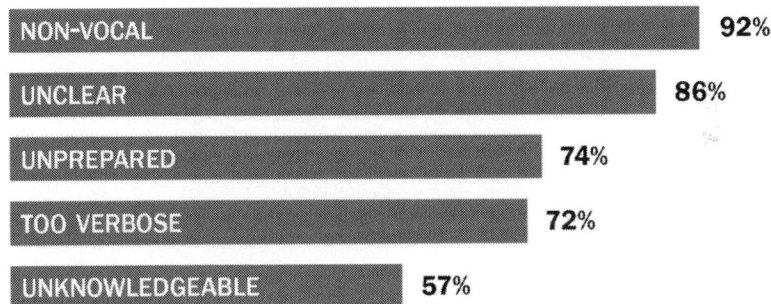

Behavior	%
NON-VOCAL	92%
UNCLEAR	86%
UNPREPARED	74%
TOO VERBOSE	72%
UNKNOWLEDGEABLE	57%

Source: GEC Research Center Survey, Poll of 1,400 U.S. Workers.

Not speaking up or being concise is the quickest way to undermine your executive presence. These are the two most easily noticeable of the nine EP competencies. You really stand out when you lack them—either by being quiet and completely unknown, or by being long-winded and rambling. However, these are also the easiest to fix of all the EP qualities. At meetings, you can quickly begin speaking up more and practicing being concise.

> Not speaking up or being concise is the quickest way to undermine your executive presence.

Comparison of qualities that cultivate or undermine expression.

Take a look at the following qualities. The ones on the left enhance the competency of expression, while the ones on the right diminish it. You need to embody the qualities on the left in all your interpersonal interactions, from group presentations to one-on-one discussions. When you've mastered these qualities, you'll show up as a leader who excels in communication.

15 WAYS TO BUILD OR UNDERMINE EXPRESSION

QUALITIES THAT CULTIVATE EXPRESSION	QUALITIES THAT UNDERMINE EXPRESSION
VOCAL • Forthright • Opinionated • Communicative • Outspoken • Projecting	**NONVOCAL** • Uncomfortable sharing • Unopinionated • Hesitant to communicate insights • Withdrawn • Soft-spoken
INSIGHTFUL • Knowledgeable • Experienced • Innovative • Intelligent • Prepared	**UNINFORMED** • Lacking knowledge • Inexperienced • Unimaginative • Simpleminded • Unorganized
CLEAR • Articulate • Coherent • Candid • Polished • Concise	**UNCLEAR** • Inarticulate • Confusing • Meandering • Unfocused • Rambling

To understand expression in action, let's look at the example of Greta Thunberg. Despite her young age—she earned global recognition for her efforts to bring about a halt to climate change as a young teenager—her poignant statements and articulate delivery have made it impossible to ignore her message. Whether she inspires or strikes a nerve, her candor is undeniable. She is filled with passion and conviction for what she says, but she often speaks softly and deliberately to accentuate the gravity of her words. She never shies away from speaking her truth, even to sympathetic political allies whom she perceives as not taking bold enough action, telling them, "You are too scared of being unpopular" and that it's time to pull "the emergency brake."[ii] She is, above all, forthright. Thunberg is also an introvert who has publicly discussed having Asperger's syndrome, calling it her "superpower," which affirms that people who fall outside of the stereotypical mold of a gregarious leader often possess incredible strengths.[iii]

Now we'll delve into each of the three core competencies of expression outlined in the 3x3 Model: vocal, insightful, and clear. Together, they synthesize the key expression competencies highlighted in the results of our survey. The following chapters will walk you through what each of these three qualities looks like, and how you can take action to develop it now.

Chapter 12

Vocal

Expression Competency #1

"Your time for participating is now.
You owe it to the company and you owe it to yourself.
Your criterion for involvement should be that you're heard and
understood."

– Andy Grove

Your company needs leaders who are vocal. Leaders who speak up regularly make themselves a vital part of every meeting and interaction. They don't settle for sitting on the sidelines and simply observing others. They make their presence felt by making their voices heard.

However, research shows that about half of all employees don't speak their minds on a regular basis—not even to peers.[i] They let things happen around them without shaping the conversation or their team's plans. Thus, this quality remains in high demand.

Your senior leadership expects you to make the effort to become a vocal leader, even if this doesn't come naturally to you. If you don't speak up, your knowledge, experience, and critical thinking capacity remain locked away. When you candidly share your thoughts, you'll deliver more value to your company rather than suppressing your ability to think strategically, communicate, and lead. Your organization will then more fully leverage your talents, knowledge, and intelligence.

> Your company needs leaders who are vocal.

Behaviors of vocal leaders.

Vocal leaders share their thoughts and ideas without hesitation. They're forthcoming with their opinions, making their voice and presence visible to others. In doing so, they make their expertise, competence, and talents known, recognizing that they are a subject matter expert in a particular domain, which gives them knowledge that those above them don't possess. When they have something to contribute, they express it. People view them as comfortable speaking up and standing in the spotlight, which underscores their leadership ability. Speaking up also bolsters innovation, challenging the status quo and expanding what is possible for a team to accomplish.

> Vocal leaders share their thoughts and ideas without hesitation.

By speaking up frequently, you'll multiply your influence and open the door for new opportunities. Senior leaders will notice you more, perceive you more favorably, and assign you to projects that make full use of your strengths. "The number of senior executives who know you and have a good impression of you will directly correlate with your career success," writes Robert Chen in *Fast Company*.[ii] Becoming vocal will give you a chance to prove that you're capable of handling high-priority tasks rather than standing in the shadows.

Furthermore, people will better understand your ideas when you present them assertively. When voiced confidently, your ideas will truly make a splash.

You'll also help your team navigate times of transition or crisis more adeptly as you learn to voice your perspectives more. "When employees feel comfortable candidly voicing their opinions, suggestions, or concerns, organizations become better at handling threats as well as opportunities," write Hemant Kakkar and Subra Tangirala in HBR.[iii]

Here's a quick look at vocal competencies in comparison with characteristics that undermine the ability to be vocal.

VOCAL QUALITIES	QUALITIES THAT UNDERMINE BEING VOCAL
Forthright	Uncomfortable sharing
Opinionated	Unopinionated
Communicative	Hesitant to communicate insights
Outspoken	Withdrawn
Projecting	Soft-spoken

If you hold back on sharing your ideas, it conveys fear or disconnection—which undermines your capacity to lead. But you're in good company—a recent study found that 17.5% of employees don't speak up at all, while 47.1% speak up on 5 or fewer issues, which usually relate directly to their work.[iv] Only 13.6% voice their opinions on more than 10 topics.

Staying silent means remaining underutilized as a resource, which affects your whole organization. A full 60% of employees say they have trouble getting their colleagues to share essential information with them, a recent study found.[v] Their silence undermines the effectiveness of their whole team.

"There are some people whose confidence outweighs their knowledge, and they're happy to say things which are wrong. And then there are other people who probably have all the knowledge but keep quiet because they're scared of saying things," says Helen Jenkins in *The New York Times*.[vi] Far more of us fall into the second category than the first. Ask yourself how often you've remained silent in the past couple of weeks because you felt uncomfortable or unprepared to jump into the conversation.

Many people avoid speaking up to address interpersonal problems, too—which just leads them to fester. In one study, 40% of respondents said they've wasted at least two weeks ruminating over whether to speak up when a colleague was not meeting expectations.[vii] "Instead of speaking up, people report engaging in resource-sapping avoidance tactics including complaining to others, doing unnecessary work and ruminating about the problem," write the researchers. "In extreme cases of avoidance, the bottom line is hit especially hard."

If you're an introvert, don't panic! Extroverts aren't the only people who can become vocal leaders. People who are naturally more reserved can learn strategies for becoming more vocal. If you don't tend to have a lot to say at meetings, we'll be discussing some ways to change that.

People who are naturally more reserved
can learn strategies for becoming more vocal.

Even the quietest people can learn to become more vocal. As you make your voice heard regularly, you'll increasingly grow your influence. By speaking your mind in every situation, you'll develop a strong presence. In turn, others will ask you to lead new initiatives or head meetings. Peers and leaders will look at you with respect and trust you with higher-level responsibilities. You'll also find new ways to collaborate with individuals who have complementary skills, including those in other functions. As you learn to lay your capabilities on the table to make them known, you'll launch new partnerships that expand the value you bring.

Staying silent means remaining underutilized as a resource.

Being vocal at meetings.

As a leader, you probably spend the majority of your time in meetings. Most people have a calendar that looks something like this:

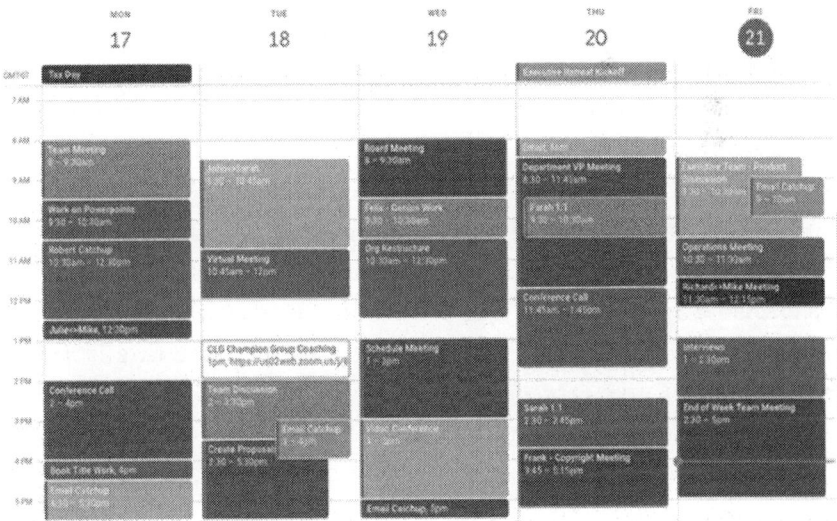

Leaders typically spend 60–75% of their day in meetings. Thus, it's extremely important to show up fully in meetings. Most people don't think about how they are being perceived in meetings—and if they do, they aren't focusing on their executive presence. However, when people lack EP, others really notice it. They stand out in ways they don't want to stand out. And not speaking up is a sure way to present yourself as lacking EP.

It's vital for your success to speak up at every meeting you attend. Make your voice heard in order to radiate executive presence in all your meetings. Expressing your thoughts will also spark more productive group discussion. Regardless of whether your idea rises to the top in a particular meeting, your participation will foster more productive dialogue and brainstorming sessions. Bringing energy to the conversation will prompt others to share ideas more freely.

When people self-censor simply because they don't know if their thoughts are good enough, the team misses out on some potentially brilliant ideas. When they voice half-formed thoughts, they give the team a chance to flesh them out in creative ways, which often leads to ingenious solutions.

Vocal people also know how to voice their ideas in ways that get attention rather than getting lost in the shuffle. Few things are more demoralizing than quietly voicing an idea that gets no attention, only to hear someone else receive ecstatic praise after reiterating it a few minutes later. By voicing ideas in ways that get them noticed, you'll gain recognition and improve your job satisfaction rather than feeling frustrated.

Speaking up in meetings can feel daunting when you're first trying to hone this ability. The solution is coming in overprepared. Barbara Adachi, Regional Head of Human Capital Consulting at Deloitte (and the first woman to hold this position) says overpreparation helped her transform from never speaking up in meetings to confidently speaking her mind. "I used to go to meetings and just not say a word," she recalls. "People wondered why I was even there. Unless asked to comment, I wouldn't volunteer. Speaking up was so hard for me. And I still need to push myself in new situations. But if I go in well-prepared and knowing I know more than I need to, I find it easier to speak up and not go back to my cocoon."[viii]

Self-evaluation: Assess your ability to be vocal.

Vocal leaders consistently demonstrate a particular set of behaviors that make their ideas known and their presence felt. Through these actions, they make themselves highly visible throughout their organization. As you read through the following list of behaviors of vocal leaders, place a checkmark by any that describe you.

I present myself as a vocal leader by ...

1. Making sure my opinions and ideas are heard by voicing them regularly.
2. Taking up air time at meetings consistently.
3. Vocalizing ideas even when they aren't fully baked.
4. Often being the first to speak up at a meeting, guiding the conversation.
5. Being direct and specific in my communications.
6. Sharing my opinions with senior-level leaders rather than just among peers.
7. Advocating for my ideas and making my rationale heard.
8. Interjecting with new and creative ideas that no one expects to hear.
9. Being the first to share my perspective when someone asks a question.
10. Enhancing others' ideas with great suggestions.
11. Projecting my voice with the appropriate volume so I'm sharing my ideas with power.
12. Driving the discussion, asking pointed questions and making thought-provoking comments.
13. Highlighting the problems that I see in a plan or idea so the team can fix them.
14. Sharing constructive feedback directly and continually with a broad range of people.
15. Giving real-time feedback whenever possible.
16. Speaking up when I disagree with an idea or decision.
17. Listening carefully so I can fully participate in the discussion with relevant comments and questions.

18. Interjecting, in a constructive way, to bring the discussion back on track.

19. Knowing how to insert my comments in the discussion even when dealing with dominant personalities who take up a lot of space.

20. Listening carefully to others' ideas so I can fully participate in the discussion.

If you scored above 17, you are highly vocal in your organization, although you may have some room to improve. If you scored below 14, you struggle with being vocal, and if your score falls below 8, this represents an especially critical area for growth.

Look over the areas you haven't checked off. Which ones represent your greatest areas for improvement? We'll review action steps for strengthening them later in this chapter. You'll learn strategies for speaking up often in meetings and other interactions, and making yourself heard—even if you sometimes feel tongue-tied. For now, choose up to five areas to focus on over the next few weeks.

In the words of Kerone Vatel from Goldman Sachs,[ix] "When you have a seat at the table, use it." By proactively placing your opinions in the spotlight, you'll make yourself known to both peers and senior leadership. By being direct and honest, you'll showcase your ability to be a candid leader who is committed to developing others' abilities and the group's ideas.

"When you have a seat at the table, use it."
Kerone Vatel

Teresa Gets Proactive about Participation in Meetings

Problem:

Teresa didn't speak up very often. Quiet and passive, she even hesitated to ask questions. She was taken aback to learn that her male subordinate had been mistaken for her superior in a meeting because he exuded more executive presence than she did. A senior-level executive pulled her aside and told her, "I want you to have more of an executive presence. To communicate your positions articulately and hold firm to them. Stand behind your viewpoints; hold your ground. You are an expert who needs to own what you know."

Her boss affirmed this advice, saying he wanted to hear from her more. She needed to stop letting others dominate meetings and actively work to add more substance to the discussions taking place.

Action:

Teresa had believed that as an introvert, she would always come across as more reserved in meetings. She didn't see that as something she could change. But her boss had seen other introverts learn to take up more space and make their voices heard, and he knew Teresa had valuable opinions to share. And he was right—through executive coaching, Teresa learned that her beliefs about what she was capable of had been holding her back. We discussed different ways in which she could contribute to the discussion, and she set goals for participation in each meeting that would allow her to track her progress.

Results:

By applying strategies she learned in the coaching sessions, Teresa became more outspoken and guided the direction of conversations rather than sitting back and listening. She didn't have to relinquish power to the extroverts; instead, she was taking up the space she deserved.

Behaviors that undermine a leader's ability to be vocal.

To establish yourself as a vocal leader, first identify whether you're engaging in the following non-vocal behaviors. They are each quite common, and they tend to persist until a person gets serious about consciously changing them. Put a checkmark by any of the following behaviors that describe you.

I undermine my ability to be a vocal leader by ...

- ✦ Not sharing my thoughts and ideas with others.
- ✦ Taking up little air time during meetings.
- ✦ Letting others dominate meetings and do the majority of the talking.

- ✦ Shying away from vocalizing new and creative ideas.
- ✦ Avoiding asking questions in meetings.
- ✦ Holding back from engaging in discussions and debates.
- ✦ Not articulating a strong point of view or advocating for my perspectives.
- ✦ Not sharing ideas until they're fully baked.
- ✦ Talking in a soft, quiet voice; not projecting.
- ✦ Letting others speak over me; taking a back seat to more assertive group members.
- ✦ Not being able to find a way into the conversation.
- ✦ Speaking tentatively.
- ✦ Staying outside or on the periphery of discussions.
- ✦ Only speaking if spoken to or asked questions.
- ✦ Not being willing to give honest feedback.

Make a note of the behaviors from this list that most undermine your ability to show up as a vocal leader. Engaging in these behaviors is a red flag that you're undermining your executive presence, although it's incredibly common.

If you're not vocal, you position yourself as more of a participant than a driver of discussions. At the rare times when you *do* speak up, others are likely to quickly forget your ideas—or not even hear them. They need to see you as a key player in your organization. Fortunately, you can quickly begin to remedy the situation by speaking up regularly in all your meetings and interactions. By doing so, you'll make yourself more visible and receive the recognition you deserve.

> If you're not vocal, you position
> yourself as more of a participant than a
> driver of discussions.

Paul Stops Second-Guessing His Ideas

Problem:

Paul delivered brilliant insights in one-on-ones with his boss, Don, yet would hardly say a word in their team meetings. He was making himself appear smaller and less capable than he actually was. "It's time to get serious about having a presence in meetings," Don told him one day. Paul admitted that he feared his ideas being rejected. He would usually second-guess himself when he thought of something to say, convincing himself it didn't measure up to others' contributions. "That's a normal fear to have, but it's far from the reality," Don said. "In actuality, you have some of the best ideas on this team—and your internal filter is silencing them."

At other times, Paul remained silent because he felt others had already voiced his opinions or raised critiques of an idea. If he agreed with the idea on the table, he'd say nothing. He didn't want to be like the obnoxious coworker who trailed on and on just to hear himself talk. "People assume you're neutral or against an idea if you say nothing," Don told him. "Speak up so others can hear your excitement about the idea. Or, share an opinion about a nuance of the plan, or why we should go in this direction. And don't make others have to voice the contrary opinions every time. If you disagree, or see room for improvement, be the one to speak up."

Action:

Paul set a goal of speaking up three times per meeting. He gathered his thoughts before the next meeting and met his goal with confidence. At the meeting after that, it was five times, and after that, he lost count.

Results:

Paul now enjoyed actively participating in team meetings and even looked forward to them. As a result, he became more visible both within his team and among company leaders. He began influencing decisions and shaping strategy. Paul knew he was paving the way to a more advanced position, and as he shaped team discussion and ideas, he could envision himself stepping into a senior leadership role.

> You have some of the best ideas on this team—
> and your internal filter is silencing them.

Do others perceive you as vocal?

This exercise will give you a better sense of how others view you. Assign yourself a score of 1 to 10 for each of these statements, with 1 being the lowest and 10 being the highest:

+ In a meeting, the conversation often focuses on ideas I have voiced.
+ People seem interested and attentive when I speak.
+ In meetings, others often look at me when they speak as though talking to me directly.
+ Others give me credit for my ideas, remembering that they came from me.
+ People respond to my words in ways that show they heard me clearly.

If you scored above 43, others likely view you as a vocal leader. Otherwise, leverage the exercises and action steps in this chapter to develop this competency.

Action steps to become more vocal.

If you're not vocal enough in your workplace, now is the time to correct course. Speak often, and every time you speak, use it as a chance to raise your profile. These action steps will empower you to become more vocal, establishing yourself as a strong, insightful, and expressive leader. By being vocal, you'll make all of your other executive presence qualities more visible as well.

1. Schedule and spend time exploring what holds you back from speaking up at work.

In your reflection time, answer these questions:

+ Why am I not speaking up more at work?
+ What excuses am I making to not speak up?

+ What obstacles are holding me back from speaking up?
+ What fears are preventing me from speaking up?
+ Do I have certain limiting beliefs about myself that stop me from speaking up?

2. Set a goal for how many times you'll speak at a meeting.

For example, you could decide to speak up three times: making a comment you've prepared ahead of time, asking a question, and voicing a thought that comes to mind in the moment.[x]

3. Voice ideas to someone you trust before bringing them to the meeting.

You'll feel more confident and prepared as a result.

4. Read over the meeting agenda in advance and think about what you'd like to say.

Jot down notes about the contributions you want to make for each topic. Consider whether you have an important topic to add to the agenda, too. Do you have an announcement to make about your project, or a new initiative to propose?

5. Overprepare for the meeting.

This can help you become quicker to speak up—and more articulate when you do. Bring questions, thought-provoking comments, and insightful points of view. Have two talking points to share at each meeting. Thorough preparation will eliminate the dread of voicing your thoughts and the struggle to find just the right moment to jump in.

6. Do some outside research on your topic to learn about industry trends or the latest studies.

Knowing you're well informed will help you to speak up with confidence.

7. Choose an agenda topic to focus on.

Take ownership of that topic, preparing detailed thoughts you want to share. Pick something you feel strongly about, so you can speak with strength and conviction.

8. Avoid planning back-to-back meetings.

Or, if you *must* plan them back-to-back, leave five minutes early to give yourself at least a small window of time to collect your thoughts and prepare talking points for the upcoming meeting.

9.   Read an article on a topic related to one of the agenda items.

Bringing fresh insights from a respected outside source can greatly enhance the discussion and show your investment in the topic.

10.   Speak up first.

Be the first to respond to an idea or voice your thoughts on an issue. Have a goal of saying something, even if it's a small comment, within the first several minutes of the meeting. That will help you break the ice and feel more comfortable speaking up again.

11.   Let others adapt to your point of view.

Don't just listen to everyone else's arguments and then weigh in with your opinion. Instead, state your opinion first to let it shape discussion.

12.   Say the first thing that comes to mind.

Instead of censoring yourself, practice trusting your gut reaction. It's okay to be wrong—others are wrong all the time!

Remember, you don't need to sound perfectly polished all the time. Insisting on perfection only hinders dialogue and the development of ideas. Instead, focus on becoming an active participant in the conversation.

While vocal leaders do strive to speak articulately and concisely—as we'll discuss in the upcoming chapters—they establish their presence in every interaction. They are agile communicators who know how to be valuable contributors without taking up too much air time by rambling. Think of the vocal leaders you know, and consider how they model these behaviors in their daily work. Emulate them as you begin working to practice these behaviors on a daily basis.

Arianna Reshapes Her Boss's Perception of Her Competence

Problem:

Arianna received outstanding performance reviews, and people respected her. However, she was naturally soft-spoken. She didn't usually speak up very much in meetings. When I interviewed her boss to learn how she was perceived, we learned that her boss saw her as "not confident" even though this wasn't the case—she was just quiet. Her boss felt hesitant to give her higher-visibility projects, believing they needed a more dominant personality who could influence and persuade others. Arianna actually could do all of this, because others *did* respect her, but her boss remained stuck on the idea that a soft-spoken person couldn't do those things.

Action:

Arianna began learning to project her voice and to speak up more. She began challenging herself to speak off the cuff more often, voicing ideas before she'd fully thought them through. She vocally supported ideas she believed in and provided constructive critiques of those she didn't.

Results:

Leaders began to see Arianna in a different way as she took these actions. They began asking her to take part in higher-profile initiatives where her talents could really make an impact. Now, they more fully understand who she is and what she can offer her organization.

Bonus section: Tips for interjecting in meetings.

If some of your coworkers are engaged in a robust dialogue, it can be challenging to find the right moment to speak—or the right thing to say. These tips and strategies for how to interject will give you a little more guidance if you're feeling flummoxed about how to make yourself heard among your more vocal colleagues.

Learn how to insert yourself into a conversation.

Whether you're struggling to interject in a meeting, or unsure of what to say in the first place, these tips will help you take an active role in the discussion.

5 tactics for making your voice heard.

What if you've been *trying* to speak up, but you can't get a word in? Here are some surefire solutions to this all-too-common problem.

- **Lead with an authoritative statement.** Phrases like "here's my idea," "I strongly suggest," and "I completely support that plan, and here's why" command attention, signifying that you're going to say something important.[xi] They also give you a moment to gather your thoughts as you take the floor.
- **Continue speaking if someone tries to interrupt you.** Don't cede the floor. If need be, say something like, "Let me just finish my thought."
- **Interrupt tactfully as the other person begins to trail off.** Ask, "Can I just add a point?" so your interruption doesn't feel rude. In many workplace cultures, interrupting is the only way you'll ever make yourself heard.[xii] Saying something that affirms the value of the other person's thoughts as you interrupt can also have the same effect. For example, "I agree, Dawn, and to add some perspective on that issue ..." or "To build on that point ..."
- **If the discussion has moved on from the topic you wanted to speak on,** reel it back in and make your point heard.
- **Use your body language.** Leaning forward or using a gesture can help you claim space when it's your turn to speak.

Put these tips to use routinely, and they'll become second nature.

10 ways to interject in meetings

What if you're motivated to speak up, but you're having trouble thinking of a valuable comment to make? First, remember that every statement you make doesn't have to be jaw-droppingly memorable. Comments that don't have earth-shattering importance are crucial to the flow of conversation.[xiii] Having these strategies in your back pocket will help you become a more dynamic part of the conversation, contributing in a variety of ways throughout meetings.

> The more you speak up at meetings,
> the more natural it will feel.

1. Supporting someone else's idea.

Providing enthusiastic support for someone else's idea will help the best ideas to rise to the top of the discussion. It will also help you to build mutually beneficial alliances with coworkers. For example:

- "I think that's an excellent point because …"
- "I think that idea has a lot of promise and we should flesh it out a bit more."
- "Susanna, you've clearly done your homework, and I feel confident in this plan."

2. Asking questions.

Good questions can prompt a more robust conversation on the issue being discussed:

- "What about the challenge of __?"
- "How will stakeholder X view this idea?"
- "What hurdles will we have to overcome to implement this idea?"
- "I like idea X—do others agree?"

3. Voicing your own idea.

This could be a big idea or a simple amendment to a larger plan. Announce it with enthusiasm so others will grow excited about it too.

- "I have a proposal: That we …"
- "I think we should make one key amendment."
- "I think we should focus our energies on …"

4. Paraphrasing an idea.

Confirm you've understood the speaker's idea correctly by simply paraphrasing it and asking if that's what she meant. Particularly with complex or outside-of-the-box ideas, this helps make sure everyone is on the same page. For instance:

+ "Are you saying that …"
+ "Did I understand correctly that …"
+ "So in a nutshell …"

5. Sharing expertise.

Maybe you've done some reading on one of the agenda topics, and you have some outside insights to contribute. Or maybe you already possess expertise in that area. Here are some examples of how you can share what you know:

+ "I just read a really interesting study on this topic. It suggests that …"
+ "Even though Y has been a popular approach, some companies are finding it beneficial to return to X, because …"
+ "Here are the results of the project Bob was referring to …"

6. Synthesizing ideas.

Synthesizing the ideas discussed or what the group has agreed upon is an extremely valuable contribution, keeping the group focused and productive. Often it helps people realize that they *do* have consensus on their goals and can move forward into the specifics of planning. Here are some examples of how to do that:

+ "Just to recap, we have agreed that X would be beneficial but only if we can find a solution to Y."
+ "So the key ideas we're looking at are X, Y, and Z, with X being the most viable and Z the most risky."
+ "It sounds like we want to find a disruptive solution rather than playing it safe."

7. Raising concerns.

If you fear appearing rude by disagreeing with others or bringing concerns to light, it's time to get over it. A healthy debate will help your team arrive at the best options. Plus, you can be diplomatic by framing your response "as a question rather than a challenge," says workplace strategist Lisa Barrington.[xiv] (That is especially effective if the answer isn't "yes" or "no.") Here are some ways to interject by disagreeing:

+ "I think idea B is feasible but just too safe. How can we take a smart risk that could really pay off?"
+ "That sounds promising, but don't the results from Project A show it's not quite so straightforward?"
+ "You've shared some solid insights, but I think the opportunity cost is just too great."
+ "I wish that were true, but I've found that … "

8. *Asserting the significance of a point.*

Maybe someone has alluded to an important point without emphasizing it adequately. Hone in on that point, expressing why it's so pivotal. For instance:

+ "That is a crucial point, because …"
+ "That idea is vital to our success, so let's dig in deeper."
+ "I'd like to see us focus on __ a bit longer, because it's central to the plan."

9. *Clarifying the next steps.*

Illuminating the next steps in a plan will help the group to move forward productively. Check in with the group about how the key elements of the plan will be carried out:

+ "Who else do we need to gain buy-in from before starting?"
+ "Who will present the idea to them?"
+ "Can we go over the workflow process for this project?"

10. *Pointing to someone else with expertise.*

Did you notice that a colleague with expertise on the topic at hand has remained silent? Direct a question specifically to that person. For example:

+ "Joanne, I'd really love to hear your thoughts on this topic."
+ "Bernie is the resident expert on this, so let's see what he thinks."
+ "Maggie, I think you have a lot of insight on this topic because ..."

The more you speak up at meetings, the more natural it will feel. A positive feedback loop will take shape: As you grow more comfortable, you'll gain more positive feedback about your value and performance in meetings. In turn, you'll enjoy these conversations and become an even more vocal contributor. Continue encouraging your employees to become more outspoken as well, so you'll have a strong flow of communication among everyone on your team.

Help your employees become more vocal.

As Todd's boss knew, developing vocal employees is a vital part of strengthening the organization. Vocal employees bring more value to their team through their consistent contributions.

How will helping your employees become more vocal build a stronger team?

If your direct reports and many on your team aren't being vocal, they'll be constantly undermining their own potential as well as the team's collective potential. Shy and reserved employees often possess a wealth of knowledge and ingenuity that remains scarcely utilized, which poses a major issue in most workplaces. Here are some key reasons to cultivate this ability in everyone on your team.

- They will make sure everyone knows their areas of specialization, so others know where to turn when they need their expertise and leaders know how to leverage them.
- Information will flow more freely across functions, rather than getting bottlenecked. Thus, decision-makers and teams will have access to the knowledge they need.
- You'll gain valuable insights that can influence your company's marketing, client relationships, and other aspects of business. Companies are desperate for new ways to generate revenue, improve customer service, streamline operations, and reduce expenses. By speaking up consistently, employees will give your organization access to these insights. They'll help you keep your finger on the pulse of operations, giving you a close-up view of what is actually happening on the ground.
- They'll get credit for their great ideas, leading to greater job satisfaction.

+ When employees are forthright and assertive, they can quickly correct mistakes they notice rather than failing to speak up about an issue.

+ Ensuring that diverse voices feel empowered to speak up will enhance the quality of your team's decision-making. "Minority viewpoints have been proven to aid the quality of decision making in juries, by teams, and for the purpose of innovation," writes Nilofer Merchant in HBR.[xv] "Even when the minority points of view are wrong, they cause the rest of the group to think better, to create more solutions, and to improve the creativity of problem solving."

Employees who voice their ideas to colleagues and collaborate on them together are far more likely to bring them to fruition than those who work alone, say researchers from Rotterdam School of Management (RSM), Erasmus University.[xvi] "Business leaders should understand that working in teams increases the chances of success of an idea by at least three times—so they should be encouraging employees not to work alone when generating innovative plans, products, services or processes," they explain.

How to help your employees become more vocal.

Many employees feel intimidated about speaking up in a big group, especially when certain personalities tend to dominate meetings. As a leader, you can take steps to help all your employees feel more comfortable speaking up. As a result, you'll have more ideas on the table and more minds working together at full capacity.

Here are some key ways to help your employees become more vocal. This list is longer than those for many of the other competencies because speaking up and making themselves heard is so vital for employees at all levels. Their ideas and insights are your company's competitive advantage, yet a large proportion of employees self-censor their valuable opinions. Here's how to help them unleash their contributions in order to dramatically extend their impact.

+ Tell your employees you want to hear from all of them. Emphasize this at every meeting, and say it to employees individually when they need to hear it. Affirm that all ideas are welcome and must be heard. This creates a culture of sharing rather than holding back.

+ Encourage them to share half-formed ideas rather than second-guessing themselves. Share stories of when a half-baked idea became a game-changer.

+ Don't dismiss ideas too quickly, even if they seem implausible at first glance. Give your team a chance to mull them over. It could be that a merger of two ideas, or an amendment to the seemingly impractical one, could make all the difference.

+ Assign meeting roles. Giving employees the responsibility to introduce particular topics that they have a stake in will help break the ice.

+ Prior to the meeting, let quiet employees know you plan to ask for their input on a particular topic. That way, they can collect their thoughts in advance.

+ Start the meeting with a new rule: People aren't allowed to interrupt each other. This will help quieter employees to feel more comfortable speaking up. When interruptions are eliminated, people will feel more heard and respected.

+ Ask for suggestions to add to the meeting agenda. This will encourage employees to take more ownership of a topic.

+ Send out your meeting agenda well in advance. Encourage less vocal employees to prepare their thoughts on particular agenda items where they have a lot to contribute.

+ Ask employees what they think when they've been silent on an issue. If an employee has a lot of knowledge on the topic, ask directly for his input.

+ When certain people are dominating the conversation, take a moment to pause, saying you'd like to hear from those who haven't shared yet.

+ Hold a breakout session. Have employees pair up and brainstorm on an idea for five minutes. Then, ask each pair to share what they came up with.

By taking these steps, you'll foster a more collaborative team that knows how to more fully draw upon each person's knowledge and strengths.

Chapter 13

Insightful

Expression Competency #2

"Nothing is more terrible than activity without insight."
— Thomas Carlyle

Leaders with executive presence deliver powerful insights that shape strategic direction and implementation of plans. They make great recommendations. They ask excellent questions and share ideas precisely, confidently, and with conviction. They are known for their smart thinking and critical analysis.

Your company's senior leadership is looking for insightful leaders who bring thoughtful advice and ideas to the table. Their trust in you will increase as you consistently deliver great insights. You'll make yourself known as a leader with well-grounded ideas that others should take seriously. As a result, others will come to you for guidance, leveraging your expertise and reflective capabilities.

Insightful leaders allow their wisdom, experience, and intelligence to shine.

Behaviors of insightful leaders.

Insightful leaders allow their wisdom, experience, and intelligence to shine. They often bring forward novel solutions that enhance an existing plan or open new doorways for their organization. They are thought leaders who offer a fresh perspective.

As you become an insightful leader, the people around you will see you as incredibly proficient and knowledgeable. Others will want to get your input before implementing a new project, knowing you're adept at fine-tuning an idea. Thus, you'll prove yourself to be an extremely valuable team member who shines not just for the projects you spearhead, but for the ways you help others refine their ideas.

Further, you'll identify and seize upon new opportunities for disruption and innovation. Your organization will reap greater rewards from the initiatives your team pursues as the quality of ideas and collaboration rises. Thus, you'll expand what is possible for your team to accomplish. As a creative thinker, you'll envision and direct your team toward new horizons rather than doing things the way they've always been done.

Here's a quick comparison of qualities that insightful leaders possess, in contrast to characteristics that undermine insightfulness. Master the qualities on the left to become known as an insightful leader.

INSIGHTFUL QUALITIES	QUALITIES THAT UNDERMINE INSIGHTFULNESS
Knowledgeable	Lacking knowledge
Experienced	Inexperienced
Innovative	Unimaginative
Intelligent	Simpleminded
Prepared	Unorganized

Being an insightful leader means devoting time to critical and strategic thinking, which allows you to bring your best ideas to the table. As you do so, others will perceive you as knowledgeable, intelligent, and innovative. They'll rely on your experience and trust you to prepare thoroughly for important discussions.

As an insightful leader, you'll also lead problem-solving initiatives that leverage the creativity of all participants. You'll often contribute your own valuable solutions while drawing upon the wisdom of the group.

Importantly, you'll also push yourself to back up your assertions with evidence based on your own experience and knowledge. You'll strive to ground your suggestions in a foundation of solid proof, so others will take you seriously. Doing your homework before making a suggestion will allow your knowledge and intelligence to shine.

A recent Gartner study found that design thinking and strategic management are the two most integral "soft skills" that today's leaders need to develop.[i] That means all leaders should be working to cultivate their insightfulness, in part through big-picture thinking.

Sergey Brin and Larry Page, co-founders of Google, serve as excellent examples of innovative thinkers who refuse to stop honing in on game-changing ideas. They developed the concept of ranked search results in the mid-'90s, along with the technology to make this idea feasible.[ii] Their efforts at encouraging employees to voice their own insights have led to innovations like Google Earth, AdWords, and self-driving car technologies, as TED says. They also co-founded X, the Moonshot Factory (formerly Google X), a division of the company that explores the most outlandish ideas their innovative team can imagine. X has pioneered technologies like Wing, a drone-based delivery service; Makani, a system of harnessing energy from kites; and Brain, which aims to bring AI to many everyday products, among numerous other initiatives.[iii] As Brin and Page exemplify, great leaders not only share powerful insights; they also draw out the best insights from the people around them and champion their groundbreaking ideas.

As you can see, being insightful isn't about always having the best idea or advocating solely for your own ideas. Rather, as an insightful leader, you'll also illuminate the key ideas that others need to hone in on. You won't always have all the answers (though you'll quite often have great ones), but you'll know how to shine light on a pathway forward. You'll put the most relevant ideas on the table and draw smart conclusions that inform your choices. Your great questions and suggestions will prompt further inquiry and discussion among the whole team. In this way, you'll help everyone around you become more insightful and inventive. Sharing your insights regularly will make your work more engaging and enjoyable as well.

Insightful leaders help identify and seize upon new opportunities for disruption and innovation.

Self-evaluation: Assess your level of insightfulness.

What does insightfulness look like in practice? Think of the leaders you've known whom you would consider insightful. Chances are, they embody a particular set of qualities in their daily work. As you read through this list of behaviors that insightful leaders demonstrate, place a checkmark by the ones that describe you.

I demonstrate insightfulness by ...

1. Suggesting solutions to problems that arise.
2. Asking thought-provoking questions in meetings and discussions.
3. Sharing astute insights that reveal significant reflection.
4. Illuminating concerns or ideas that lead to improvements of a plan, even if I haven't thought of a full solution yet.
5. Making great recommendations.
6. Highlighting significant ideas that people might otherwise miss.
7. Thinking logically about all the available information and synthesizing it for the group.
8. Drawing upon diverse perspectives to solicit or hone ideas.
9. Providing sound advice to others based on credible evidence.
10. Helping others to see from a different perspective.
11. Sharing my depth of knowledge and expertise in an approachable way.
12. Igniting interactive discussions that draw out others' ideas by asking pertinent questions.
13. Backing up arguments with supporting data from credible sources.
14. Predicting questions that others may have about my ideas, so I'll be prepared.
15. Sharing outside-of-the-box ideas that no one has yet voiced.
16. Showing a clear understanding of the issues because I've spent time learning about and reflecting on them.
17. Communicating information that is directly relevant to my audience, and sharing persuasive examples that resonate with them.
18. Gathering adequate information in advance of a presentation, meeting, or important conversation.

19. Proactively seeking and sharing valuable knowledge, which provides me with fresh and relevant talking points.

20. Illuminating a pathway forward in any challenging situation.

If you scored above 17, you've established yourself as a deeply insightful person in your organization, although you may still have room to grow. If you scored below 14, you may struggle with appearing insightful at times, while if you scored below 8, this represents a critical area for growth.

Review the behaviors you did *not* check off. Which ones do you struggle with the most? Choose up to five areas to focus on over the next several weeks—we'll review action steps for strengthening them later in this chapter. You'll learn to let your insightfulness shine through by strategically preparing for meetings and other interactions, as well as engaging in big-picture thinking and exposing yourself to new ideas regularly. As your ideas increasingly help steer group discussion and your team's direction, you'll become known as an insightful leader.

> Your great questions and suggestions will prompt
> further inquiry and discussion among the whole team.

Now, let's review the behaviors that most sabotage insightfulness, so you can work to avoid them.

Behaviors that undermine insightfulness.

Think of the leaders you know who *don't* demonstrate insightfulness. They probably engage in some (or all) of the following behaviors, which sabotage their success as a leader. Place a checkmark by any of the following behaviors that describe you.

I undermine my insightfulness by ...

+ Showing up unprepared for a conversation or discussion.
+ Remaining quiet rather than sharing my views freely.
+ Communicating an unclear point of view that leaves others confused.

- Asking mainly "yes-or-no" questions that don't spark dialogue.
- Not drawing upon my experience to inform my suggestions and ideas.
- Making statements that show I don't understand the issues at hand.
- Sharing ideas and insights without evidence or proof.
- Not contributing to solutions for the problems arising.
- Getting mired in the details, preventing me from seeing the bigger picture.
- Being an unenthusiastic participant in brainstorming sessions.
- Not sharing recommendations for how to improve on a plan.
- Seeming to speak for the sake of talking rather than to contribute something useful.
- Providing poor advice that isn't grounded in reality.
- Not continuously seeking out new knowledge to inform my perspectives.
- Sharing information that is irrelevant to the audience.

Being insightful doesn't necessarily mean being smarter than everyone else in the room. It simply means taking the time to reflect on and nurture your ideas. If you don't give yourself space to reflect, you won't come across as a person with valuable insights. It's as simple as that.

Review the points in this list that you didn't check off, making a note of them for later reference. We'll address how to turn these weaknesses into strengths in just a moment.

Josh Takes Initiative to Develop Insights

Problem:

Josh had a major reality check in his 360 review. His coworkers expressed that he didn't seem to prepare well for meetings. He often didn't share his thoughts or ideas, remaining disengaged from the conversation. When others asked for his input, his ideas lacked substance. The comments he made were surface-level. He did ask questions at times, but they were basic and uninteresting. When he made a point, others had trouble understanding it. He acted as if he didn't fully grasp the key ideas being discussed and had no real investment in the conversation.

Action:

In discussing these issues with Josh, it became clear that he hurried into meetings rather than taking time to prepare for them. He always seemed to be just barely hanging on by the seat of his pants. He needed to unload some of the mundane tasks and unnecessary meetings from his schedule and block out time for reflection—which he did. And then he had to follow through, making strategic thinking a core priority. Frequent check-ins with his boss about how he was using his time helped him stay accountable to himself.

Results:

As Josh took these steps, his coworkers noticed a big difference, marveling at the quality of his input. "I never knew you had so much knowledge," one of them remarked to him privately. He continued receiving appreciative remarks about the quality of his insights after meetings, which emboldened him and made him feel more deeply engaged in group discussions. His boss put him in charge of an exciting initiative, saying she needed the most creative minds on the job.

Do others perceive you as insightful?

This exercise will help you understand how others view you. Assign yourself a score of 1 to 10 for each of these statements, with 1 being the lowest and 10 being the highest:

- ✦ Others routinely share appreciation for my novel ideas.
- ✦ People often seem pleasantly surprised by ideas I share.
- ✦ Colleagues turn to me for help with figuring out a solution or fine-tuning an idea.
- ✦ Group discussion often changes course after I share an idea, focusing on what I've expressed.

- Leaders at or above my boss's level have reached out to me for help with solving a problem.

If you scored above 43, others likely view you as an insightful leader. Otherwise, focus on the action steps and exercises in this chapter to develop this competency.

Action steps to become more insightful.

Tap into your own capacity to be insightful with these actionable steps. By doing so, you'll make a name for yourself as a key player with winning ideas.

1. Block out time to explore what holds you back from being insightful at work.

Answer the following questions:
- Why am I not being more insightful at work?
- What excuses am I making to not be insightful?
- What obstacles are holding me back from being insightful?
- What fears are stopping me from being insightful?
- Do I have certain limiting beliefs about myself that stop me from being more insightful?

2. Gain more knowledge in your subject area.

Do you need more technical knowledge to rise to the next level of prowess in your field? Or could you stay more up-to-date on current trends and new research? Consider taking a course, scheduling time to catch up on the latest industry articles, or contacting expert colleagues in your domain.

3. Partner with a peer mentor who can teach you about a relevant area you're less familiar with.

Learning about cross-functional areas of business is a sure way to broaden your perspective. Groundbreaking ideas about how to leverage skills and resources from different functions may emerge when you have a strong grasp of what each of them does.

4. Build your problem-solving muscles.

The more you seize opportunities to solve problems, the better you'll be at doing it. You'll learn to think creatively about problem-solving rather than feeling intimidated by these situations.

5. Schedule time to reflect regularly.

Journal about your ideas if you think best in writing. Or, bounce ideas off of someone you respect. Devote a specific time each week to reflection.

6. Seek out opportunities to work with new people who will challenge your existing thinking patterns and ways of doing things.

Shaking up your routine will help you awaken to new possibilities.

7. Get away from your desk from time to time.

Go for a walk. Be active. The best insights often arise when you aren't grinding away at your computer, but when you're taking a breather and allowing your mind to wander freely.

8. Be curious about how others have done things.

Facing a serious problem? Someone else has probably gone through the same thing. Do your homework on how they worked to solve it. Ingenious solutions often aren't totally novel.

9. Talk to someone new.

Enrich your perspective by having in-depth conversations with people you don't normally talk to. Expanding your social circle—either outside of work or in your organization—will bring new food for thought. Talking to someone in a different field or function about ideas you're both interested in can sometimes spark groundbreaking innovations.

10. Read voraciously.

Soak up new ideas from books, articles, and news reports. Read about pioneers in other fields as well as your own, looking for opportunities for cross-pollination or adaptation of ideas.

11. Spend time on absurd ideas.

Like Brin and Page, delve into ideas that sound too "out-there" to take seriously. Find out if they hold hidden promise. You just might be surprised.

12.   Take a lesson from improv groups.

"The first rule of improvisation is AGREE. Always agree and say YES," says Tina Fey in *Bossypants*.[iv] You won't always love every idea that emerges in a brainstorming session, but keep an open mind. Allow a scenario to play out fully.

"Start with a yes, and see where that takes you. As an improviser, I always find it jarring when I meet someone in real life whose first answer is no. 'No, we can't do that.' 'No, that's not in the budget,'" she continues. "What kind of way is that to live?" Then add something to the other person's idea—you're essentially saying, "Yes, AND." Focus on ways to make the idea better—things that accentuate it or resolve potential issues.

As you and your team tap into your collective insights, your organization will thrive. You'll have a wealth of excellent ideas and minds that are adept at problem-solving and critical thinking. As a result, you'll generate novel solutions ahead of the competition, fine-tune your ideas to eliminate hiccups, and adeptly soar over any bumps in the road. Your insights will allow you to triumph over any type of adversity by thinking creatively and leveraging the full brainpower of your team.

Help your employees cultivate insightfulness.

Insightfulness doesn't just benefit you as an individual—it benefits your whole company. Read on to learn why, and then how to help your whole team cultivate this competency.

Only 25% of employees feel they can
freely express their ideas at work.

How will growing your employees' insightfulness build a stronger team?

Here are a few key reasons why you should encourage your employees to cultivate their insightfulness.

- Insightful employees will build a culture of innovation. Teams will bring in a higher quality of ideas from all directions, not just from the top down.
- Your team will master the art of decision-making as people learn to candidly share insights steeped in experience and evidence.
- People will break free from traditional silos, recognizing and seizing opportunities to collaborate across functions. As they discuss ideas with people outside of their immediate circle, they'll come up with breakthrough solutions.
- Employees will gain more satisfaction from their work as they exercise their creative potential and gain recognition for it. Thus, overall morale will improve, and you'll have a culture in which everyone feels appreciated and integral to the organization.
- Your insightful thinkers will notice emerging trends and come up with brilliant ways to respond to them rather than allowing opportunities to pass them by.

By harnessing the full brainpower of your team, you'll move toward more ambitious goals, enhance your bottom line, and increase everyone's job satisfaction.

Leaders must work to draw out their team's insights and create a culture of sharing them. According to research by the communications firm Smarp, only 25% of employees feel they can freely express their ideas at work.[v] A quarter of all employees often don't speak up even when they feel they have something valuable to say. Nearly half of employees are not asked to voice their ideas regularly, which depletes their confidence about sharing them.[vi] Leveraging their insights can pay off in a big way. When Toyota took over an unproductive GM facility in California, it decided to ask the employees how they'd improve operations, Smarp explains. Toyota ended up implementing 80% of their suggestions. "As a result, the plant went from the industry's worst to being a shining star example," the firm asserts.

Employee insights are vital across industries. "Frontline employees especially are intimately familiar with the problems in systems, internal processes and day-to-day operations that manifest as difficulties for the customer. It's hard to make an intelligent correction without their insights," says TLNT.[vii] "Most employees have frontline insight that top management just doesn't. Top management may devise the operational and business strategy, but the employees execute it, and therein lies success or failure."

How to help your employees become more insightful.

Cultivating insightfulness will make a tremendous difference for your employees in their careers.

Encourage your employees to unleash their own insightfulness through the following steps.

+ Share your feedback regularly. Through feedback, employees can learn which types of suggestions and ideas are most valuable. Let them know where they've really made an impact.
+ Ask courageous questions: open-ended questions that have a targeted focus rather than being overly vague, as researchers with Let's Grow Leaders and the University of Northern Colorado explain. Courageous questions show you want an honest (and insightful) answer, even if the truth is surprising or hard to hear. Instead of asking, "How can we improve?" ask a more specific question like one of these:[viii]
  o "What are our biggest customer's greatest frustrations?"
  o "What is a problem we have that no one talks about?"
  o "What must I do better as a leader if we are to be successful?"
  o "How are we sabotaging our success in this project?"
+ Create forums for idea-sharing. Having a few different options (like a virtual idea box) will help all employees get more comfortable with sharing their ideas—even the shy ones. Hold brainstorming sessions in which you assert there is no such thing as a bad idea, and set up an "innovation zone" (virtual or in-person) for discussion and collaboration.[ix]
+ Don't steer the discussion away from an idea just because it seems unfeasible. Instead, encourage people to remain open-minded and explore options not considered before.
+

- Change the composition of teams from time to time. "Repurposing the same teams for similar tasks may seem like the easiest approach to resource allocation, but switching things up can stimulate new brainstorming ideas," says Seamas Egan of j2 Global, who suggests rotating desk arrangement, teams, and assignment types to spark new interactions and ideas.[x]
- Ask pointed questions that help people arrive at the truth themselves, or as a group. Share your own thoughts after others have had a chance to speak.

When you ask thought-provoking questions that ignite discussion, be prepared to hear new ideas. "Courageous questions also require the asker to listen without defensiveness," the researchers at *Let's Grow Leaders* explain.[xi] "This is where well-intentioned leaders often get into trouble. They ask a good question, but they weren't prepared to hear feedback. When you ask a courageous question, allow yourself to take in the response: Take notes, and thank everyone for taking the time—and having the confidence—to share their perspectives." As you genuinely welcome these questions and take the other steps described here, you'll foster a team of insightful thinkers.

Chapter 14

Clear

Expression Competency #3

"Executive presence is not necessarily about being formal or abundant in your communication, but rather straightforward and brief."
– Kerrie Peraino

Your company needs leaders who are clear, because they effectively deliver messages throughout the organization. These efficient communicators make themselves understood quickly. Thus, a leader with executive presence communicates clearly at all times so that others will truly hear the message.

Learning to clearly present your ideas in every type of interaction will make people take you more seriously as a leader. You'll more effectively give directives and share ideas with others. Senior leaders will take note of your improved self-expression and will increase their trust in you as a result. They'll perceive you as more professional and equipped to lead a team at a high level when you articulate your ideas clearly.

Clear leaders are succinct and to the point. They present a crisp message in a straightforward and direct style.

Behaviors of clear leaders.

Think about the leaders you know who communicate especially well. Do they drone on and on in a meeting, or do they get right to the point? Do they meander slowly toward a conclusion, or are they extremely direct?

Whenever they communicate, clear leaders are succinct and to the point. They present a crisp message in a straightforward and direct style. They express themselves in a polished way by avoiding qualifier or filler words. People remember what they have said long after the conversation. There's no struggling to understand their meaning or instructions.

As you become a clear communicator, you'll make yourself heard and understood. To convey the importance of your message, you'll speak in a straightforward and candid manner. Instead of slowly rambling toward your main point, you'll speak in a polished, succinct way that lets listeners immediately understand what you mean. You won't waste time on a long-winded speech that ultimately leaves the audience confused. When you communicate instructions, you'll move people to take immediate action. When you describe a problem, you'll ensure people grasp what you're saying so you can drive toward a solution together.

You'll also understand that a miscommunication by a leader can have reverberating effects throughout the organization, causing people to put their efforts into the wrong course of action or creating interpersonal conflict. Struggling to understand a message laden with complex terminology also wastes time.

Take a look at this comparison of the characteristics of leaders who are clear and those who are not:

QUALITIES OF A CLEAR COMMUNICATOR	QUALITIES THAT UNDERMINE CLEARNESS
Articulate	Inarticulate
Coherent	Confusing
Candid	Meandering
Polished	Unfocused
Concise	Rambling

As a clear communicator, you'll show consideration for your audience by embodying all of the qualities on the left. You'll strive to understand what information is most pertinent to your audience before addressing them. You'll tailor your message to the people you're speaking to. Further, you won't make your audience struggle to understand your rationale or comprehend the point you're making. You won't strive to impress people by making ideas sound overly complex. Additionally, you'll pay attention to your pacing, speaking slowly enough for the audience to understand what you're saying but varying your cadence at times to build interest. You'll place emphasis on key points by varying your tone to highlight certain ideas as well.

As a leader with executive presence, you'll understand how important clarity is to organizational efficiency. Delivering messages as succinctly as possible will use your time more efficiently. Teams will quickly move toward their goals when given clear directives, too. When discussing a problem, they'll arrive at decisions more swiftly because they'll understand the situation more clearly.

"Simplify and be direct. Say what you mean," urges the Center for Creative Leadership (CCL).[i] "Don't hide behind complexity or pile on a ton of information. Simple communication can be smart communication."

McCormack's BRIEF Lab found that most people don't have long attention spans when the speaker doesn't quickly get to the point:[ii]

+ They spend just 30 seconds reading an email.
+ They tune out after 15 seconds when colleagues are speaking.
+ They stop listening to presentations in a minute or less.

That means a lot of what people say (and write) goes unheard. In a study by Gartner, 46% of leaders said they view audience overload as a major problem to overcome in their communications.[iii] Strong communicators cater to their audience's limited attention span and time constraints by distilling a message into succinct, easily understandable language. These clear, concise speakers are *much* more likely to get their point across than people who don't choose their words carefully. Thus, they grow their influence and impact. Since people don't have long attention spans, brevity ensures they hear the full message. When speaking with senior leaders, clear speakers recognize that they have a small window of time to get their point across, so they make their message crisp, brief, and poignant.

Strong communicators cater to their audience's limited attention span and time constraints by distilling a message into succinct, easily understandable language.

As a leader with executive presence, you'll brand yourself as a person who shares important and relevant messages. When you are consistently succinct, others will trust that when you speak, you're going to deliver a message with a clear purpose. Thus, they'll listen more intently. In contrast, when a person known for rambling speaks up at a meeting, people may begin to zone out before she's even opened her mouth.

As you establish yourself as a clear communicator, employees and colleagues will also feel they can reach out to you for information. They'll know that you'll give them a quick answer to a question, so they won't delay or avoid communicating. Similarly, you'll have more productive conversations with people at all levels because you'll immediately let them know what you want from them personally.[iv] You won't leave them guessing, "What are you asking *me* to do here?" or "Why are you telling this to *me*?" In turn, employees will set priorities effectively because they'll understand what their leader wants.

For all of these reasons, people perceive their leaders as more capable and reliable when they communicate with clarity. Strive to become a clear leader, and you'll greatly boost your effectiveness and enhance how others perceive you.

Since people don't have long attention spans, brevity ensures they hear the full message.

Self-evaluation: Assess your level of clearness.

Let's take a closer look at how clear leaders work in action, so you can fully grasp which behaviors to hone in on. Consider how leaders you admire speak and act with clarity in all of these ways outlined below. And place a checkmark by any of these behaviors that describe you.

I demonstrate that I am a clear, communicative leader by ...

1. Providing just the right amount of information, communicating with precision and simplicity.
2. Collecting my thoughts before speaking rather than thinking aloud.
3. Delivering well-structured presentations that share a logical progression of ideas.
4. Being direct, candid, and straightforward.
5. Getting right to the main point.
6. Summarizing the most important points.
7. Connecting each supporting point to the main point.
8. Mentally rehearsing what I'm going to say, especially before explaining a complex concept.
9. Leveraging the power of the pause so listeners can absorb what I've said.
10. Concisely communicating important details and essential elements.
11. Using easy-to-understand language that listeners can grasp immediately, especially when approaching complex concepts.
12. Checking for expressions or body language that suggest confusion, and quickly clarifying the message if need be.
13. Being succinct in email communications.
14. Providing the right level of detail when sharing an idea.
15. Delivering relevant messages to the target audience so I'm not wasting their time with information they don't need.
16. Providing information in a format preferred by the audience whenever possible.
17. Sharing a compelling and easy-to-understand point of view in my messaging.
18. Letting people know where they can find more information rather than stating it all upfront.
19. Expressing myself in a polished way, avoiding qualifier and filler words.
20. Tailoring communications to the audience's level of authority.

If you scored above 17, you're communicating clearly and making yourself understood, although you may have room to grow. If you scored below 14, you probably struggle with being clear, and if your score falls below 8, this is a critical area for growth.

Reflect on the behaviors you have not checked. Which ones represent the greatest challenges for you, in terms of becoming a clear communicator? Make a note of them so you can create a plan for improving them when we discuss action steps later in this chapter. We'll explore how to be more succinct and direct in all of your communications through a combination of thoughtful prep work, a commitment to brevity, and a strong understanding of your audience.

Now let's examine behaviors that can sabotage your ability to be a clear leader, so you can steer clear of them!

Simple communication can be smart communication.

Behaviors that undermine clearness.

Conversely, leaders who haven't mastered the art of clarity are setting themselves up to be misunderstood, diminishing what they can accomplish. If you're engaging in any of these behaviors, it's a red flag that you're undermining your executive presence by not being a clear communicator. Place a checkmark by any that describe you.

I demonstrate a lack of clearness by ...

+ Rambling instead of getting to the point.
+ Elaborating too much, overwhelming my audience with information.
+ Repeating similar points over and over.
+ Thinking out loud, sharing my unedited train of thought.
+ Using convoluted phrasing rather than simple language.
+ Communicating with indecisive, weak language and filler words.
+ Going too deep into the details.
+ Spending too much time ramping up to the important points.
+ Making ideas sound more complex than they actually are.
+ Overdoing the amount of data and facts needed to get the message across.

- Overusing business jargon, idioms, or corporate speak.
- Not adapting my communication style to the audience's level of authority.
- Failing to notice that the audience isn't paying attention.
- Focusing too much on processes and background details.
- Not checking in to gauge understanding and give people a chance to ask questions.

Most of us have room to grow when it comes to clarity. Simply make a note of your areas of weakness in this regard, and we'll discuss how to overcome them shortly.

"The more you keep speaking, or explaining yourself, the more you cloud or dilute your core message," says Kerrie Peraino, the head of international HR for American Express.[v] Being long-winded and providing too many details detracts from your message. You might think you're being diligent and thorough, but everyone doesn't need to know every aspect of the issue. Don't try to impress people with the volume of information you know about a topic, or with complex language. They simply can't absorb it all at once, and they'll tune it out. Providing the most vital points in a concise way will leave others feeling more impressed. Let them know they can speak to you if they want further details. That way, you'll have a chance to share details later if need be, but they won't derail your main point.

> "The more you keep speaking, or explaining yourself, the more you cloud or dilute your core message."
> Kerrie Peraino

Unclear communicators also tend to overuse filler words and phrases, like these:

- **"Noise words,"** like "umm," "ah," "like," and "you know."
- **Filler phrases** like "I was thinking," "In my opinion," "I'm not sure, but I think," "I'm not the expert, but," and "Sorry, but I just want to explain my point of view," which weaken speech. It's already obvious that you are sharing your own opinion, and you should never act as though you need to apologize or justify your speech.

- **Qualifiers** like "usually," "sometimes," and "probably," which tend to soften your statements. While they have their place, ask yourself if you can make your point without them. They can make you sound like you're hedging your bets just in case you're wrong, rather than exuding certainty.

These unnecessary words take up unnecessary air time. They also indicate that you're not exactly sure what you're going to say next, which makes you sound less confident. Thus, clear communicators strive to avoid them in their speech.

Diana Refines Her Delivery

Problem:
Diana was insightful and very good at her job, but she didn't communicate in a concise and clear way. When she spoke to executives, she didn't realize they were anxiously waiting for her to arrive at her point. They didn't have time to listen to her slow ramp up that she believed built anticipation.

Her boss took her aside one day. "Diana, these executives don't have all day," he said. "You need to hook them in the first thirty seconds by getting to the main idea. Lead with your recommendation, and then give your rationale. Your important ideas are getting lost in the muddle, and I want them to be heard. Senior leadership needs to hear them."

Action:
Diana practiced her delivery with her boss, pretending she was giving a presentation to a group of top leaders. Her boss gave her feedback on what she could cut out, and she fine-tuned her notes. When she gave it another try, he said she sounded ten times better. They did this exercise regularly in weekly check-ins, and Diana began getting the hang of it. She needed less and less guidance from her boss on how to phrase her ideas and what to leave out.

Results:
The next time Diana spoke to high-level leaders, she held them in rapt attention. "That was astounding," said her boss. "They were riveted. You

spoke for only five minutes, but you really showed the full importance of the project you're proposing—and I think they want you to lead it." Indeed, it turned out, they did.

Do others perceive you as clear?

This exercise will give you a better sense of how others view you. Assign yourself a score of 1 to 10 for each of these statements, with 1 being the lowest and 10 being the highest:

+ When I speak, people look highly attentive.
+ My team carries out my directives in a manner that shows they fully understand them.
+ People typically respond to my emails rather than ignoring them.
+ When people reply to me in conversation, it's clear they understood the point I was making.
+ When I speak with senior leaders, they are engaged, fully present, and appreciative.

If you scored above 40, others likely view you as a clear leader. Otherwise, use the action steps and exercises in this chapter to develop this quality.

Remember the power of "less is more."

Action steps to become a clearer communicator.

What can you do to become clearer in your communication? Here are some action steps to begin taking now.

Remember the power of "less is more" by striving to be a minimalist communicator. Do away with unnecessary details, only providing what is most relevant. Here are some concrete ways to do that in all your interactions.

1. Block out and spend time exploring what holds you back from being a clearer communicator at work.

As you get to the root of the issue, the obstacles will become less restricting and you'll embrace new possibilities. Answer these questions in your reflection time:

- Why am I not being a clear communicator at work?
- What excuses am I making to not be a clear communicator?
- What obstacles are preventing me from being clear?
- What fears are stopping me from being clear?
- Do I have limiting beliefs about myself that stop me from being a clear communicator?

2. Pause to accentuate key points rather than rushing and rambling through your speech.

A story by *The New York Times* illuminates the importance of silence in music.[vi] Just as pauses play an essential role in a musical composition, well-placed pauses add eloquence to a leader's speech.[vii]

Just as pauses play an essential role in a musical composition, well-placed pauses add eloquence to a leader's speech.

---

3. Consider why you're speaking to a particular audience.

That will help you frame your message, sharing the most relevant info and giving the appropriate call to action. Put yourself in your audience's shoes to determine what they really want to know.

4. Begin with the main idea, and tell them why you're telling them about it.

Avoid a lengthy buildup to the main point—arrive at it in the first 30 seconds of speaking.

5. State the 5 Ws of journalism–the *who*, *what*, *when*, *where*, and *why*.[viii]

That will help you ensure that you haven't left out anything crucial or added too much fluff. "Before you initiate any communication, ask yourself, 'What am I trying to accomplish?' Even chitchat should have a purpose, even if it's just to build camaraderie," writes Geoffrey James in *Inc.*[ix] "If somebody else is initiating the conversation, ask yourself, 'Why is this conversation taking place?' If the answer isn't obvious, guide the dialogue to the 'why' of it."

6.   Especially when speaking to senior leaders, lead with your recommendation and then provide your rationale—not the other way around.

You'll not only hold their attention; you'll sound more commanding as well.

7.   Consider how much space you take up in meetings and conversations.

If you're speaking more than your fair share, start dialing it back and spending more time listening.

8.   Pay attention to people's nonverbal communication as you speak.

Does their eye contact, expression, and other body language show that they're intently listening? Or are their eyes beginning to glaze over? Learn to read the room and adjust accordingly. This vital feedback will help you prepare for your next conversation, comment, or presentation as well.

9.   Don't try to impress others by sharing everything you know on the topic at hand.

Share a couple tidbits of information to establish credibility, but don't go off on a tangent.

10.   Keep your emails short.

Write five sentences or less. Review them before sending and weed out any superfluous words, sentences, or even paragraphs. Leave nothing but the essential message you're trying to communicate.

11.   Edit your slides thoroughly before delivering a presentation to senior executives (or anyone else, for that matter).

Put your most important points—your key recommendations and calls to action—on your first slides, so the audience knows what your presentation will be about. Next, include summary slides that give quick overviews of your key points, followed by an appendix of slides. Follow the 10% rule: If the appendix is 40 slides, include 4 summary slides.

12. Avoid "uptalk" and "downspeak."

Uptalk makes you sound like you're asking a question rather than confidently making a statement. Steer clear of "downspeak," too, which means allowing your volume to taper off as you finish your statement.

13. Choose phrases that succinctly convey your confidence in your own judgment.

"I believe" and "I know" have much more power than "I think," asserting clarity and conviction. "While 'I think' makes us feel that the person speaking is still unsure or thinking it over, 'I believe' is a persuasive declaration," explains Judith Humphrey in *Fast Company*.[x] "I assure you," "I am confident," and "I envision" are also strong word choices that build your audience's confidence in your thinking, she adds.

As you become a clear communicator, your words will have more power and impact. Speaking and writing with clarity will enhance how others perceive you in every other dimension of executive presence. You'll show up with more confidence, expand your influence, and appear more insightful once you've learned to present your thoughts clearly.

Help your employees become more clear.

As a leader, it's your duty to help your whole team become more succinct, to the point, and clear. Read on to learn how this will benefit your organization and how to help your direct reports express themselves clearly.

How will helping your employees communicate with clarity build a stronger team?

Increased clarity doesn't just benefit individuals in their careers; it benefits whole organizations. Here are the main reasons why.

- Communication will flow far more clearly in all directions. Subordinates will understand their leaders' instructions; colleagues will work together more smoothly.
- Teams will improve their efficiency by avoiding wasted time. Clarity creates well-oiled teams that quickly launch into the

correct course of action and drive toward results. They also have more mental energy for what matters most.

+ You'll gain valuable information from all directions when people understand how to communicate with you efficiently. You don't have time to wade through lengthy emails or sit through a long presentation on something that may not even be relevant to you.

+ Meetings won't take more time than necessary, allowing teams to put more time into high-priority tasks. Discussions will be as efficient as possible.

+ Colleagues will effectively share feedback and guidance with one another. Work will flow more smoothly because people will accurately hear one another.

+ Morale will increase because everyone will feel heard and will know their time is being respected. People will feel more engaged in debates and discussions since they can easily understand one another's ideas.

For all of these reasons, clear communicators have immensely positive effects throughout an organization. Teams will improve their ability to decide on the best plan of action, implement it smoothly, and discuss any modifications needed.

How to help your employees communicate with clarity.

Through the following steps, you can coach your employees on how to become clear communicators.

+ Encourage them to edit their speech before they begin talking. Extroverts are particularly prone to thinking *as they speak* instead of *before they speak*.[xi] Work to spot this tendency in your employees and coach them on how to speak in a more polished way. By mentally rehearsing what they're going to say—or practicing saying it aloud—they'll make themselves heard more effectively. Asking a trusted friend or colleague to provide feedback is a great idea.

+ For employees who are prone to rambling (which can apply to both introverts and extroverts[xii]), consider why they might overtalk. Are they long-winded because of nervousness, or do they mistakenly believe that by taking up more airspace, they'll make themselves seem more important? Help them get to the root of the issue so they can overcome this tendency.

+ Urge them to finish one thought before they begin the next. They must consider how to structure their message before they begin, so they're not interrupting *themselves* time after time by beginning a new idea before they arrive at the first point.

+ Provide feedback on their communication style after they deliver a presentation. Stay positive, but point out ways they could strengthen their performance next time.

+ Prompt them to slow down their speech to give the audience time to absorb what they're saying. Many people rush through their speech, causing important points to get lost. Presenting the most vital information more slowly will help others to truly grasp what they're saying.

+ Set up a "buddy system" in which employees give each other pointers on how to strengthen their communication in meetings. This can be a friendly way to suggest easy improvements and gauge progress on an ongoing basis.

+ Encourage employees to avoid the filler words and phrases discussed earlier in this chapter. Eliminating weak words from their vocabulary will make them more articulate speakers.

Through all of these steps, you'll help your employees develop into clear and effective communicators whose words and ideas get results.

Bonus section: Speaking down.

If you don't have any issue speaking *up*, making your opinions and ideas heard, then this is a special section just for you. This is for the people who never hesitate to vocalize ideas and express themselves—the extroverted and outspoken members of the team.

We've talked a lot about speaking *up* in the chapter on becoming more vocal because it tends to present more of a challenge to most people.

However, a select few people do tend to dominate meetings and interactions by speaking up *too much*. If you're one of them, you need to learn how to speak *down*.

This issue deserves its own special section because many of the traits of dominant personalities don't pertain to *everyone* who struggles with clarity—just a select few. If you're one of them, I have some specific advice just for you.

"On a team of eight people, one or two members
often do up to 70 percent of the talking."
Leigh Thompson

Do *you* need to learn to speak down?

First ask your peers for feedback on your behavior in meetings to determine whether you're truly being too vocal. Tell them you're genuinely trying to understand how you can improve, assuring them that you want honest feedback. Then listen.

If you are a person who needs to learn how to speak down, you are a naturally expressive, talkative, wordy, and loquacious person. You don't want to be contained. You don't want to stop talking. You're comfortable excessively asserting yourself in both groups and one-on-one interactions. In meetings, you can't stop your ideas and convictions from coming out—and often taking up more time than necessary. You may not even realize that you are dominating a meeting by doing most of the talking.

Why talkative people need to learn how to speak down.

In meetings, a small proportion of people often control the conversation. They may not intend to do so, but they prevent their quieter colleagues from sharing their valuable ideas. "On a team of eight people, one or two members often do up to 70 percent of the talking," says Leigh Thompson of the Kellogg School of Management.[xiii] "The topper is that the dominant people do not realize this," she explains in *Fortune*.[xiv] "In fact, they vehemently argue that the meetings are egalitarian. They lack self-awareness."

Talkative people too often aren't aware of the others in the room who remain quiet. They are very poor at discerning when to stop speaking, be silent, and listen. They don't know how to get out of the way by taking up less room so that others have the space to step in and share.

The truth is that the quieter employees should get as much airtime as the talkative ones. However, they find it nearly impossible to get a word in. They don't know how to speak over or interrupt the dominant talkers. Even when they try to speak, they are talked over. The message they internalize is, "My input and ideas aren't wanted," which leads them to undervalue their own recommendations.

> Quieter employees should
> get as much airtime as the
> talkative ones.

The talkative person who is dominating meetings lacks a heightened sense of situational awareness. If you dominate meetings, you need to strengthen your observational skills, consciously paying attention to what people say, who is driving the discussion, and why more people aren't actively sharing.

Take a look at this comparison of qualities. People who display the traits on the right-hand side of the table need to learn how to speak down by cultivating the qualities on the left side.

OBSERVANT	UNAWARE
Attentive	Self-absorbed
Cognizant	Oblivious to others' reactions
Plugged in	Disconnected
Perceptive	Unobservant

Strong communicators have exceptional situational awareness. They continuously read the room and accurately perceive how others are feeling. They know exactly how to reach their audience, when to respond to any discomfort that people are experiencing, and when to be quiet. If you tend to dominate the conversation in groups, tune into what is happening around you in a meeting. It's just as important as the things you want to say. By becoming more observant and attuned to others' contributions, you'll become a more effective communicator and strengthen your executive presence.

Not having this awareness directly undermines your executive presence by making you less clear as well as less supportive of those around you. Discouraging others from speaking (intentionally or unintentionally) diminishes your charisma, making you a less likeable and inspiring leader. Great leaders draw others out and make them feel good, not the reverse. And they don't have to share every thought that arises—they select the most important ones and voice them in a tight, succinct way.

If you're a leader, tapping into your employees' potential means learning how to draw them out. That means being highly attuned to how much airtime you and each member of the team are consuming. Creating space for your quieter employees to share their insights will expand what your team is capable of achieving together.

> Strong communicators have exceptional situational awareness. They continuously read the room and accurately perceive how others are feeling.

Action steps for speaking down.

Here are the key steps you can take to dial back your speech while remaining assertive and bold. You'll also greatly benefit from following the action steps for becoming a clear communicator that we've already discussed.

1. Focus on active listening.

Before a meeting, affirm to yourself that it's an opportunity to practice your active listening skills.

- Set listening goals for yourself. For example, "I want to hear Mary's detailed thoughts about the topic she's presenting on, so we can have an in-depth discussion over lunch," or "I really want to understand all the pros and cons of this idea, from everyone's point of view."
- Take notes. Having your pen on paper will remind you of your goal to listen much more than you speak.

2.   Mentally survey the room periodically during meetings to gauge how many people are engaged in the conversation.

Who hasn't shared yet? Do your part to give others equal time so a variety of ideas will be heard.

3.   Practice pausing before you speak.

Count to five and collect your thoughts.[xv] This will help you focus your ideas, making you less prone to rambling.

4.   Speak more slowly.

When you speak slowly, you give more weight to your words. Moreover, slowing your tempo will encourage you to choose your words more carefully and express your message more concisely.

5.   Prepare your thoughts beforehand.

Choose several key topics for which you have something important to contribute. Ask yourself which topics are most vital for you to speak on, and which information is most critical to share. Jot down notes to help you stay on message. By doing so, you'll make your message more crisp and concise.

6.   Pay attention to how much you're speaking about yourself.

Personal examples can be extremely useful, but if you've fallen into a pattern of continuously talking about yourself, it's time to self-censor.

7.   Pause after stating an important or unexpected idea.

This will make the audience pay even more attention to what you've just said. It will also act as a speed bump to slow you down.

8.   Watch your audience's expressions and body language closely.

Even when you're speaking, you should be noticing how they're responding. You may *think* your long-winded explanation is fascinating, but are they truly hanging on your every word?

Again, use the action steps for speaking clearly and concisely as well. They will absolutely help you to establish the kind of presence you want to have in a meeting. By focusing on the most vital information, you'll ensure that people truly hear you. And by keeping it simple, you'll help them retain your important points.

As you become more aware of all the audience members in the room, you'll witness the quality of the discussion increasing. The more actively involved everyone is, the more elevated the learning between participants will become. When more equal participation occurs, the meeting will leverage all the experts in the room and achieve the best outcome possible.

Alan Learns to Listen More Than He Speaks

Problem:

Alan talked a *lot* at meetings and didn't pay attention to how other participants were reacting and feeling toward him. Greg, one of his coworkers, finally approached him. "I have a hard time cutting in when you're speaking during meetings," Greg told him, "and quite frankly, that's a lot of the time."

"I never realized I did that," said Alan. He felt embarrassed, and he knew he needed to change his behavior. How many others felt the same way Greg did? He could sense Greg's annoyance, and he knew he'd become "that guy"—dominating, opinionated, and arrogant. He also knew it had taken a lot of courage for Greg to share this input with him.

Action:

Alan immediately became more self-aware after hearing Greg's comment. While speaking, he would realize that he'd been rambling. He stopped always being the one to speak first, noticing that others seemed eager to voice their thoughts too.

About a week later, he caught himself starting to dominate the meeting and stopped himself, looking to Greg and the rest of the group. "Does anyone have something to add?" he asked.

Alan also considered which colleagues were assertive yet not domineering, then tried to emulate their example. His coworker Yvonne really seemed like a pro at this, though he hadn't paid much attention to her skill at integrating others into the conversation in the past. When more timid coworkers wanted to join a conversation, she would notice and invite their input. He spent more time being silent and observing how she conducted herself, and she became his new role model. He asked Greg and Yvonne to both give him regular feedback so he could gauge his progress, and they were delighted to do so.

Results:

Alan soon became much less overbearing and learned to engage in genuine dialogue with everyone in the room. He shared gratitude for his coworkers' continued mentoring and was glad to also have a closer relationship with them both as a result. Team dialogue improved considerably now that everyone had a voice at the table, too.

Overly expressive people like Alan need to learn how to modulate themselves. They need to work to install an internal dimmer switch that they know how to turn down so it's not always set on high. The more they can regulate themselves, the easier it will be to achieve equal participation.

If you're one of these loquacious people, practice ceding space to the others in the room. Let them speak up and state their opinions and ideas. Remind yourself that you don't need to be constantly speaking to be valued and appreciated. Let others ask questions, give input, and provide direction. Let them experience what it feels like to have impact in a meeting.

Practice ceding space to the others in the room.
Let them speak up and state their opinions and ideas.

How to help your employees learn to speak down.

As you learn to speak down, also work to help your employees develop this competency. Here are some key ways to use strong facilitation to help make all voices heard.

+ Ask talkative speakers to wait. It may feel uncomfortable to silence someone, but that's your role as the facilitator. When a quieter person tries to jump in, ask more vocal people to wait for him to speak. Using the talkative person's name can gently get her attention and show you're serious.[xvi]

+ Tell the group that all opinions matter. Assert upfront that you expect to hear everyone's viewpoint in the meeting.

+ Do a round-robin-style check-in, giving each person a minute to share their thoughts. Go around the room, beginning midway to avoid having the most dominant speaker go first or last, suggests Barbara MacKay of North Star Facilitators.[xvii]

+ Stop people when they've gone off topic. Ask ramblers to concisely complete their point or save their thoughts for later if they don't pertain to the topic at hand.

+ Set clear ground rules at the beginning of the meeting. For instance, state a maximum length of time for comments and note that if people digress from the current agenda topic, you'll ask them to hold their thoughts.

+ Utilize a timer to keep comments from becoming too long. This will help give equal time to all participants and prevent long-winded speeches.

+ Ask for input from specific participants. Rather than singling them out because they've been quiet, ask for their opinions on areas reflecting their strengths and expertise.

+ Speak to dominant personalities outside of the meeting. Enlist their help in making space for more reserved group members. Give them direct feedback on ways they can improve their performance in groups in a positive, tactful manner.

+ Ask questions on areas of knowledge directly relevant to quieter employees. Focusing the discussion toward their areas of specialty will boost engagement and bring in a greater variety of ideas.

+ Limit your responses to dominators' comments. Don't inadvertently encourage them to be more vociferous by replying in depth to all of their comments. You could nod and say something like, "Thanks, Brian. Does anyone else want to share their thoughts on that?"

+ Give people the chance to work together in different sizes of groups. In a smaller working group of three, a quieter employee might take up more space than in a large group. This will build their confidence for participating in larger groups as well.

Through these steps, you can create a culture that frowns upon letting one or two people dominate a meeting. Instead of normalizing that behavior, you'll set the expectation that all voices must be heard and valued. With attentive facilitation, you'll continue reinforcing that standard. As a result, you'll develop a team of individuals who know how to effectively communicate and collaborate, not just sharing their own ideas but also drawing out one another's best insights.

Set the expectation that all voices must be heard and valued.

Conclusion

Now and for the duration of your career,
executive presence will be the key ingredient
to your success.

We've now discussed each of the nine key executive presence competencies that together make up the three domains of executive presence: gravitas, authority, and expression. Let's take a moment to briefly review what you've learned.

First, you know how to develop your gravitas so you can radiate the commanding, self-assured presence of a high-level leader. We've also unpacked what charisma truly is, so you can cultivate and leverage it in all your interactions. Whether you're loud and bubbly or quiet and reflective, you have what it takes to become a charismatic leader who makes others feel valued and important. As you cultivate these three core competencies, you'll carry yourself with gravitas in every situation, whether you're meeting with direct reports or a panel of senior leaders.

Second, you know how to grow your aura of authority by becoming decisive, bold, and influential. You've studied how to step outside of your comfort zone by trusting your instincts, making quicker and bolder decisions, and holding your ground. Similarly, you know how to assert a compelling point of view that persuades others to adopt your ideas. Your assertiveness and ability to convince others of the merits of your ideas will grow your influence throughout your company.

Finally, you know how to enhance your expression by presenting yourself as vocal, insightful, and clear. You've learned actionable strategies for becoming more visible in meetings and other group settings by speaking up clearly. You know how to develop and share meaningful insights that will guide group discussion. As you hone your ability to be succinct and polished in your speech, you'll become a more powerful communicator whose ideas are heard and valued.

Mastering these qualities won't happen overnight, but you will see progress more quickly than you probably think. Until now, many of these qualities may have remained a mystery to you, as they do to most people. Being commanding, decisive, or vocal may have seemed out of reach. But now you know how to cultivate these qualities step by step. You can refer back to the various chapters in this book as your blueprint for success as you move forward on this journey. Through continued practice, you'll gradually expand your comfort zone and capabilities until you are radiating executive presence in every scenario, no matter how high the stakes.

As you work to develop these nine executive presence competencies, you'll see your potential expand in a way you may never have imagined. Your influence will grow in every direction, causing senior leaders, coworkers, and peers in other functions to look to you for ideas and guidance. New doors will open all around you as a result. It will be up to you to decide which ones to walk through. Strive to know yourself fully as you undergo this incredible transformative process, so you can make the decisions that bring you to where you truly want to be.

The 3x3 Executive Presence Model is the way forward.

Earlier in your career, you learned the value of executing tasks with precision and skill. You learned to excel in your projects and meet deadlines promptly. You learned to be reliable. As you now know, being a dependable employee will not take you to the levels where you aspire to go. You can't rely on what worked in the past to bring about your future success. Instead, you need to find a new way of operating.

The 3x3 Executive Presence Model is the way forward. Now and for the duration of your career, executive presence will be the key ingredient to your success. Begin to master it through the 3x3 Model, and it will serve you for the rest of your life.

Stepping into the shoes of a leader with executive presence takes courage. You're expanding your identity, which inherently means taking risks. Have the courage to envision yourself succeeding in each step you take, which will propel you forward. Nelson Mandela wisely said, "I learned that courage was not the absence of fear, but the triumph over it. The brave man is not he who does not feel afraid, but he who conquers that fear."

Having courage will drive you to take chances that guide you to become an inspiring leader who exudes confidence in every situation. Allow your courage to shine in all of these ways:

- Fully SHOW UP with EP.
- COMMAND the room or command a situation when the opportunity presents.
- In the face of fear, be CONFIDENT.
- Be BOLD and assertive even when you have doubt.
- When you aren't sure, be DECISIVE.
- Be SUCCINCT and know your words are enough.
- PUT A STAKE IN THE GROUND and own your position.
- Radiate GRAVITAS, act with AUTHORITY, and EXPRESS yourself fully.

You may have been undervalued and overlooked as a leader when you began reading this book. Now, though, you are becoming a leader who knows how to exude a world-class executive presence. Your executive presence is a powerful tool. Use it. It allows you to show up as your actual size, not a lesser or watered-down version of yourself. Don't diminish yourself in any way. You now have the ability to fully express yourself and radiate all of your essence so that others grasp your full value and impact. Allow your executive presence to shine, and your success truly will have no limits.

Book Review Request

We'd love your feedback. If you enjoyed this book, please leave a brief review at your favorite online bookstore: Amazon, Apple, Barnes & Noble, or Goodreads? A good review is very important to authors these days, as it helps other readers know a book is worth their time. It doesn't have to be long or detailed. Just a sentence saying what you enjoyed, and a five-star rating is all that's needed. Many thanks.

Buy Executive Presence for Your Employees

This book helps you to not only cultivate your own executive presence (EP), but it can also be gifted to your employees so they can step into their power, convey confidence, and lead with conviction. People who will benefit from receiving this book, include:

+ **Employees with a solid performance who are ready for the next level.**
  Gift this book to these employees with a strong foundation of performance and results, who are now ready to begin developing their executive presence.
+ **Future company leaders.**
  This book is for the fast-rising, high-potential employees who are the up-and-coming stars of the organization.
+ **Managers who want to help employees grow into leaders.**
  As a manager, buy this book for your direct reports to develop executive presence and elevate their potential and impact.
+ **Marginalized employees.**
  Buy *Executive Presence* for the women, people of color, introverts, and others who live outside of the dominant societal norm. All these groups are prone to being overlooked and undervalued. Cultivating executive presence will help them show the world their full potential.
+ **People in the STEM professions.**
  Leaders in fields like engineering, research, IT, and science, often have an extremely high level of technical proficiency

but lack the presence to lead. Their executive presence skills have been underutilized and underdeveloped.

+ **Top-level leaders and senior executives.**
  The higher leaders rise in an organization, the more executive presence becomes a necessity.

Bring Executive Presence into Your Organization

Executive coaching services: https://garfinkleexecutivecoaching.com/

Joel's Executive Presence Coaching Program is for senior leaders, mid-level managers, and high-performing employees. This program unleashes the potential of to step into their power, convey confidence, and lead with conviction. These services are especially helpful to introverts, women, and minorities.

"I highly recommend him."
Jairaj Sounderrajan, **MICROSOFT**

"Joel is an outstanding coach."
Priya Swamy, **NBC UNIVERSAL**

"Joel's coaching helped me take my career to a new level."
Scott H., **AMAZON.COM**

"Joel has helped me become a more confident leader."
Laurie Hanover, **LEVI STRAUSS**

"Joel's coaching helped me to direct and lead people."
Andrew Peters, **CISCO SYSTEMS**

"Working with Joel was the best decision I've made in my career."
Ray Kauffman, **IBM, SETERUS**

"Joel is one of the most effective and innovative executive coaches."
Amalia Sterescu, **ORACLE**

Corporate training / keynotes / webinars: https://joelinspirationalspeaker.com

Joel is a sought-after keynote speaker and corporate trainer on executive presence. He provides a systematic step-by-step process on how to build, develop and grow an executive presence. His motivational skills inspire potential leaders to higher levels of achievement.

"Thanks for the excellent training."
Chris Grim, **ORACLE**

"The training with Joel was great."
Kevin Spindler, **TOYOTA**

"We hope to bring him back every year."
Kathy Weiner, **CISCO SYSTEMS**

"Best workshop I've attended in 30 years."
Kieran Major, **AMERICAN AIRLINES**

"Over 96% of employees wanted to hear him speak again."
Karen Habegger, **GENSLER**

Executive Presence 360° Feedback Assessment Tool

This multi-rater assessment is an essential tool that provides individuals with an in-depth understanding of their effectiveness as a leader, specifically in terms of executive presence. This feedback is firmly planted in measuring the 9 behaviors that identify a leader with executive presence.

Learn more at: https://garfinkleexecutivecoaching.com/executive-presence-360-assessment

Learn How You Are Perceived at Work in Regard to Executive Presence

Many employees don't know how they are perceived at work. This Executive Presence 360 Assessment provides an opportunity to learn how you are perceived by your colleagues, direct reports, superiors, and others in the area of executive presence.

Who will benefit from the Executive Presence 360 Assessment?

- Top-level leaders and senior executives who are underutilizing their executive presence.
- Fast-rising, high-potential employees who are realizing their skill and expertise isn't enough to succeed in advanced positions.
- Women, people of color, and other employees from marginalized groups, who are too often overlooked and underappreciated.
- The hidden talent in an organization—the high-potential employees who fly under the radar.
- Introverts who have questioned whether they have the personality type of a leader.

Additional Resources for You

Sign up for Fulfillment@Work newsletter (10,000+ readers)

1-min read full of best-practice articles, famous leader profiles, and 2-min inspiring videos.

Sign-up and receive a FREE e-book, *41 Proven Strategies to Get Promoted Now* https://garfinkleexecutivecoaching.com/fulfillment-at-work-newsletter

Subscribe to Joel's YouTube channel

View 150+ of Joel's 2-min motivational videos.
Subscribe: https://www.youtube.com/user/joelgarfinkle

Read Joel's 11 books

Purchase any of Joel's 11 books: https://garfinkleexecutivecoaching.com/products

Review over 300 free articles at Joel's website

Read free leadership development articles that provide practical how-to information: https://garfinkleexecutivecoaching.com/executive-coaching-articles

Acknowledgments

Melanie Martin, editor, proofreader, and writer. You were with me every step of the way. Your attention to detail, editing, and development of concepts is outstanding.

The Alliance for Leadership Excellence (Alexcel), an exclusive group of highly experienced executive coaches and talent management consultants. I've valued the advice, guidance, and vulnerability shared by this group. When I look at the success I've achieved, I know that I am standing on your shoulders. Your friendships mean so much to me.

George Stevens, who designed the book cover, your strong creative drive is invaluable.

To my wife, Jueli. I'm so lucky to have you as a life partner. The depth of who you are reveals itself to all who know you. Thank you for reviewing the manuscript and providing invaluable insights and perspectives.

To my two kids, Ariella and Haydn, who loved being part of the acknowledgments for my other book, *Getting Ahead*, and often asked, "When can we be in it again?" You are both growing up to be young adults who are thoughtful, insightful, curious, confident, fun-loving people on this planet. I'm a father to two beautiful people whose unique presence strongly impacts this world.

About the Author

RECOGNIZED AS ONE OF THE BEST: Acknowledged as one of the top 50 executive coaches in the U.S. — Global Gurus named Joel #14 on its list of the top 30 global coaching experts.

MASTER CERTIFIED COACH: Only 2% of the 30,000 coaches worldwide achieve this distinction — the highest accreditation in the profession of coaching from the International Coaching Federation.

CLIENT LIST: *Google, Amazon, Starbucks, Microsoft, Oracle, Deloitte, The Ritz-Carlton, NBC, NBA, Nissan, Citibank, Eli Lilly, Visa, and more.*

YEARS OF EXPERIENCE: 25 years of executive coaching and speaking experience as a keynote speaker and corporate trainer.

AUTHOR: Has written 11 books and over 300 articles on leadership.

Joel has written 11 books that are read in 25 countries. He has also contributed to the book *The Art and Practice of Leadership Coaching* (John Wiley & Sons), as well as *Leader to Leader*, the award-winning quarterly journal launched by the Peter F. Drucker Foundation. His books include:

Executive Presence: *Step into Your Power, Convey Confidence, and Lead with Conviction*

Getting Ahead: *3 Steps to Take Your Career to the Next Level*

16 Essential Qualities That Define Great Leaders: *Learn the Ideal Behaviors, Mindset, and Habits of the Most Successful*

Time Management Mastery: *Stress-Free Productivity in the 7 Key Areas of Life*

Difficult Conversations: *Practical Tactics for Crucial Communication*

How to Be a Great Boss: *Learn the 7 Traits All Great Bosses Have*

Are You Always Stressed and Hurrying at Work? *Learn to Break Your Rush Syndrome Cycle*

Love Your Work: *Make the Job You Have the One You've Always Wanted*

Get Paid What You're Worth: *How to Negotiate a Raise or Higher Starting Salary*

Land Your Dream Job: *Define it. Land it. Live it.*

Job Searching Made Easy: *A Practical Guide to Finding the Job You Need Fast*

References

Part 1

The Importance of Executive Presence

Introduction: Executive Presence Is a Prerequisite to Leadership Success

i   Sally Williamson & Associates. n.d. "Executive Presence Is a Top Priority for Leadership."
https://sallywilliamson.com/executive-presence-top-priority-leadership/

ii   Knowledge@Wharton. 2003. "Why Everyone in an Enterprise Can—and Should—Be a Leader."
https://knowledge.wharton.upenn.edu/article/
why-everyone-in-an-enterprise-can-and-should-be-a-leader/

iii Sally Williamson & Associates. n.d. "Executive Presence Is a Top Priority for Leadership."
https://sallywilliamson.com/executive-presence-top-priority-leadership/

iv Hidden Brain. 2016. "Too Sweet, or Too Shrill? The Double Bind for Women." NPR, October 18, 2016.
https://www.npr.org/2016/10/18/498309357/
too-sweet-or-too-shrill-the-double-bind-for-women

v   Fisher, Annie. 2006. "Ask Annie: Kickstart Your Career." *Fortune*, August 15, 2006.
https://archive.fortune.com/2006/08/14/news/economy/annie_0814.fortune/index.htm

vi Bloomberg. 2003. "Leadership Lessons from Roger Enrico." October 6, 2003.
https://www.bloomberg.com/news/articles/2003-10-06/
leadership-lessons-from-roger-enrico

vii Davis, Scott and Connor Perrett. 2020. "Kobe Bryant Was Known for His Intense Work Ethic—Here Are 24 Examples." *Business*

Insider, January 26, 2020. https://www.businessinsider.com/
kobe-bryant-insane-work-ethic-2013-8

viii   Viral Hoops. n.d. "18 Motivational Kobe Bryant Work Ethic Stories
from Other NBA Players & Coaches."
https://www.viralhoops.com/kobe-bryant-motivational-stories/

ix   MacMullan, Jackie. 2010. "Kobe Bryant: Imitating Greatness." ESPN,
June 4, 2010. https://www.espn.com/nba/
playoffs/2010/columns/
story?columnist=macmullan_jackie&page=kobefilmstudy-100604

x   Dubash, Arish. 2020. "8 Ways to Immortalize Kobe Bryant's Work Ethic
into Your Daily Life." Medium, February 6, 2020. https://medium.
com/@arishdubash/8-ways-to-immortalize-kobe-bryants-work-ethic-
into-your-daily-life-f22c570748a9

xi   Lyttleton, Ben. 2019. "Scoring Under Pressure." Strategy + Business,
January 4, 2019.
https://www.strategy-business.com/blog/
Scoring-under-Pressure?gko=43ac8

xii   Lane, Kevin, Alexia Larmaraud, and Emily Yueh. 2017. "Finding
Hidden Leaders." *McKinsey Quarterly*, January 4, 2017. https://
www.mckinsey.com/business-functions/organization/our-insights/
finding-hidden-leaders\

Chapter 1: How Executive Presence Enhances Leadership

i   Petor, Jessica, and Paul Glatzhofer. 2018. *Executive Presence: The Three
Dimensions*. PSI. https://content.psionline.com/hubfs/Talent%20
Management%20White%20Papers/WP_PSI%20Executive%20Presence.pdf

ii   Feser, Claudio, and Nielsen, Nicholai. 2019. "What Is Leadership:
Moving Beyond the C-Suite." McKinsey & Co., February 28,
2019. https://www.mckinsey.com/featured-insights/leadership/
what-is-leadership

iii   Association for Talent Development. 2018. "83 Percent of Organizations
Have Skills Gaps, According to ATD Research." December 19, 2018.
https://www.td.org/press-release/83-percent-of-organizations-have-
skills-gaps-according-to-atd-research

iv   Robert Half Management Resources. 2018. "Survey: Nearly Half of
CFOs Don't Have a Succession Plan." Robert Half, December 20, 2018.

https://rh-us.mediaroom.com/2018-12-20-Survey-Nearly-Half-Of-CFOs-Dont-Have-A-Succession-Plan

v   Beck, Randall J., and Jim Harter. 2018. "Why Great Managers Are So Rare." Gallup, June 18, 2018. https://www.gallup.com/workplace/231593/why-great-managers-rare.aspx

vi   Bowness, Anita. 2019. "Finding and Keeping Your High Potential Employees." TLNT, December 19, 2019. https://www.tlnt.com/finding-and-keeping-your-high-potential-employees/

vii The Society for Human Resource Management. 2006. "Employee Engagement and Commitment: A Guide to Understanding, Measuring and Increasing Engagement in Your Organization." https://www.shrm.org/hr-today/trends-and-forecasting/special-reports-and-expert-views/Documents/Employee-Engagement-Commitment.pdf

viii Catalyst. 2020. "Women in the Workforce—United States: Quick Take." October 14, 2020. https://www.catalyst.org/research/women-in-the-workforce-united-states/

ix   U.S. Bureau of Labor Statistics. 2021. "Labor Force Statistics from the Current Population Survey [2020]." https://www.bls.gov/cps/cpsaat18.htm

x   Dillon, Bernadette, and Juliet Bourke. 2016. "The Six Signature Traits of Inclusive Leadership." Deloitte University Press. https://www2.deloitte.com/content/dam/Deloitte/au/Documents/human-capital/deloitte-au-hc-six-signature-traits-inclusive-leadership-020516.pdf

xi   Sally Williamson & Associates. n.d. "Executive Presence Is a Top Priority for Leadership." https://sallywilliamson.com/executive-presence-top-priority-leadership/

Chapter 2: What Executive Presence Entails

i   Melfi, Theodore, dir. 2016. *Hidden Figures*. Los Angeles, CA: Fox 2000 Pictures.

ii   Forbes, Moira. 2014. "Are You Leadership Material?" *Forbes*, June 10, 2014.

https://www.forbes.com/sites/moiraforbes/2014/07/10/
are-you-leadership-material/?sh=18f1bc0225ab

Chapter 4: Avoid Undermining Your Executive Presence

i   Westfall, Chris. 2019. "C-suite Secrets: Four Steps to Developing
Executive Presence." *Forbes*, February 7, 2019.
https://www.forbes.com/sites/chriswestfall/2019/02/07/c-suite-
secrets-developing-executive-presence/?sh=3f3f1
4f44fb1

ii   Page, Danielle. 2017. "How Imposter Syndrome Is Holding You Back at
Work." NBC News, October 25, 2017.
https://www.nbcnews.com/better/health/
how-impostor-syndrome-holding-you-back-work-ncna814231

iii   Weir, Kirsten. 2013. "Feel Like a Fraud?" *gradPSYCH Magazine* 11 (4):
24. https://www.apa.org/gradpsych/
2013/11/fraud

iv   Kinsey Goman, Carol. 2019. "How Leadership Presence Is Different for
Women." *The Ladders*, September 18, 2019. https://www.theladders.
com/career-advice/how-leadership-presence-is-different-for-women

v   Hewlett, Sylvia Ann, Noni Allwood, Karen Sumberg, Sandra Sharf,
and Christina Fargnoli. 2013. *Cracking the Code: Executive Presence and
Multicultural Professionals: Executive Summary.* New York: Center for
Talent Innovation. https://www.talentinnovation.org/_private/assets/
CrackingTheCode_EPMC-ExecSummFINAL-CTI.pdf

vi   Clance, Pauline Rose. 1985. *The Impostor Phenomenon: When Success
Makes You Feel Like a Fake.* Toronto: Bantam Books. https://
paulineroseclance.com/pdf/IPTestandscoring.pdf

vii   Johnson, W. Brad, and David G. Smith. 2019. "Mentoring
Someone with Imposter Syndrome." *Harvard Business
Review*, February 22, 2019. https://hbr.org/2019/02/
mentoring-someone-with-imposter-syndrome

viii   Leadem, Rose. 2017. "12 Leaders, Entrepreneurs, and Celebrities Who
Have Struggled with Imposter Syndrome." *Entrepreneur*, November 8,
2017. https://www.entrepreneur.com/slideshow/304273

ix   McCammon, Ross. 2016. *Works Well with Others.* New York: Dutton, p.
xvi.

x McGregor, Jena, and Rachel Siegel. 2018. "Why Are There Still So Few Minority Women CEOs?" *The Washington Post*, August 8, 2018. https://www.washingtonpost.com/business/2018/08/09/why-there-are-still-so-few-minority-women-ceos/

xi Matthews, Gail, and Pauline Rose Clance. 1985. "Treatment of the Impostor Phenomenon in Psychotherapy Clients." *Psychotherapy in Private Practice* 3, no. 1 (November): 71–81. https://doi.org/10.1300/J294v03n01_09

xii Katan, Tania. 2019. "4 Ways to Quiet Imposter Syndrome and Start Believing in Yourself." TED, May 21, 2019. https://ideas.ted.com/4-ways-to-quiet-imposter-syndrome-and-start-believing-in-yourself/

xiii Johnson and Smith. 2019. "Mentoring Someone with Imposter Syndrome."

Chapter 5: Know If Others Perceive You As Having Executive Presence

i Nasher, Jack. 2019. "To Seem More Competent, Be More Confident." *Harvard Business Review*, March 11, 2019. https://hbr.org/2019/03/to-seem-more-competent-be-more-confident

ii Temin, Davia. 2016. "What They're Saying about You When You're Not in the Room—and What You Can Do to Influence It." *Forbes*, April 4, 2016. https://www.forbes.com/sites/daviatemin/2016/04/04/what-theyre-saying-about-you-when-youre-not-in-the-room-and-what-you-can-do-to-influence-it/?sh=bfe323971ac3

iii Sally Williamson & Associates. n.d. "Executive Presence Is a Top Priority for Leadership."

iv Brown, Brené. 2015. *Daring Greatly: How the Courage to Be Vulnerable Transforms the Way We Live, Love, Parent, and Lead.* New York: Penguin Random House, p. 201.

v Zenger Folkman. 2013. "Zenger Folkman Offers a New Free Feedback Assessment on *Harvard Business Review*." PR Newswire, December 17, 2013. https://www.prnewswire.com/news-releases/zenger-folkman-offers-a-new-free-feedback-assessment-on-harvard-business-review-236189781.html

vi Musser, Chris. 2019. "The Most Effective Feedback Is the Kind You Ask For." Gallup, December 20, 2019.

https://www.gallup.com/workplace/271184/effective-feedback-kind-ask.aspx

vii Goldsmith, Marshall. n.d. "Want to Give Feedback? Rather Try Feedforward!" University of Michigan Medical School. https://faculty.medicine.umich.edu/sites/default/files/resources/feedforward.pdf

Part 2: Gravitas, Authority, Expression

Section 1: Gravitas

Introduction: Understanding Gravitas

i   Cuddy, Amy. 2015. *Presence: Bringing Your Boldest Self to Your Biggest Challenges*. New York: Little, Brown Spark, p. 131.

ii   Hewlett, Sylvia Ann, Noni Allwood, Karen Sumberg, Sandra Scharf, and Christina Fargnoli. 2013. *Cracking the Code: Executive Presence and Multicultural Professionals*. New York: Center for Talent Innovation.

iii Ketchum. 2014. *Ketchum Leadership Communication Monitor*. https://www.uwcentre.ac.cn/haut/wp-content/uploads/2015/03/2014_klcm_reportleadership.pdf

iv   Denning, Stephanie. 2018. "Oprah: The Secret to Her Success." *Forbes*, January 8, 2018. https://www.forbes.com/sites/stephaniedenning/2018/01/08/what-makes-oprah-oprah-her-thoughts-on-her-exceptional-success/?sh=752b7a8b5a05

v   Goudreau, Jenna. 2010. "How to Lead Like Oprah." *Forbes*, October 22, 2010. https://www.forbes.com/sites/jennagoudreau/2010/10/22/how-to-lead-like-oprah-winfrey-own-rachael-ray-dr-oz-phil/?sh=734427655825

Chapter 6: Confident

i   Folkman, Joseph. "How Self Confidence Can Help or Hurt Leaders." *Forbes*, February 12, 2019. https://www.forbes.com/sites/joefolkman/2019/02/12/how-self-confidence-can-help-or-hurt-leaders/?sh=3ea5241c5990

ii   Gartner. 2019. "Gartner Survey Shows Only Half of Business Leaders Feel Confident Leading Their Teams Today." July 23, 2019. https://

www.gartner.com/en/newsroom/press-releases/2019-07-22-gartner-survey-shows-only-half-of-business-leaders-fe

iii   Association for Psychological Science. 2013. "Appearances *Really* Count When Rising to the Top." https://www.psychologicalscience.org/news/minds-business/appearances-really-count-when-rising-to-the-top.html

iv   Beck, Julie. 2016. "The Running Conversation in Your Head." *The Atlantic*, November 23, 2016. https://www.theatlantic.com/science/archive/2016/11/figuring-out-how-and-why-we-talk-to-ourselves/508487/

v   Okura, Lynn. 2013. "Brené Brown: You Can't Get to Courage Without Walking Through Vulnerability." *Huffington Post*, September 9, 2013. https://www.huffpost.com/entry/brene-brown-vulnerability_n_3909420

vi   Brown, Brené. 2015. *Daring Greatly*, p. 37.

Chapter 7: Commanding

i   Scroggins, Clay. 2017. *How to Lead When You're Not in Charge: Leveraging Influence When You Lack Authority*. Grand Rapids, MI: Zondervan.

ii   CliftonStrengths. 2018. "Understanding and Investing in Your Command Talent." Gallup, May 25, 2018. https://www.gallup.com/cliftonstrengths/en/249803/understanding-investing-command-talent.aspx

iii   IEDP Editorial. 2016. "Passive Leadership and the Damage Done." IEDP, November 3, 2016. https://www.iedp.com/articles/passive-leadership-and-the-damage-done/

iv   Gallo, Carmine. 2014. "Steve Jobs and Winston Churchill Didn't Start Out as Great Speakers." *Forbes*, November 25, 2014. https://www.forbes.com/sites/carminegallo/2014/11/25/steve-jobs-and-winston-churchill-didnt-start-out-as-great-speakers/?sh=68fa7707296a

v   BBC News. 2020. "Winston Churchill's Inspiring Wartime Speeches in Parliament." May 8, 2020. https://www.bbc.com/news/uk-politics-52588148

vi   Zeng, Hao, Lijing Zhao, and Yixuan Zhau. 2020. "Inclusive Leadership and Taking-Charge Behavior: Roles of Psychological Safety and Thriving at Work." *Frontiers in Psychology* 11 (February): 62. https://doi.org/10.3389/fpsyg.2020.00062

Chapter 8: Charismatic

i   Economy, Peter. 2018. "This Study of 300,000 Leaders Revealed the Top 10 Traits for Success." *Inc.*, March 30, 2018. https://www.inc.com/peter-economy/this-study-of-300000-businesspeople-revealed-top-10-leader-traits-for-success.html

ii   Thompson, Loren. 2020. "Marillyn Hewson Finds a Timely Successor to Lead Lockheed Martin." *Forbes*, March 16, 2020. https://www.forbes.com/sites/lorenthompson/2020/03/16/marillyn-hewson-finds-a-timely-successor-to-lead-lockheed-martin/?sh=61900593575b

iii   *Fortune*. 2020. "Most Powerful Women." https://fortune.com/most-powerful-women/2019/marillyn-hewson/

iv   Hewson, Marillyn. 2016. "The 4 Traits You Need to Be a Great Leader." *Fortune*, October 18, 2016. https://fortune.com/2016/10/18/mpw-leadership-lockheed-martin/

v   McGregor, Jena. 2017. "Introverts Tend to Be Better CEOS—and Other Surprising Traits of Top-Performing Executives." *The Washington Post*, April 17, 2017. https://www.washingtonpost.com/news/on-leadership/wp/2017/04/17/introverts-tend-to-be-better-ceos-and-other-surprising-traits-of-top-performing-executives/

vi   Clifford, Catherine. 2018. "Why This Tech CEO Says Being an Introvert Is Good for Business." CNBC, September 10, 2018. https://www.cnbc.com/2018/09/10/lanzatech-ceo-being-an-introvert-is-good-for-business.html

vii   Hogue, Wayne. 2013. *Elements of Leaders of Character: Attributes, Practices, and Principles*. Bloomington, IN: WestBow Press, p. 60.

viii   Hoffeld, David. 2016. "7 Scientifically Proven Habits of Charismatic Leaders." *Fast Company*, February 3, 2016. https://www.fastcompany.com/3056232/7-scientifically-proven-habits-of-charismatic-leaders

ix   Schulz, Jodi. 2017. *Emotions Are Contagious: Learn What Science and Research Has to Say about It.* Michigan State University Extension, August 16, 2017. https://www.canr.msu.edu/news/emotions_are_contagious_learn_what_science_and_research_has_to_say_about_it

Section 2: Authority

Introduction: Understanding Authority

i   Association for Psychological Science. 2018. "Dominant Leaders Are Bad for Groups. Why Do They Succeed?" https://www.psychologicalscience.org/news/minds-business/dominant-leaders-are-bad-for-groups.html

ii   Jacobs, Harrison. 2014. "Why Hot-Air Ballooning Is Richard Branson's Favorite Way to Travel." *Business Insider,* October 12, 2014. https://www.businessinsider.com/richard-branson-on-hot-air-ballooning-2014-10

iii   Coleman, Alison. 2018. "How Entrepreneurs Like Richard Branson Handle Risk." *Forbes,* December 21, 2018. https://www.forbes.com/sites/alisoncoleman/2018/12/21/how-entrepreneurs-like-richard-branson-handle-business-risk/?sh=6e8a25e2462b

iv   Branson, Richard. 2018. "The Audacious Project." Virgin, April 11, 2018. https://www.virgin.com/branson-family/richard-branson-blog/audacious-project

v   Eudaily, Chris, and Michael Sheetz. 2021. "Virgin Galactic to Launch Richard Branson on July 11, Aiming to Beat Jeff Bezos to Space." CNBC, July 1, 2021. https://www.cnbc.com/2021/07/01/virgin-galactic-to-launch-richard-branson-on-july-11-aiming-to-beat-jeff-bezos-to-space.html

Chapter 9: Decisive

i   Botelho, Elena Lytkina, Kim Rosenkoetter Powell, Stephen Kincaid, and Dina Wang. 2017. "What Sets Successful CEOs Apart." *Harvard Business Review* (May–June). https://hbr.org/2017/05/what-sets-successful-ceos-apart

ii   Monarth, Harrison. 2020. "What Does Being Decisive Say about You?"
      Personal Excellence 25 (10): 10.
      https://www.hr.com/en/magazines/personal_excellence_essentials/
iii   Bezos, Jeff. 2017. "2016 Letter to Shareholders." Amazon, April 17,
      2017. https://www.aboutamazon.com/news/
      company-news/2016-letter-to-shareholders
iv   Trammell, Joel. 2018. "Leadership Matters: The Power of Decisiveness."
      CU Management, June 20, 2018.
      https://www.cumanagement.com/articles/2018/06/
      leadership-matters-power-decisiveness
v   Monarth, Harrison. 2019. "3 Ways to Make Better Decisions for Your
      Career." *Fast Company*, September 20, 2019. https://www.fastcompany.
      com/90406795/3-ways-to-make-better-decisions-for-your-career
vi   Botelho et al. 2017. "What Sets Successful CEOs Apart."
vii   Onley, Dawn. 2019. "How Leaders Can Make Better Decisions." The
      Society for Human Resource Management, August 29, 2019. https://
      www.shrm.org/hr-today/news/hr-magazine/fall2019/pages/how-
      leaders-can-make-better-decisions.aspx
viii Folkman, Joseph. 2019. "The Art to Becoming a Decisive Leader." *Forbes*,
      September 16, 2019.
      https://www.forbes.com/sites/joefolkman/2019/09/16/
      the-art-to-becoming-a-decisive-leader/?sh=38ca3bc05211
ix   Zipursky, Michael. n.d. "21 Productivity Tips for Consultants."
      Consulting Success.
      https://www.consultingsuccess.
      com/21-productivity-tips-for-consultants
x   The Oracles. 2017. "11 Genius Tips to Be More Decisive."
      SUCCESS, January 31, 2017. https://www.success.
      com/11-genius-tips-to-be-more-decisive/
xi   Robbins, Tony. n.d. "Be Decisive: Leadership Is about Making
      Decisions."
      https://www.tonyrobbins.com/stories/unleash-the-power/be-decisive/
xii   The Oracles. 2017. "11 Genius Tips to Be More Decisive."
      https://www.success.com/11-genius-tips-to-be-more-decisive/

Chapter 10: Bold

i   Folkman, Joseph. 2016. "How Bold Leadership Can Hurt or Help You." *Forbes*, August 12, 2016.
https://www.forbes.com/sites/joefolkman/2016/08/12/how-bold-leadership-can-help-you-or-hurt-you/?sh=2270fc3d35ea

ii   Deloitte. 2016. *The Future Belongs to the Bold*. Deloitte LLP. https://www2.deloitte.com/content/dam/Deloitte/ca/Documents/insights-and-issues/ca_Deloitte_Courage_report2016_online_v31_AODA.pdf

iii   Hintze, Arend, Randal S. Olson, Christoph Adami, and Ralph Hertwig. 2015. "Risk Sensitivity as an Evolutionary Adaptation." *Scientific Reports* 5, no. 8242 (February). https://www.nature.com/articles/srep08242

iv   Zetlin, Minda. 2017. "Here's Why Employees Don't Tell You Their Best Ideas (and How to Get Them to Start)." *Inc.*, February 21, 2017. https://www.inc.com/minda-zetlin/heres-why-employees-dont-tell-you-their-best-ideas-and-how-to-get-them-to-start.html

v   Bryant, Adam. 2013. "Using Just One Word, Try to Describe Your Career DNA." *The New York Times*, April 18, 2013. https://www.nytimes.com/2013/04/19/business/salesforcecom-executive-on-seeking-out-challenges.html

vi   Leibowitz, Glenn. 2017. "Steve Jobs Used This Insanely Simple Strategy for Getting What He Wanted (and You Can Too). *Inc.*, January 12, 2017. https://www.inc.com/glenn-leibowitz/how-to-use-steve-jobss-insanely-simple-strategy-for-getting-what-you-want.html

vii   Isaacson, Walter. 2012. "The Real Leadership Lessons of Steve Jobs." *Harvard Business Review* (April). https://hbr.org/2012/04/the-real-leadership-lessons-of-steve-jobs

viii   Ibid.

ix   Fabrega, M. n.d. "How to Be More Daring, Bold and Audacious." Daring to Live Fully. https://daringtolivefully.com/be-daring-bold-and-audacious

x   Ibid.

xi   Williamson, Tameka. 2018. "How to Build a Culture of Bold and Courageous Leaders." *Forbes*, April 30, 2018. https://www.forbes.com/sites/forbescoachescouncil/2018/04/30/how-to-build-a-culture-of-bold-and-courageous-leaders/?sh=70b49b4d2566

xii Deloitte. 2016. *The Future Belongs to the Bold.*

Chapter 11: Influential

i Edelman. 2019. 2020 B2B *Thought Leadership Impact Study.* https://
   www.edelman.com/research/2020-b2b-
   thought-leadership-impact-study
ii Keller, Scott, and Mary Meaney. 2017. *Leading Organizations: 10
   Timeless Truths.* London and New York: Bloomsbury Business. https://
   www.mckinsey.com/~/media/McKinsey/Business%20Functions/
   Organization/Our%
   20Insights/Leading%20Organizations%20book/Leading-
   Organizations-Ten-Timeless-Truths.pdf
iii Haudan, Jim. 2018. *What Are Your Blind Spots? Conquering the 5
   Misconceptions That Hold Leaders Back.* New York: McGraw-Hill.
iv Taylor, Chloe. 2019. "Elon Musk Is the Most Inspirational Leader in
   Tech, New Survey Shows." CNBC, September 17, 2019. https://www.
   cnbc.com/2019/09/17/elon-musk-named-the-most-inspirational-
   leader-in-tech.html
v Milner, Yuri. 2018. "Elon Musk: The Visionary." *Time,* April 19, 2018.
   https://time.com/collection-post/5217614/elon-musk/
vi Goleman, Daniel. n.d. *The Power of Influence.* Korn Ferry.
   https://www.kornferry.com/insights/this-week-in-leadership/
   influence-emotional-intelligence
vii Laker, Ben, and Charmi Patel. 2020. "Strengthen Your Ability to
   Influence People." *Harvard Business Review,* August 28, 2020. https://
   hbr.org/2020/08/strengthen-your-ability-to-influence-people
viii Goulston, Mark, and John Ullmen. 2019. "Are You Listening?" American
   Management Association.
   https://www.amanet.org/articles/are-you-listening-/
ix Clark, Dorie. 2012. "A Campaign Strategy for Your Career." *Harvard
   Business Review* (November).
   https://hbr.org/2012/11/a-campaign-strategy-for-your-career
x Cialdini, Robert B. 2006. *Influence: The Psychology of Persuasion.* New
   York: Harper Business.

Section 3: Expression

Introduction: Understanding Expression

i   Shambaugh, Rebecca. 2017. "To Sound Like a Leader, Think about What You Say, and How and When You Say It." *Harvard Business Review*, October 31, 2017. https://hbr.org/2017/10/to-sound-like-a-leader-think-about-what-you-say-and-how-and-when-you-say-it

ii   Buranyi, Stephen. "Greta Thunberg's Enemies Are Right to Be Scared. Her New Political Allies Should Be Too." *The Guardian*, September 30, 2019. https://www.theguardian.com/commentisfree/2019/sep/30/greta-thunberg-enemies-inaction-climate-crisis

iii De Luce, Ivan, and Rebecca Aydin. "The Art of Activism: How Greta Thunberg's Matter-of-Fact Way of Speaking and Taking Action Turned Her into a Global Icon and *Time*'s 'Person of the Year.'" *Business Insider*, December 11, 2019. https://www.businessinsider.com/how-greta-thunberg-speaks-protests-communicates-2019-9

Chapter 12: Vocal

i   Wilkie, Dana. 2017. "Afraid to Speak Your Mind at Work? So Are Many of Your Colleagues." The Society for Human Resource Management. https://www.shrm.org/resourcesandtools/hr-topics/employee-relations/pages/communication-.aspx

ii   Chen, Robert. 2015. "Three Strategies for Introverts to Speak Up in Meetings." *Fast Company*, October 23, 2015. https://www.fastcompany.com/3052599/the-top-3-reasons-introverts-dont-speak-up-in-meetings

iii Kakkar, Hemant, and Subra Tangirala. 2018. "If Your Employees Aren't Speaking Up, Blame Company Culture." *Harvard Business Review*, November 6, 2018. https://hbr.org/2018/11/if-your-employees-arent-speaking-up-blame-company-culture

iv   Burris, Ethan, Elizabeth McCune, and Dawn Klinghoffer. 2020. "When Employees Speak Up, Companies Win." *MIT Sloan Management Review*, November 17, 2020. https://sloanreview.mit.edu/article/when-employees-speak-up-companies-win/

v   Jiang, Zhou. 2019. "Why Withholding Information at
    Work Won't Give You an Advantage." *Harvard Business
    Review*, November 14, 2019. https://hbr.org/2019/11/
    why-withholding-information-at-work-wont-give-you-an-advantage

vi Jenkins, H. 2021. "The U.S. Is Getting a Crash Course in Scientific
    Uncertainty." *The New York Times*, August 22, 2021. https://www.
    nytimes.com/2021/08/22/health/coronavirus-covid-usa.html

vii VitalSmarts. 2016. "Costly Conversations: Why the Way Employees
    Communicate Will Make or Break Your Bottom Line." https://www.
    vitalsmarts.com/press/2016/12/costly-conversations-why-the-way-
    employees-communicate-will-make-or-break-your-bottom-line/

viii Thought Leadership Zen. n.d. "Leadership Communication Primer."
    https://thoughtleadershipzen.blogspot.com/2016/07/leadership-
    communication-primer.html

ix Ericson, Cathie. 2017. "Voice of Experience: Kerone Vatel, Managing
    Director, Risk Division, Goldman Sachs." The Glass Hammer. https://
    theglasshammer.com/2017/12/kerone-vatel-goldman-sachs/

x   Garfinkle, Joel. n.d. "10 Ways to Increase Visibility in Meetings."
    Garfinkle Executive Coaching. https://garfinkle
    executivecoaching.com/articles/
    stand-out-and-get-noticed/10-ways-to-increase-visibility-in-meetings

xi Heath, Kathryn, Jill Flynn, and Mary Davis Holt. 2014. "Success on the
    Corporate Stage: Why Meetings Matter Even More for Women." Flynn
    Heath Holt Leadership. https://www.flynnheath.com/wp-content/
    uploads/2016/01
    /Why-Meetings-Matter-Even-More-for-Women_FHH-Report_June-
    2014.pdf

xii Mitchell, Olivia. n.d. "The Introvert's Ultimate Guide to
    Speaking Up in Meetings." Speaking About Presenting.
    https://speakingaboutpresenting.com/presentation-skills/
    speaking-up-in-meetings-for-introverts/

xiii Kaye, Jezra. 2018. "How to Speak Up More in Meetings
    by Saying Inconsequential Things (and Yes, That's a Good
    Idea!)" LinkedIn. https://www.linkedin.com/pulse/
    how-speak-up-more-meetings-saying-inconsequential-things-jezra-kaye/

xiv   Wotapka, Dawn. 2017. "How to Stand Out in Meetings." AICPA, July 18, 2017. https://www.aicpa.org/interestareas/youngcpanetwork/resources/stand-out-at-meetings.html

xv   Merchant, Nilofer. 2011. "Your Silence Is Hurting Your Company." *Harvard Business Review*, September 7, 2011. https://hbr.org/2011/09/your-silence-is-hurting-your-company

xvi   Rotterdam School of Management. 2018. "Why Employees Resist Sharing New Ideas with Teams—Even If It Means Failure." HR Dive, November 20, 2018. https://www.hrdive.com/press-release/20181120-why-employees-resist-sharing-new-ideas-with-teams-even-if-it-means-failur/

Chapter 13: Insightful

i   Wiles, Jackie. 2019. "Top 10 Emerging Skills for the C-Suite." Gartner, May 24, 2019. https://www.gartner.com/smarterwithgartner/top-10-emerging-skills-for-the-c-suite/

ii   TED. n.d. "Sergey Brin." https://www.ted.com/speakers/sergey_brin

iii   X – The Moonshot Factory. 2018. "We Create Radical New Technologies to Solve Some of the World's Hardest Problems." https://x.company

iv   Fey, Tina. 2011. *Bossypants*. New York: Little, Brown and Company, p. 84.

v   Martic, Kristina. 2019. "Corporate Communications: Your Employees' Voice Matters." Smarp, December 17, 2019. https://blog.smarp.com/corporate-communications-your-employees-voice-matters

vi   Dye, David, and Karen Hurt. 2019. "How Can I Encourage My Employees to Share Their Ideas?" U.S. Chamber of Commerce, December 6, 2019. https://www.uschamber.com/co/good-company/ask-the-board/how-to-encourage-employees-to-share-ideas

vii   Møllerop, Frank. 2017. "Employee Insights Can Drive Your Business Success." TLNT, July 13, 2017. https://www.tlnt.com/employee-insights-can-drive-your-business-success/

viii   Dye and Hurt. 2019. "How Can I Encourage My Employees to Share Their Ideas?"

ix   Forbes Communications Council. 2018. "15 Ways to Encourage Creative Idea Sharing from All Team Members." *Forbes*, May 21, 2018. https://www.forbes.com/sites/forbescommunicationscounci l/2018/05/21/15-ways-to-encourage-creative-idea-sharing-from-all-team-members/?sh=308b4f57ce0a

x   Ibid.

xi   Dye and Hurt. 2019. "How Can I Encourage My Employees to Share Their Ideas?"

Chapter 14: Clear

i   Leading Effectively Staff. 2020. "Why Communication Is So Important for Leaders." Center for Creative Leadership, November 24, 2020. https://www.ccl.org/articles/leading-effectively-articles/communication-1-idea-3-facts-5-tips/

ii   Dishman, Lydia. 2014. "Mastering the Fine Art of Getting to the Point." *Fast Company*, January 22, 2014. https://www.fastcompany.com/3025114/mastering-the-fine-art-of-getting-to-the-point

iii   Gartner. 2019. "Lead a World-Class Communications Team." https://www.gartner.com/en/corporate-communications/role/communications-leaders

iv   Shambaugh, Rebecca. 2017. "To Sound Like a Leader, Think about What You Say, and How and When You Say It." *Harvard Business Review*, October 31, 2017. https://hbr.org/2017/10/to-sound-like-a-leader-think-about-what-you-say-and-how-and-when-you-say-it

v   Egnal, Bart. 2016. *Leading Through Language: Choosing Words That Influence and Inspire*. Hoboken, NJ: John Wiley & Sons, Inc., p. 191.

vi   da Fonseca-Wollheim, Corinna. 2019. "How the Silence Makes the Music." *The New York Times*, October 2, 2019. https://www.nytimes.com/2019/10/02/arts/music/silence-classical-music.html

vii   Gallo, Carmine. 2019. "How to Look and Sound Confident During a Presentation." *Harvard Business Review*, October 23, 2019. https://hbr.org/2019/10/how-to-look-and-sound-confident-during-a-presentation

viii   Dishman, Lydia. 2014. "Mastering the Fine Art of Getting to the Point."

ix   James, Geoffrey. 2014. "5 Ways to Communicate More Clearly." *Inc.*, September 5, 2014.

https://www.inc.com/geoffrey-james/5-ways-to-communicate-more-clearly.html

x   Humphrey, Judith. 2019. "6 Phrases That Will Help You Sell Your Ideas." *Fast Company*, May 16, 2019. https://www.fastcompany.com/90346485/6-phrases-that-will-help-you-sell-your-ideas

xi   Ni, Preston. 2019. "Do You Talk Too Fast? How to Slow Down." *Psychology Today*, November 16, 2019. https://www.psychologytoday.com/us/blog/communication-success/201911/do-you-talk-too-fast-how-slow-down

xii   Ibid.

xiii   Quoted in Walsh, Dylan. 2016. "5 Strategies for Leading a High-Impact Team." KelloggInsight, July 1, 2016. https://insight.kellogg.northwestern.edu/article/five-strategies-for-leading-a-high-impact-team

xiv   Thompson, Leigh. 2013. "How to Neutralize a Meeting Tyrant." *Fortune*, February 11, 2013. https://fortune.com/2013/02/11/how-to-neutralize-a-meeting-tyrant/

xv   Tracy, Brian. n.d. *The Power of Pausing*. Brian Tracy International. https://www.briantracy.com/blog/sales-success/the-power-of-pausing/

xvi   BRI. n.d. "How to Control Dominators in Meetings." https://booherresearch.com/control-dominators-meetings/

xvii   MacKay, Barbara. 2019. "People Who Talk Too Much in Meetings—Respectfully Dealing with Dominance." North Star Facilitators. https://northstarfacilitators.com/2019/04/people-who-talk-too-much-in-meetings-respectfully-dealing-with-dominance/

Printed in France by Amazon
Brétigny-sur-Orge, FR

14198960R00189